JUN -9 1993

D0409721

NO LONGER THE
PROPERTY OF
ELON UNIVERSITY LIBRARY

Making Peace Possible

THE PROMISE OF ECONOMIC CONVERSION

Titles of Related Interest

BROCK-UTNE Educating for Peace

CHESTNUT Contributions of Technology to International Conflict Resolution

GRAHAM Disarmament and World Development

LALL Multilateral Negotiation and Mediation

Pergamon Reference Works

BRECHER, WILKENFELD & MOSER: Crises in the Twentieth Century, Volumes I and II

LASZLO & YOO World Encyclopedia of Peace

Making Peace Possible

THE PROMISE OF ECONOMIC CONVERSION

Edited by

LLOYD J. DUMAS

and

MAREK THEE

PERGAMON PRESS

OXFORD · NEW YORK · BEIJING · FRANKFURT
SÃO PAULO · SYDNEY · TOKYO · TORONTO

930095

U.K.	Pergamon Press plc, Headington Hill Hall, Oxford OX3 0BW, England
U.S.A.	Pergamon Press, Inc., Maxwell House, Fairview Park, Elmsford, New York 10523, U.S.A.
PEOPLE'S REPUBLIC OF CHINA	Pergamon Press, Room 4037, Qianmen Hotel, Beijing, People's Republic of China
FEDERAL REPUBLIC OF GERMANY	Pergamon Press GmbH, Hammerweg 6, D-6242 Kronberg, Federal Republic of Germany
BRAZIL	Pergamon Editora Ltda, Rua Eça de Queiros, 346, CEP 04011, Paraiso, São Paulo, Brazil
AUSTRALIA	Pergamon Press Australia Pty Ltd., P.O. Box 544, Potts Point, N.S.W. 2011, Australia
JAPAN	Pergamon Press, 5th Floor, Matsuoka Central Building, 1-7-1 Nishishinjuku, Shinjuku-ku, Tokyo 160, Japan
CANADA	Pergamon Press Canada Ltd., Suite No. 271, 253 College Street, Toronto, Ontario, Canada M5T 1R5

Copyright © 1989 Lloyd J. Dumas and M. Thee

All Rights Reserved. No part of this publication may be reproduced, stored in a retrieval system or transmitted in any form or by any means: electronic, electrostatic, magnetic tape, mechanical, photocopying, recording or otherwise, without permission in writing from the publishers.

First edition 1989

Library of Congress Cataloging-in-Publication Data
Making peace possible: the promise of economic conversion/[edited]
by Lloyd J. Dumas and Marek Thee.—1st ed.
p. cm.
Includes index.
$19.90 (est.)
1. Disarmament—Economic aspects—Case studies.
I. Dumas, Lloyd J. II. Thee, Marek, 1918– .
HC79.D4M35 1988 338.4'76234—dc19 88-38436

British Library Cataloguing in Publication Data
Dumas, Lloyd J.
Making peace possible: the promise of economic conversion
1. Disarmament. Economic aspects
1. Title II. Thee, Marek, 1918–
327.1'74

ISBN 0-08-037252X (Hardcase)
ISBN 0-08-037253-8 (Flexicover)

This is Peace Research Monograph No. 19 from the International Peace Research Institute, Oslo.

Publication of this book has been made possible by the Miriam and Ira D. Wallach Foundation.

Printed in Great Britain by BPCC Wheatons Ltd., Exeter

Contents

Preface
Conversion: The Idea Whose Time Has Come

A long time has been required for 'conversion' to become 'the idea whose time has come'. There are, however, indications that the many obstacles put in the way of common sense on this matter might be overcome.

I am well aware that much immensely valuable work by independent-minded scientists, not least in the United States, has contributed highly to this turn of events. But I hope to be justified also to say that the many years of efforts within the United Nations to clarify the character and the intensity of the relationship between resources used for the arms race and economic and social underdevelopment on the one hand and—to put it in positive terms—the relationship between a genuine disarmament process and resources released for economic, social and human development on the other, have played their role.

I state with great pleasure, therefore, that this is reflected in an important chapter of this book. Much to my satisfaction, studies carried out in Scandinavian countries have been given a chapter of their own as well.

We live, as I have said symbolically on many occasions, in an over-armed and undernourished world. And governments seem so far not to have had the capacity and/or the will to understand the tremendous dangers for our common future that are inherent in this situation and the need to act to avert these dangers.

The UN International Conference on the Relationship between Disarmament and Development (ICRDD) that finally took place in August-September 1987 represents the first step at the intergovernmental level to define—and act upon—the relationship between the over-armament of the world and the under-nourishment of its peoples. It was preceded by a thorough preparatory process, including an excellent updating of facts, figures and analyzes, based mainly on the 1981 UN report.

Among the contributions to the efforts for a positive outcome of the ICRDD was the convening of a panel of 'eminent personalities' in April 1986, which succeeded in issuing, after 2½ days of work, a unanimously adopted Declaration on Disarmament and Development. The moderator of the panel—the author of this preface—is immodest enough to maintain that this short document is a good summary of many years of work within the United Nations on the disarmament-development relationship. This is also evidenced by the fact that the Declaration has been repeatedly quoted in the Final Document of the ICRDD.

I should like to reproduce here the final paragraph of the Declaration:

> Our small planet is getting endangered: by the arsenals of weapons which could blow it up; by the burden of military expenditures which could sink it under; and by the unmet basic needs of two-thirds of its population which subsists on less than one-third of its resources. We belong to a near universal constituency which believes that we are borrowing this Earth from our children as much as we have inherited it from our forefathers. The carrying capacity of Earth is not infinite, nor are its resources. The needs of national security are legitimate and must be met. But must we stand by as helpless witnesses of a drift towards greater insecurity at higher costs?

The ICRDD had not aroused great advance expectations, even if peace movements and a number of other organizations of concerned citizens had prepared themselves thoroughly for their participation and their contributions.

The main reason for doubts about the final outcome of three weeks of deliberations was the fact—which I have referred to briefly already—that governments of UN member states had shown themselves singularly indifferent to the repeated urging of the UN General Assembly: to study, prepare, and plan, at the national level, for conversion of resources used for military purposes to constructive civilian use in an international disarmament situation. One major power even went so far as to refuse to recognize any link between disarmament and development and, consequently, stayed away from the conference.

However, the conference turned out much better than expected. I consider the main reason to be the fact that the relationship issue was the only substantive item on the conference agenda. That forced governments of the 150 participating states to think, not about disarmament or development per se, but the relationship between them. The result was that in the general debate, as well as in the Final Document, there is a beginning of a new thinking, a new language, and a new vocabulary.

In other words, it was for obvious reasons that so many delegates, including foreign ministers, spoke about an historic conference, a landmark conference.

A few words need to be said on the content of the Final Document. It does not appear to contain very much of concrete substance in terms of action-oriented proposals, nor could that have been expected. The task that the conference had been given was to examine and negotiate the principles based on the texts of the drafts submitted to it by the preparatory committee—and, I will have to add, the declaration by the panel. On the other hand, the Final Document was intended to serve as a guideline for the next steps to follow on the conclusion of the conference, being itself the first step forward. As such, it contains much more substance than I had believed possible.

In addition, many delegations expressed regret that the document did not explicitly endorse the proposal of establishing an International Disarmament Fund for Development. I do not share this concern, for what are, very briefly, the following reasons. In my view, the fund is not a magic formula for implementing, in concrete terms, the relationship concept. One has to compare the possible importance of additional financial transfers from the industrialized and weapon-producing countries in the North in a disarmament situation—possibly rather small—with the importance of the necessary and fundamental change in the structural relationship between countries in the world economy including world trade. This is, after all, the aim, purpose, and content of the New International Economic Order. And this can only be brought about, in a disarmament situation, through the conversion and the transfer of human talents and skills as well as material resources from military to constructive developmental purposes, thus forming a step towards the New International Economic Order. After all, this was the basic thinking behind the UN General Assembly mandate to the Governmental Expert group for its three-year study (1978-81) on the relationship to have its conclusions and recommendations placed into the framework of the NIEO. Therefore we have to deepen our thinking and our analysis of the relationship issue. How do the interdependencies among peoples and issues really function in today's world?

At its 42nd Session, the UN General Assembly took decisions which include the approval of the Final Document of the conference, including its Action Programme, as well as the placing of the issue on the agenda of the Assembly's 3rd Special Session on Disarmament in June 1988.

This could have meant that the future life of the disarmament-development relationship in its international context would be secured. In this respect as in many others, however, the 3rd Special Session on Disarmament turned out to be a disappointment. The major power which stayed away from the ICRDD firmly refused to have the relationship issue even referred to in a final document of the Session. This proved to be one of several reasons why the Session failed to produce such a document. Consequently, it is now, more than ever, up to governments of member states to show their willingness to be true to what they said at the ICRDD and to follow up through practical political action.

In conclusion, let me widen the perspective somewhat. Governments must be made to understand that in our age some realities must be recognized and made to influence practical policies:

—the globality of crucial issues, and
—the commonality of crucial issues.

So far, the concept of security has not been defined in too narrow terms. So far, disarmament negotiations have been carried out in isolation and based on outdated traditional concepts of security.
    After all:

—We are in the midst of a common crisis
—We have, all of us, common interests
—We share the need for common security
—We all look forward towards a common future.

Maybe 'new thinking' along these lines might still contribute to make disarmament, conversion, and development an idea whose time has indeed come.

INGA THORSSON

I. Economic Conversion for Disarmament and Development

Economic Conversion: The Critical Link

LLOYD J. DUMAS

1. Costs of the arms race

Since the close of World War II, the arms race has become a centrepiece of international relations. Though attention is often focused on the arms competition between the US and the USSR, particularly in the arena of nuclear weapons, there is no question that the arms race is a worldwide phenomenon. Its dogged pursuit over the last half of the twentieth century has undermined the productive competence and economic wellbeing of even the strongest and most developed economies among its participants. The damage it has done to the prospects of those nations still struggling to develop has been correspondingly more severe, and more painful. It is a sobering thought that the nations of the Third World have not merely kept pace with the vast expansion in military expenditures of the more developed nations, but have actually doubled their share of world military spending since the early 1960s.[1]

More importantly, the international arms race has led to a massive reduction in national and world security. It has played no small part in the hundred plus wars that have been fought since the end of World War II, making them increasingly destructive and increasingly likely to lead to wider war. Now we all live in one world, sharing the ever present threat of the termination of human society and perhaps the extinction of the human species by global nuclear war. Whether such war comes by intention, escalation or accident, it is the logical end that the arms race will impose on us, if we do not find the wisdom to impose an end to the arms race.

Both our physical security and our economic wellbeing require that a significant fraction of the productive resources currently being poured into the militaries of the world be shifted to productive, civilian-oriented activity. To do this efficiently and smoothly, with minimal disruption and pain during the transition, is the mandate of economic conversion.

2. Arms and the economy

Both those of the far Right and those of the far Left have often vociferously argued that military spending conveys real economic benefits to

3

capitalist economies. It creates jobs and provides an additional source of demand to stimulate economic activity (an argument which seems particularly obvious to those who work in the military economy or live in militarily dependent areas). It drives the discovery of new technology with important application to civilian purposes, technology that ultimately results in rising productivity and better products. And by the threat it poses to other nations, a high level of military expenditure guarantees access to both needed raw materials and profitable product markets.

All the pieces of this argument are partly true. Yet what is missing from these half truths is far more powerful than what is there. Yes, military expenditures create jobs, but nearly every other form of public expenditure creates more jobs, dollar for dollar.[2] And the jobs produced by military spending do not create economic value, as I will shortly explain. Yes, military spending does inject money into the economy and can therefore be used as a tool for short run economic stimulation. But when high levels of military expenditure persist for an extended period, the continuing drain of resources interferes with critical economic processes required to keep production efficient. The result is a long term deterioration in the ability of the economy to function.

Yes, military research and development does result in technologies that 'spinoff' to civilian application. But heavy emphasis on military R&D creates a kind of internal 'brain drain' that tends to retard the progress of civilian technology far more than can be compensated by this spinoff. And finally, the threat posed by a large military may at times be an effective form of coercion. But it is often far less effective than nonmilitary, noncoercive means of assuring access to materials or markets, as is well illustrated by the ability of the powerful Japanese economy to effectively achieve these objectives without any significant accompanying military threat capacity.

Taken together then, these missing parts of the truth rather dramatically reverse the ultimate conclusion. Military spending is an economic burden, not an economic boon. Furthermore, the long-term structural damage that tends to be created by persistent, high levels of military expenditure is not merely a feature of capitalist economies—it is common to every form of economic organization. Why is military spending so peculiarly and fundamentally damaging to economic wellbeing? The answer lies in the very nature of economic activity itself.

The economy is that part of the society whose central function is to provide material wellbeing. It generates and distributes both the goods and services that directly satisfy material needs (i.e., consumer goods, such as televisions and automobiles) and the means required to supply them (i.e., producer goods, such as industrial machinery and factory buildings). Thus, it makes sense to consider that a good or a service has economic value only to the extent that it contributes to the material standard of living.

The various systems and institutions of society serve many social goals. Providing material wellbeing is only one of them: physical security, political coordination and control, spiritual guidance are others. Many social activities are carried out in pursuit of these various goals. To the extent that they are successful, they generate differing kinds of value—moral, political, psychological. But only those activities that contribute to the material standard of living generate *economic* value. In keeping with the analysis elaborated in my recent book, *The Over-burdened Economy*, activities that result in economically valuable goods and services will be referred to as 'contributive', while those that do not will be called 'noncontributive'.[3]

Yet even noncontributive activities often require goods and services that can only be produced with the same labour, machinery and equipment needed to produce economically valuable goods and services. Consequently, though noncontributive activities are without *economic value*, they do have *economic cost*. This cost is measured by the economic value that could have been created by using this same labour, machinery and equipment to produce goods and services that do have economic value.

Economically productive resources (e.g., labour, machinery) that are used for noncontributive activity can be said to have been 'diverted', since they have been directed to other than economic purposes. The 'theory of resource diversion' holds that an economy in which significant amounts of critical economic resources have been persistently diverted to noncontributive activities will tend to experience a secular decrease in its ability to produce efficiently.[4] Such declining productive competence will surely lead to a deteriorating standard of living over time.

The production of military goods and services is clearly a noncontributive activity. Whatever else may be said for such products, they neither add to the present standard of living (as do consumer goods) nor are they tools that add to productive capacity and thus to the future standard of living (as are producer goods). Many other forms of noncontributive activity exist, but military-oriented activity is clearly dominant in today's world. And the voracious appetite of modern military sectors for both technologists and capital creates a kind of resource diversion that is particularly damaging to present day economies.

The majority of the population in virtually every country earns the largest part of its money income in the form of wages and salaries. Therefore, creating widespread improvement in the economic condition of the general population requires continuing increases in wages and salaries that outrun increases in the prices of products people buy. But since higher wages and salaries mean higher labour costs, it is necessary to find some way of offsetting these costs or they will push prices up so much that higher pay will not translate into greater purchasing power. (This problem is in a sense more severe in the more developed countries because labour costs tend to loom so large there.) The ability to offset these costs depends crucially on the rise of labour productivity. Rising labour productivity, in turn, depends primarily on improving the techniques of production and the quantity and quality of the capital available to workers.

Improvements in the techniques of production come primarily from research and development aimed at discovering and applying new civilian-oriented technology. Such R&D activity cannot be successful without a sufficient quantity and quality of engineers and scientists to perform the work. Furthermore, unless enough capital is available, it may be difficult to provide the required research facilities or to widely apply the results of successful research throughout the relevant industries.

A sufficiently large diversion of engineers and scientists and/or capital will reduce the availability of these critical resources to the civilian economy. This will tend to undermine productivity growth, reducing the ability of producers to offset rising labour costs. The result will be cost-push inflation that will wear away the value of the nominally higher pay, or direct downward pressure on wages and salaries. In either case, the effect will be the same—a relative if not absolute decline in the standard of living over time.

How large has the diversion of resources been as a result of the arms race? In the US, for example, roughly 30% of the nation's engineers and scientists have been engaged in military-oriented R&D for about the last three decades. As to capital diversion, as of 1983, the book value of physical capital directly owned by the Department of Defense was nearly half as large as the book value of all the physical capital owned by all manufacturing establishments in the United States combined![5]

In terms of financial capital in the Third World, the combined military expenditures of the less developed countries over only the six years from 1977-82 were cumulatively greater than the total Third World debt outstanding in 1982. If the Third World's *share* of world military spending had been the same in those years as it was in the early 1960s, the less developed nations as a group would have saved enough money from this one source to finance repayment of nearly two-thirds of their outstanding debt.[6]

Even by these rough indications, it is clear that resource diversion has been large enough to cause considerable economic damage to at least the largest military spenders. The standard of living in the US has been declining now for about ten years; the problems of chronic and acute shortages of consumer goods in the USSR are well known; the failure of two 'Decades of Development' (declared by the UN) has led to a widening gap between the richer and poorer nations of the world. Though many things have contributed to this array of problems, there is little doubt that the arms race has been and continues to be one of the most important. The redirection of substantial quantities of people and facilities from military to civilian-oriented activity has always been a nice idea. It is rapidly becoming an economic necessity.

3. The changing nature of the conversion problem

Immediately after the end of World War II, the US economy underwent a remarkably successful large-scale transition from military to civilian-oriented production. In the words of Kenneth Boulding,

> . . . in one year, 1945-46, we transferred 30% of the GNP from the war industry into civilian uses, without unemployment ever rising above 3%, an astonishing testimony to the flexibility of the American economy and also to some wise planning by the Committee for Economic Development at the local level.[7]

It is clear from this experience that even massive redirections of a heavily war-oriented national economy are feasible without extraordinary disruption. Yet this experience must be interpreted with great care if it is to guide present day policy. For the US in that period underwent what is most accurately called 'reconversion', and this is quite different from the problem of 'conversion' that faces most highly military-oriented economies today.

As the US involvement in World War II expanded, firms normally involved in civilian production began to switch to producing military equipment instead. All of the labour force at such firms, from production and maintenance workers to engineers and managers, were accustomed to serving civilian commercial markets. That is what they had spent most of their working life doing. Though production equipment and facilities were modified, they had been originally designed and configured for effective civilian production. When the War ended, these firms went back to doing what they were used to doing. They 'reconverted'. For them, military production was a temporary aberration from the norm of the civilian commercial marketplace.

The situation is quite different today. There are generations of managers, engineers, scientists, production and maintenance workers whose employment experience includes little or nothing but military-oriented work. Many contemporary military industrial firms have never operated in civilian commercial markets. Even those firms that are major producers of both military and civilian products (e.g., Boeing and Rockwell International) typically have operationally separate, insulated divisions which in effect function as wholly owned subsidiaries reporting to the same overall top management. For the major modern military producers, serving the military is no short-lived aberration—it is the norm.

It is also important to note that during World War II, both the means of production and the technologies involved in designing and producing military goods were still fairly similar to those in the civilian sector. Over the past forty years, these facilities, equipment and technologies have rapidly diverged. The physical plant, machinery and technologies applied in a modern military industrial firm are markedly different from what is common in a modern civilian manufacturer. The technologies embodied in the designs of the products themselves are even more different. The problem of shifting from military to civilian production has accordingly become one of 'conversion', shifting to something new, rather than 'reconversion', returning to something familiar.

Forty years of the arms race have made the problem of transition from military production more difficult, but there is no need to be discouraged. There is little question that it can be done, and done smoothly and efficiently. It is simply necessary to approach the problem more carefully.

4. Conversion and macroeconomic policy

Despite the fact that persistent high levels of military spending tend to be fearsomely damaging to any economy, a simple minded policy of sharply cutting back military expenditures would create considerable economic distress. Not only would the workers who lose their jobs in military industry suffer, but their loss of income would cause a drop in consumer spending that would also generate further job loss in industries supplying consumer goods. Similarly, reduced purchases of equipment and the like by the military industrial firms whose projects are cut back would generate job loss in producer goods industries.

In the market economies, government decision makers have a variety of so-called 'macroeconomic' policies available to them to counter problems of rising unemployment: cutting taxes, increasing government spending, increasing money supply, etc. While these policies can in general be quite effective, they are not sufficient to cope with the economic problems generated by military cutbacks. Why not?

The effects of the kinds of macroeconomic policies mentioned above tend, in rough terms, to be averaged over the economy. Of course, not all areas of the country or all sectors of the economy are affected equally. But these policies are not directed at specific industries or areas, and consequently their effects tend to spread out across the economy and across the nation. Military industry and bases, however, tend not to be spread evenly throughout the nation. They tend instead to be located in concentrated pockets, though these pockets may themselves be located in a variety of geographic regions. And military production tends to be highly concentrated in a relatively small number of industries.

Consequently, economic policies that average their stimulating effects across the nation and the various sectors of the economy cannot reach deeply into these specific areas and sectors. The effects of the policies in these particular places and sectors could easily prove to be too weak to prevent their becoming sites of deep recession or worse in the event of major military cutbacks. Advanced planning for conversion on a contingency basis can avoid such problems by preparing military-serving facilities and their workforces to move efficiently into productive and profitable civilian-oriented activity. It is structural enough to prevent the economic anguish that has been suffered by the workforces and surrounding communities dependent on military spending in past downturns.

That such conversions can convey substantial local as well as national economic benefits is, for instance, illustrated by a report done by the US Department of Defense covering the conversion of some 94 military bases in the US over the period 1961-1981.[8] The study shows that 123,777 new civilian jobs were created after these bases were converted to a wide variety of alternative uses to replace the 87,703 jobs lost when the bases were initially closed.[9] The flavour of the local impact of these base conversions is illustrated by the following, taken from a *New York Times* article reprinted in that same Pentagon document:

> Mobile, Alabama—When Brookley Air Force Base was closed in 1969 with the loss of 13,600 civilian jobs, there were bitter protests and acute apprehension . . . a decade later, . . . many leaders in this city would not have Brookley back even if the Government came begging. The base has turned into a prospering industrial-aviation-educational complex; the city government has become an industrial landlord with a major new source of revenue, and the departure of so large a military presence has made the city more diverse and independent.[10]

There is yet another reason why macroeconomic policies are insufficient to deal with the economic transition problems created by large-scale cutbacks in military spending. A significant fraction of the workforce at military-oriented facilities is hampered by a 'trained incapacity' to function in civilian-oriented activity. This is particularly true of managers, engineers and scientists.

Trained incapacity results from having learned, both on and off the job, to adapt to the peculiar world of military-oriented activity. Put concisely, the military world is characterized by selling essentially to a single (government) customer, extreme pressure for maximum product performance capability and relatively little attention to cost. The world of civilian production, on the other hand, is characterized by multi-customer markets, attention to good but not extreme performance capability, and very great emphasis on minimizing costs. Whether it is harder or easier to function in one environment or the other is not really the issue—the fact is, it is very different. Retraining and reorientation of managers, engineers and scientists is therefore critical to successful conversion.

There are many cases of military companies in the US trying to produce civilian products without undergoing this retraining/reorientation process so crucial to real conversion. The results were inevitably poor. The most common problems were excessively high cost, product over-design, and the inability of the civilian goods produced to function properly under normal conditions of civilian operation. Interestingly enough, in a recent conversation with a group of analysts from the People's Republic of China, I was told of similar problems there. In particular, it was made clear that attempts to convert military production without retraining/reorientation had encountered serious problems of excessive product cost. There is in fact no reason to suspect that these problems would necessarily be radically different in socialist and market economies. Shifts in centralized economic plans in socialist economies will not cope with the conversion problem any better than the macroeconomic policies available to market economies, for much the same set of reasons.

Macroeconomic policy does, however, have a role to play in successful large-scale conversion. In general policies that stimulate will tend to make the transition easier. Keeping interest rates low, for example, will tend to facilitate the financing of the substantial capital investments likely to be necessary in modifying facilities and equipment. Economic stimulation will also avoid undercutting demand in markets to which military firms are converting. It might not be necessary or wise to stimulate an economy that happens to be in a 'boom' phase when conversion is taking place, but it would still be worth bypassing unduly strong policies of restraint.

The long term economic decay that results from persistent high levels of military expenditure is a direct consequence of the economic burden imposed by large-scale noncontributive use of a society's productive resources. It is superordinate, damaging any economy no matter how it is organized. Likewise, undoing this damage requires basically similar structural shifts in economic systems as different as centrally planned socialism and market capitalism.

5. Conversion as a critical link

The making of constructive social change requires a combination of vision and pragmatism. It begins by looking at the world and seeing, thinking, feeling that something is very wrong. But it is given life when, to paraphrase Robert Kennedy, rather than just asking 'Why?', we construct a vision of how the world should be, how it could be, and ask 'Why not?' The importance of 'the dream' should not be underestimated—it motivates, directs, encourages. Yet it cannot, by itself, create real social change. That also requires a sense of pragmatism, the determination to find practical ways to get there from here. It is not enough to have a vision of the Emerald City; there must also be a workable plan for building the yellow brick road.

Those who advocate conversion are perhaps driven by one or both of two differing, though certainly compatible visions: that of an economic system unburdened of the debilitating effects of excessive military spending, able to make greater strides in improving the material condition of life; and that of a world turned away from an obsession with the means of destruction and coercion, whose talents and energies are directed instead to the nourishment of life and the living. Yet advocacy of economic conversion is very much grounded in practicality.

The pragmatism of conversion has a number of different dimensions. On the one hand, it involves the carefully thought out planning of precisely how to change the product line of a given factory from weapons and related products to some particular good or collection of goods serving civilian markets. The profit potential of various possible alternative products must be evaluated. Specifics of required modifications of plant and equipment, details of workforce retraining/reorientation and a plan for financing all of this must be worked out. Finally, a coordinating schedule for this complex of interconnected conversion activities must be developed and implemented. None of this is very esoteric or visionary.

On the other hand, conversion is a practical political strategy. Advanced planning for conversion should reassure those whose livelihood currently depends on continued funding of military projects that the curtailment or elimination of these activities will not cost them their jobs. Consequently, neither those who directly work in the military sector nor those who live in areas heavily dependent on military spending will feel compelled to equate cutting military spending with cutting their throats economically. This in turn should help to free legislators who must vote on military appropriations from being held hostage to the military budget. Without advanced planning for conversion, voting against military programmes, no matter how poorly conceived or irrelevant to the nation's security, is seen as a vote against jobs. Particularly for those representing militarily dependent districts, political damage, if not political suicide is likely to be the result. Thus, advocacy of conversion is a clear political strategy for removing at least an important part of the internal pressure that keeps the arms race alive.

There is yet another dimension to conversion, more psychological and sociological than political or economic—the issue of empowerment. There is a fundamental difference between the 'shut it down' approach and the conversion approach. Slogans like 'Stop the B1 Bomber', 'Close Rocky Flats' (nuclear weapons plant), have a certain power and simplicity to them. They are clear statements of opposition to the state of things. But they are final; they go no further. Moving from 'Close Rocky Flats' to 'Convert Rocky Flats' does not lose clarity or power, but it immediately opens another whole realm of discussion. For you cannot say 'convert' without raising the question 'convert to what?'

That is an exceedingly powerful question. For while it involves the specifics of new products and alternative civilian uses, it also involves issues of decision making, redirection of national priorities and the ability to influence one's own future. Shall the specific decisions of plant conversion be made by government officials, bureaucrats, plant managers, affected workers or some combination of these? Should funds saved by reductions in military programmes be returned directly to the public through tax cuts, transferred to local governments or used to expand other programmes of the central government? And if they are to be kept within the sphere of government, which programmes should they be used to create or expand?

To the extent that a conversion process is structured to involve a wider public—particularly affected workers and local communities—in the making of these decisions, there is a great potential for breaking through the feelings of helplessness that have become common in complex modern society. There is perhaps no greater affliction of the human spirit, nothing more destructive to the flowering of creativity and the full development of human potential than the self-fulfilling conviction of individual powerlessness. An appropriately structured decentralized conversion process can be a clear and concrete demonstration to ordinary individuals that they can take a hand in directly shaping their own future, and less directly, that of the nation.

6. Varied thought and analysis

Many of the points I have raised here are elaborated in various ways by the contributors to this book. No attempt has been made to be comprehensive or to eliminate differences in perspective, judgement or emphasis. In a sense, each contribution stands by itself and is very much the product of the individual author. Yet taken together, these papers represent a collection of varied thought and analysis focused on a number of critical dimensions of the common theme of conversion that links them to each other.

Michael Renner's contribution explicitly raises the question of 'conversion to what?', presenting his views on the role economic structures play in driving the arms race and the characteristics of a desirable, peaceful economy. Lisa Peattie considers conversion as a political movement addressing the economic base of the international arms race and domestic militarism. Jonathan Feldman's paper looks at the issue of local conversion projects, asking two basic questions: what opportunities and obstacles face non-federal conversion initiatives; and should local conversion advocates push for constraints as well as incentives?

Greg Bischak considers some of the problems of converting the facilities actually involved in the production of nuclear weapons, arguing that detailed planning for conversion of these facilities is prerequisite to effective inspection and verification of potential nuclear disarmament agreements. Robert Krinsky looks at the degree of militarization that has taken place in universities in the United States, the implications of that process for unfettered inquiry and debate, and the nature of the conversion problems it presents. Mario Pianta's paper compares three large-scale high technology projects with sharply different degrees of military/civilian emphasis: the entirely military Strategic Defense Initiative ('Star Wars') programme of the US: the initially civilian but increasingly militarily applicable European 'Eureka' programme; and Japan's completely civilian Human Frontiers Science Program.

Paul Quigley argues that neither the conversion nor the arms trade literature has focused broadly enough to bring out the connections between the internal economic dynamics of military industry and the international flow of arms. Seymour Melman, for all practical purposes the 'father' of economic conversion, analyzes the value of economic conversion law. Finally, Tom Woodhouse, Steve Schofield and Peter Southwood discuss a considerable variety of conversion related developments in the United Kingdom.

The Nordic countries have played an important role in pressing for greater international attention to the advantages and problems of disarmament. In 1977, they officially proposed that the United Nations study the relationship between disarmament and development. Excerpts from the report of that landmark effort, written by a specially designated group of experts chaired by Inga Thorsson, are reprinted here. Following this, Nils Petter Gleditsch, Olav Bjerkholt and Ådne Cappelen present an intriguing case study of the global, national and local dimensions of conversion in Norway. Inga Thorsson follows with a case study of conversion in Sweden.

Nicole Ball then takes a brief look at the reconversion experience that immediately followed World War II, and considers some of the critical differences in the nature of the conversion problem between then and now. Finally, Marek Thee reviews the conversion issue from the perspective of Western Europe, with special attention to trade union concerns and the crucial connection between conversion and disarmament.

In part the purpose of this book is to inform. But perhaps to an even greater extent, its purpose is to encourage, to stimulate more work in this area. For much remains to be done in forging this critical link.

7. The choice between life and death

There is great potential for human betterment in the skills and capabilities of the productive resources now engaged in non-contributive activity in the service of the world's militaries. While the obstacles to productive use of this vast store of resources are not to be underestimated, they can be overcome by a well planned and carefully implemented process of conversion. Such a large pool of newly available labour and capital creates opportunities to pursue a wide variety of social objectives, whether by public or private means.

The possibilities for constructive alternative use of diverted engineers and scientists alone are nearly limitless. Simply reconnecting them with appropriate contributive R&D will revitalize civilian innovation and rebuild cost-offsetting capability, replacing economic deline with the capacity for sustained improvement in the general standard of living. Advances in the technology of pollution control in general and toxic waste treatment in particular would not solve environmental problems, but would certainly help mitigate them. A major R&D effort directed at producing cheap and abundant energy from renewable resources would convey many benefits, economic and otherwise.

Beyond this, revolutionary developments in fields such as electronics, computer science and biotechnology have created exciting new possibilities. A massive infusion of the talents of those engineers and scientists now improving the design of devices for taking life could, for example, be the key to an entirely new generation of devices for giving life—reliable implantable artificial hearts, kidneys and the like, as well as prosthetic devices that could literally let the crippled walk and the blind see.

We are rapidly approaching the last decade of the twentieth century. In many ways this century has been a sad one, one that has seen worldwide economic trauma; more than its share of racism and genocide; in excess of two hundred wars, including the two most destructive wars in human history; and of course the emergence of the growing threat of nuclear self-annihilation. It has also been a century of breathtaking advance in life saving and life enhancing medical technology, of breaking through the boundaries that for all of human history had restrained us to the surface of the planet on which we were born, a century of incredible progress in the technologies of communication and transportation that bind us to each other in one world.

There is only one more decade to finish writing the story of this century. Shall it be the final chapter in the tale of a deeply flawed species whose fear and technical brilliance outran even its instinct for survival? In what remains of this century, there is still time to find the wisdom to change the course of history. It is within our power to make the end of the twentieth century the beginning of a new era. We can choose to make this the first decade of the era in which we began to seek security in our common purpose and common humanity, and finally got down to the business of learning to manage our many conflicts without the constant threat or outbreak of mass organized violence. We can choose to direct our resources away from destructive and toward constructive purposes, and so create unprecedented prosperity to accompany our newfound security. It is literally a choice between life and death, and it is up to us. We can choose life, we must choose life, and I believe we will.

NOTES AND REFERENCES

1. Ruth Leger Sivard, *World Military and Social Expenditures, 1986*, Washington D.C.: World Priorities, 1986, p. 32.
2. See for example R. Bezdek, 'The Economic Impact—Regional and Occupational—of Compensated Shifts in Defense Spending', *The Journal of Regional Science*, Vol. 15, No. 2, 1975.
3. Lloyd J. Dumas, *The Overburdened Economy*, Berkeley: University of California Press, 1986, particularly pp. 52-77.
4. Ibid., particularly pp. 147-183.
5. Ibid., p. 221.
6. Ibid., p. 244.
7. Kenneth E. Boulding, in Foreword to L. J. Dumas, ed., *The Political Economy of Arms Reduction: Reversing Economic Decay*, Boulder: Westview Press and the American Association for the Advancement of Science, 1982, p. xiii.
8. Office of Economic Adjustment, *Summary of Completed Military Base Economic Adjustment Projects: Twenty Years of Civilian Reuse, 1961-1981*, Washington D.C.: The Pentagon, November 1981.
9. The study must be interpreted with some care, since some of the 'conversions' involved military industry taking over parts of former military bases. But on the whole, the results are quite impressive.
10. J. Herbers, 'Cities Find Conversion of Old Military Bases a Boon to Economies', *New York Times*, 26 April 1979.

International Experience of Conversion*

NICOLE BALL

1. The post-World War II experience

It is generally agreed that the most successful and widespread experience with the conversion of resources—financial, material, and human—from the military to the civil sector occurred at the end of World War II. Within a relatively short period, millions of soldiers had been demobilized, defence budgets had been sharply reduced, and many defence-related industries were producing goods for the civil market. In the United States, the first postwar year saw defence expenditure cut by 80% and some 9 million men and women released from the military services (around 14% of the total labour force). Unemployment rose as a result of this demobilization but never reached more than 4% of the labour force. Similarly, the large reduction in the defence sector caused gross national product to shrink, but only slightly as other economic activities replaced much of the economic stimulus which had previously come from the defence sector.

Statistics for the Soviet Union are harder to come by but those that exist suggest that the pattern which obtained in the US and the UK also characterized the Soviet experience. Within one year of the end of the war, millions of members of the armed forces were demobilized and defence outlays were reported to have been cut by over 40%. That this process was not entirely troublefree can be ascertained by the 16% decline in industrial output that occurred during 1946 as factories returned to the production of goods for the civil sector. Nonetheless, production in certain sectors expanded significantly during the first postwar year: 30 times more locomotives, over 20 times more freight cars, and 5 times more harvesters and hydraulic turbines were produced in 1946 than in 1945.

In the Soviet Union, the conversion to a peacetime economy took place under the aegis of the Fourth Five-Year Plan. Soviet figures show that at the end of this plan period in 1950, budget outlays on economic functions had more than doubled while those on defence functions had declined by over one-third.

* Shortened version of 'Conversion outside Sweden' from *In Pursuit of Disarmament— Conversion from military to civil production in Sweden*, Report by Special Expert Inga Thorsson, Vol. 2, Stockholm, 1984. References can be found in the original.

In the United Kingdom, the Government reported that by the end of 1946, some 4.3 million individuals had been demobilized while 3.5 million had been released from the defence-industrial sector. In 1945, unemployment was less than 1% of the labour force. By 1946, it had risen substantially to 5% but two years later it had once again dropped to 1.8%. According to conventional wisdom, postwar conversion in the industrialized market economies occurred more or less by itself, fuelled by demand from the civil market. While demand for civil goods played an important role in the conversion process, the situation was somewhat more complex than this characterization suggests.

It is not sufficient that people *want* to buy goods; they must also have the financial resources to enable purchases to be made. During the war, consumers had built up cash reserves because the emphasis on production for the war effort had left the civil market relatively starved for goods. Once civil-sector production increased in 1946, consumers were not only willing to buy a wide variety of goods; they also had the money to do so.

Another important contributing factor to the generally smooth transition from a wartime to a peacetime economy was that many people who were employed during the war—particularly women but also men beyond retirement age—voluntarily left the labour force once the war was over. For example, in the United States, the number of women employed in nonagricultural jobs dropped by two million between August 1945 and February 1946. Female unemployment, however, increased by only 110,000. In Britain, just over one million women left the labour force between 1945 and 1948 while the number of unemployed females increased by 13,000. Had women chosen to seek work outside the home after World War II in as great numbers as they did during the war, the unemployment statistics of the late 1940s would have looked rather different.

While much of the postwar conversion process was left to the operation of market forces, a number of governmental measures were undertaken to facilitate it. Some of the potential pressure on the labour market was reduced by staggered demobilizations and adult education programmes. Interest rates were reduced to deter saving and encourage investment. Investment was further encouraged by the refunding of excess profits taxes and consumption was encouraged by the reduction of income tax rates. Incentives were offered for the mass production of certain consumer durables. Still, it has been argued that, at least for Great Britain, the most important governmental activity was to channel demand into specific areas; nothing was necessary to sustain demand.

Despite the general success of the post-World War II conversion process, some problems did arise. In the United States, the more traditional industries such as steel, rubber and automobiles which had originally converted from the civil to the military sector to contribute to the war effort experienced relatively few problems in reconverting and taking advantage of the pent-up demand for civil goods which characterized the immediate postwar period. The more specialized firms— particularly the aircraft producers—never really succeeded in converting to the civil market. Different firms attempted to adapt to the civil market in different ways. Some sought to take advantage of their ability to produce light metal products by developing and marketing such diverse items such as buses, trolley cars, marine engines, bottle labellers, dry cleaning machinery, and artificial hands. Other firms became subcontractors for civil-sector firms. On the whole, however, the income from these new ventures was disappointing.

It was the Korean War which saved many of these firms. At the end of the Korean War, the conversion problems were smaller since less of the US economy had been mobilized to contribute to the war effort. In addition, some excess consumer demand had been built up during the years that the war was being fought and tax reductions encouraged consumption even more.

2. Lessons from the past

Comparing the possibility of defence industry conversion in the 1980s with the experiences of the post-World War II and post-Korean War periods, there are two important points to be made. First, conversion undertaken now would not occur with the same relative ease as it did following World War II. The second point is that, despite the differences between the late 1940s/early 1950s and the mid-1980s, conversion is far from an impossible task.

2.1. Why conversion will be more difficult today

The post-World War II and post-Korean War experiences differ in two essential respects from the current situation. The first pertains to the relative state of the economy and the second to the differences between the military and civil sectors of industry.

The economy

One important difference is that the general level of unemployment in the 1980s is much higher than it was at the end of World War II or even the Korean War.

One reason why unemployment remained so low in the late 1940s after large-scale demobilizations and cutbacks in defence production was that consumer demand was extremely strong. Many goods that had been unavailable during the war were again being produced and consumers were using their wartime savings to purchase them. In addition, there was considerable reconstruction work to be carried out in Europe in the former combatant countries. Firms that produced consumer goods were both more or less guaranteed of a market and, at least in the US, not really subject to competition from other industrialized countries.

This points to the necessity of governmental involvement if the conversion process is to be sustained. In the United States, for example, the government could usefully stimulate demand by instituting programmes and letting contracts to deal with urban poverty, the lack of public transport systems, and environmental pollution.

The situation in the Soviet Union and other WTO states may be somewhat different. For one thing, it is likely to be easier to increase the production of consumer goods in these countries. The Soviet Union, for example, is known to have serious shortages of many consumer goods and basic needs such as food and housing. For another thing, economic planning occurs as a matter of course in these countries and there is not the ideological barrier to planning which exists in some of the major Western arms producers.

The nature of the military market and military technology

The second way in which the current situation differs from that of the late 1940s revolves around the degree to which the military and the civilian sectors of industry have diverged from one another over the last 30 years.

Today, a large number of defence contractors resemble the specialized producers of the World War II period in that they were created essentially to serve the defence sector and as such have had little or no experience or producing or marketing non-military goods.

The lack of competition in the defence sector further reduces the ability of arms producers to operate in the civil market. In the United States, nearly two-thirds of all major arms contracts were awarded without any competitive bidding at all.

A final consideration is the degree to which the government assumes a portion of the financial risk involved in producing arms.

A recent survey of electronics firms producing primarily for the military market in Britain identified a number of reasons why these companies believed that they could not succeed in the civil market:

- They were largely lacking in the entrepreneurial skills required.
- The civil time scales were much shorter than those that they were familiar with in their defence work.

- It was difficult in the civil field to get customers to define clearly what they required. If only they would do so and also pay in advance for the associated development costs, the companies would be interested in undertaking the work.
- There was no long-term guarantee of the continuation of the particular class of work.
- They were likely to find themselves in head-on competition with those with a much stronger civil technology base, particularly from Japan.
- Civil and military work could not be mixed because the approach, the standards aimed for, and the relationship with the customer was very different.

For the most part, the civil applications of military technology are not readily evident and the military research and development system is not designed to foster interest in finding possible civil uses for the technology developed in the course of weapons development programmes.

2.2 Conversion is possible

Despite the differences between the current situation and that which obtained at the end of World War II, conversion in the 1980s is far from an impossible task. A good deal of research has been undertaken over the last 25 years which supports the view that military-related production accounts for a relatively small proportion of total production in countries with domestic arms industries and that a decline in such production would not have serious consequences for the economies of these countries. Particular localities and industries where defence production is concentrated would face temporary difficulties but these could be mitigated by adequate planning and compensatory measures (for example, special tax incentives for industries undergoing conversion). There is good reason to believe that in the long run, economies would benefit from the reduction of the military sector since in many cases the same amount of investment produces more jobs in the civil sector than it does in the military sector.

In addition, the release of large numbers of research and development personnel from military-related jobs and their redirection towards socially useful civil-sector goals can only be beneficial.

While conversion would be both possible and beneficial for all national economies, one cannot expect that a decline in defence-related procurement would automatically be translated into a successful expansion of the defence producers into civil markets. Cooperation between government (at the national and the local levels) and defence producers (management and workers) is vital if conversion is to occur with the minimum disruption for all concerned. Because defence technology has become increasingly specialized over the past 30 years and because the current economic situation is more problematic than the situation at the end of World War II, the more advance planning that occurs in conjunction with conversion efforts, the more successful these efforts are likely to be. Despite the need for planning, however, the difficulties associated with conversion should not be exaggerated. Modern industrial economies constantly undergo change and are thus not entirely unequipped to deal with the sorts of transitions implied in the reduction of the output of military industries.

Despite the growing activity at the grassroots level and despite the numerous studies that have been carried out to demonstrate the economic feasibility of defence industry conversion, considerably more work of a political nature must be undertaken if any serious steps towards defence industry conversion are to be made.

Economic Conversion as a Set of Organizing Ideas

LISA R. PEATTIE

1. The arms race perspective

Economic conversion is most frequently thought of as a set of essentially technical projects—implying, of course, associated problems of institutional means and of mobilizing the 'political will' essential to implement solutions.

> Economic conversion from military to civilian economy includes the formulation, planning and execution of organizational, technical, occupational, and economic changes required to turn manufacturing industry, laboratories, training institutions, military bases, and other facilities from military to civilian use.[1]

I propose here to take a somewhat broader view and to think of economic conversion as a political movement which addresses the economic basis of what in international relations is known as 'the arms race' and in domestic politics can be thought of as 'militarism', or more structurally as the 'military-industrial complex' or the 'welfare-warfare State'.

This perspective carries several analytic consequences. In the first place, we have to consider a rather wide range of activities—not only alternative use planning for shipyards and aerospace firms, but organizing around the military budget, and even dissemination of materials which have as their general thrust making military spending look wasteful, greedy, and ridiculous. 'Economic conversion' in its more usual, more technical sense, then becomes one among alternative strategies for a general end, to be compared with those others. In the second place, we will come to recognize the arguments of strategy around specific 'economic conversion' projects, like the work at the Philadelphia shipyard, as particular instances of a deep and important argument in radical thought. Finally, to set 'economic conversion' into this context is to appreciate the magnitude of the task at hand.

Seymour Melman, who has written most extensively on the permanent war economy, points out that

> war making is the single largest industry in the American economy, indeed in the economies of all the industrialized states, and even in the main developing nations.

More than six million people in the United States (including more than a third of the nation's engineers and scientists) and the largest single block of the nation's capital resources are directly engaged in the military economy. Warmaking institutions now dominate the governments and the economies of the main nation-states—certainly of the United States.[2]

Military spending has unique political implications. The management system installed under the Secretary of Defense to manage military procurement and production is, as Melman pointed out more than a decade ago, by far 'the largest and most important single management in the United States', and 'combines peak economic, political and military decision-making'.[3]

In the modern welfare-warfare state, the connection between political and economic power is mediated very directly through military spending. The largest and most technically advanced of the corporations have become directly tied to the military planning apparatus of the State, and as has been recurrently pointed out, in their internal functioning unfit for operating on any other terms. In the military segment of the economy, the terms of competition are not price and efficiency, but grantcraft and lobbying. The standards of design are responsive to a set of criteria present nowhere else outside the arms economy. Thus, the economic institutions most fitted by their size and resources to exercise power in the world become vassals of the military state. Meanwhile, the state itself becomes dependent on the military buildup as the means for inducing compliance and maintaining the existing order. The more that military spending weakens the economy by deficit financing and by diverting human and material resources into the production of military hardware, the more the state feels it necessary to brandish the threat of blowing everybody to bits as a way of showing strength in the world. At the same time, what Mary Kaldor has called the 'imaginary war', the permanent arms race with the Soviet Union and the permanent state of fear, and animosity which goes with it, becomes a way of keeping the citizenry in line. Then, in addition, military production creates vested interests around jobs among the participants. It was not for nothing that MX production was so arranged as to locate some component of the process in every state of the Union.

Finally, like any developed political economy, the political economy of the welfare-warfare state goes along with a set of ideological constructions, and the institutional means for maintaining these, which can serve to make sense of all this and rationalize it to the persons who have to live subject to the system's constraints and penalties. These include not only the ideology of the Cold War and of the 'Evil Empire' of communism, but also glamorizing technical research and development (R&D) for whatever purpose, even mass murder, as 'at the cutting edge' of cultural innovation.

A special sanitized and technical-sounding language is invented to discuss the preparations for Armageddon. Protest which breaks out of the technical framework of planning is seen as 'emotional' and 'value-laden' and therefore hardly worthy of consideration. A movement for economic conversion, thus, is one which attempts to engage central institutional and intellectual arrangements of our society. It should not be surprising to find the task somewhat difficult.

2. Confronting the prevailing political economy

There are also some special factors which make it hard to get a hearing for economic conversion proposals. One is the conceptual apparatus of economics. With painfully few exceptions, contemporary economists persist in treating the production of one kind of product as equivalent to the production of any other kind of product for accounting purposes. Bombs, butter, bridges, and baby bottles are, in the thin air of economics, all part of that great heap of output that we call the Gross National Product.

The second reason is history. From the 1940s people learned to think of military spending as a handy way to get out of economic recession. The fact that the current buildup and the gigantic deficits it brings along bids fair to destroy the civilian industrial capacity of the United States has not been able to undo an idea which comes from this history.

The third reason is everyday experience. The jobs exist. Every day people get paid for working on military contracts and take their paychecks down to the bar and grill or the toy store to bring happiness and prosperity to the rest of society. The argument that we would be better off without the military spending is counter-factual; the paychecks are here and now.

To summarize: efforts at economic conversion, whether they declare themselves openly or not, are confronting the prevailing political economy of the United States. Economic conversion is properly thought of as a political movement—not simply a set of technical or practical problems to be addressed. Part of the political strategy of this particular movement may be to emphasize the technical or practical, but this is itself a strategic choice of presentations in the world of politics.

3. Goals, organizing strategy, vision and forms of action

Political activities have multiple aspects. They have goals: that is, they strive for actual concrete changes in society. They have organizing strategy: that is, they try to create alliances between particular social groups and intensify opposition between others. They have vision: they embody, implicitly or at times quite explicitly, a normative conception of the world, and try, in accordance with this vision, to alter people's interpretations of the world and of the purposes they forward. Finally—and let's not forget this, because it might appear too obvious to notice—they have techniques, specific forms of action: alternative use planning, petitioning, lobbying, conferences, and publishing. These components are fused together into particular campaigns, or more loosely, in what we might call organizing ideas.

Goals, strategy, vision, and technique necessarily interrelate in practice. In a dynamic political movement they should support each other, but the world being as complex as it is, it often happens that they conflict and limit each other. The relationship between any pair of these components is reciprocal. Political ideas are drawn upon to raise the salience and plausibility of proposed changes, and proposals for practical change are used to heighten the relevance and plausibility of particular political visions and ideas. Political ideas and specific action campaigns are brandished like banners to build coalitions between diverse groups; but the experience and interests of the potential coalition members shape and constrain action and vision.

While each of these four components must be present to some degree in any political campaign or broader movement, campaigns and movements certainly vary quite a lot in the relative importance of each. Some segments of the peace movement, for example, are dominated by the projection of vision, and relatively underdeveloped in strategies for organizing particular constituencies. Economic conversion is, I believe, much more developed at the level of goal setting and identification of constituencies to be organized, than it is in the development of specific action techniques which could mobilize the potential constituencies and link their interests and motivations to the achievement of the movement's goals.

4. Delegitimizing the militarized economy

If we think of economic conversion as a political movement, it seems useful to look at it rather broadly, as including a variety of activities, organizations, and published materials which in one way or another focus on the economic aspect of militarism. One item to look at would be the highly successful Cambridge conference on economic conversion in June 1984, which managed to bring together peace movement activists with conversion spokesmen from the labour movement in the United States and Europe. But we would also take note of the *Pentagon Catalog*,[4] a small, exceedingly funny book which dishes up material from a variety of Congressional investigations into an imitation catalogue of parts, displaying the outrageous pricing of military contractors. There are also writings on the 'Iron Triangle' which, in their own deadly serious vein, also try to delegitimize military spending.[5] The 'Employment Research Associates' in Lansing, Michigan, distribute material like Marion Anderson's *The Empty Pork Barrel: Unemployment and the Pentagon Budget*,[6] which argue for economic conversion as a way of generating more jobs, and the Highlander Research and Education Center, an old and highly-regarded centre for movement training, has issued a manual on *How to Research Your Local Military Contractor*[7] as one step in local organizing against militarism. High Technology Professionals for Peace tries to facilitate the rejection of military work by professionals, and the Student Pugwash group at MIT organizes an annual 'Alternative Job Fair'; we might not think of these as efforts at economic conversion, but they do have a role in the spectrum of activities which aim at delegitimizing the militarized economy.

In addition, there are organizations such as the Bay State Center for Economic Conversion in Cambridge, Massachusetts, and the Center for Economic Conversion in Mountain View, California, both of which produce and distribute materials on economic conversion and try to provide support to conversion projects in particular firms and particular cities. Recently there has been organized a group called Local Elected Officials for Social Responsibility (with its seat of office, not surprisingly, in Cambridge, Massachusetts), which proposes to help municipal governments develop programmes 'which can lay the groundwork for a new national consensus—to work for peace and establish budget priorities which will truly strengthen our nation'.[8]

INFACT, an organization formed to mount a boycott campaign against Nestle's, is now mounting a campaign for boycott of General Electric's civilian products to force the corporation to disengage from weapons contracting. The campaign workers, who collect signatures and stimulate postcard writing from ironing boards in front of shopping centres and other public places, believe that through campaigns such as theirs, 'Transnational weapons corporations must be exposed for their key role as the "source of world-wide arms buildup".'[9]

A national Jobs With Peace campaign, which was founded in 1981, currently has strong local chapters in seven cities, and is developing campaigns in over fifteen other localities. It produces educational materials to make clear the local costs of military spending, does voter registration and education, and sponsors some alternative-use projects. Its major tool, however, has been the local referendum demanding a transfer of funds from the military budget into programmes for housing, health, education, and other social needs. In 1982, such resolutions were passed in 42 cities and towns in Massachusetts, 18 in California, and 6 other communities.

The Peace Commission of the City of Cambridge has found it less threatening to business and to local politicians to pursue conversion thinking under the heading of 'diversification planning', and has been approaching Cambridge military contractors on the subject of alternate use plans for their firms. It has summarized these discussions, and some other data, in a pamphlet called *The Cambridge Case for Diversification Planning: Towards Stability in an R&D Economy* (1986).[10]

Meanwhile, there have been a number of efforts to convert particular firms from military to civilian production. The Catholic diocese of Bridgeport, Connecticut, has been trying to mount a conversion study of Electric Boat, manufacturer of the Trident submarine. A Jobs With Peace group organized a conversion study for a shipyard in Philadelphia, and in Quincy, Massachusetts, a group of shipyard workers—a minority faction in the union, unfortunately—joined with a group of activists in the South Shore Conversion Project to promote alternative use planning for the shipyard there.

Legislation to facilitate economic conversion has been introduced in several states and in the Congress nationally. Meanwhile, a rider to the 1985 defence appropriation bill directed the Department of Defense to (1) present a report on the employment impact of a number of military contract programmes, and (2) to indicate the feasibility of creating an Office of Economic Conversion in the Department of Defense. The idea failed to generate necessary support,[11] but let the record show that the Defense Department already has an Office of Economic Adjustment charged with aiding local communities affected by military base closures.

The organizing ideas afloat in this variegated spectrum of enterprises are obviously quite diverse, even in the case of those which use similar techniques. Writings on the 'Iron Triangle', for example, are calculated to appeal to those who have an identification with the peace movement; while it might, in fact, turn out to be the case that the readership of the *Pentagon Catalog* is rather similar, its slant is towards a conception of the audience as taxpayers, who may be outraged at finding themselves the unwitting and even unwilling buyers of grossly overpriced military materiel. 'Alternative use planning' may be put forward as a way of moving towards worker power in the productive process, or as a way of reducing unemployment and 'transition costs' for workers, or as a way of maintaining corporate profits in the face of shifting government spending; one supposes that Pentagon economic adjustment planning is aimed at cooling-out disgruntled contractors who might easily become disgruntled constituents.

5. Three major organizing ideas

Although the general vision of economic conversion, in the broad sense of demilitarizing the economy, lends itself to a variety of approaches, we can distinguish three major organizing ideas. One organizing idea, and that usually meant by the term 'economic conversion', focuses on the economic activities themselves, and seeks to find nonmilitary uses for the firms, technologies, and human skills presently dedicated to the manufacture of weapons. It has, as its central tool, alternative use planning.

A contrasting approach looks not at the multiple firms and activities, but rather at their single source of funding, and proposes to change the Federal budget so as to reduce spending on the military. Its tools are lobbying, education, and organizing, often around citizen-initiated referenda. A somewhat similar view of the target, but with a rather different view of the critical constituency, has as its central theme the long-range damage to the economy from military spending, and hopes, via analysis and education, to persuade the business community to both look for alternative uses for current military enterprise and to reduce military spending in the Federal budget. Its terrain of action is industrial policy and economic planning.

5.1. *Alternative use projects*

There are good reasons why the alternative use projects, like Lucas Aerospace, have constituted the central focus of interest for those concerned with the militarization of the economy. In the first place, they are concrete; they deal with the real problems of real firms, rather than with the counter-factuals of macroeconomic debate. In the second place, for anyone shaped by the intellectual traditions of the Left, they seem to offer a splendid opportunity for peace movement activists to forge a bond with organized labour. Even if the hoped-for Peace/Labour coalition seems a bit slow in getting off the ground, there is still a powerful incentive to pursue alternative use planning as a way of showing the peace movement's good faith with respect to labour and concern for the worker's fear of job loss. Finally, the approach seems to offer a way in to giving Labour a bigger piece of the action in economic planning.

Nevertheless, these projects have their problems. As Schumpeter argued, and as postwar retooling has demonstrated, the flow of resources from one use to another is a normal economic process. But it is quite another thing for any firm to deliberately abandon a good thing, in the form of a military contract, for the production of some other item for which the market is as yet untested. I think it is fair to say that neither labour nor management is at all likely to initiate alternative use planning unless forced to do so by circumstance. The Cambridge Peace Commission's interviews with Cambridge military contractors make it clear how unlikely military contractors are to look for new products and new markets, as long as the Defense Department tap is flowing freely. It is not by chance that major alternative use planning projects currently going on in this country involve shipyards; commercial shipbuilding in the United States is, in effect, dead, and the yards still in operation are competing for a single buyer—the Navy—who might keep them going as they are. The struggle in Quincy is not *whether* to convert; the shipyard, as it was, is finished. It is whether the conversion should be controlled by, and in the interest of, management, which wants to convert to real estate; or of the workers and their allies, who want to make it a continuing source of employment.

In addition, it is by no means easy to manage the difficult politics of alliance between Labour and peace groups on the Left, and with management and government on the Right, in local economic planning. The conversion organizer in a military-dependent plant is likely to find the peace issue an impediment and an embarrassment; thus, we find among such organizers a tough language of material advantage, which seems to disown the very social goals with which the enterprise was begun.

Reviewing the 'alternative use' experience, Gordon Adams, of the Defense Budget Project in Washington, declares tartly that:

> Economic conversion has come to a dead end. While the idea of converting a defense-oriented facility from defense production to a commercial activity is a good one, its realization is impossible as currently framed. . . . It makes little sense for an organizer to approach the toughest target first: those who directly benefit from Pentagon spending. It is hard to imagine a more frustrating strategy, with clear implications for activist 'burnout': no victories, no sense of momentum, and an immovable objective as an organizing target.[12]

Yet this may be taking too narrow a view of the matter. As a single strategy for demilitarizing the economy, alternative use planning seems to have the problems Adams identifies, and as a single strategy, I could not but agree with his analysis. But how about the relationship between the peace movement and organized labour? How about a means by which peace organizing can learn to take seriously, and be seen as taking seriously, people's concerns for their economic security? How about some activities which make concrete the understanding that the way we live is not the only way we could live? For these purposes, the alternative use economic conversion projects still seem to be the best tools we have at hand.

5.2. Focusing on the military budget

The alternative approach of focusing on the military budget is well exemplified by the Jobs With Peace Campaign. Jobs With Peace has been engaged in a certain amount of alternative use planning; in Minnesota, the Campaign built a broad coalition which won agreement from the state legislature to use state resources and funding to develop model economic conversion projects; and in Philadelphia, a Jobs With Peace group has been strongly involved in developing other uses for a shipyard and hospital. But its main organizing focus has been around the military budget, rather than the military firm. Besides producing educational materials comparing the cost of military spending to Federal expenditures on housing, education, and other social needs, the Campaign strives to organize politically the people in cities who are most disadvantaged by budget cuts in Federal programmes, and to lead them to see their own disadvantage as connected with the expanding military budget.

Larry Frank, of the Los Angeles Jobs With Peace, thinks of this organizing enterprise as a 'triangle coalition' around: (1) economic issues of unemployment and service cuts; (2) issues of militarism involving the anti-nuclear and pro-peace groups; and (3) social justice issues around prejudice and racism. In practice, organizing around the military budget in cities seems to involve bringing together a coalition of peace activists with community organizers and social service advocates, somewhat resembling the coalition between social workers and welfare clients which Frances Piven once proposed to bring into being in order to contest against conservative Republicanism.

In contrast to the alternative use planning approach, this kind of organizing around the budget has the advantage of starting with people's direct material interests. Service recipients or would-be service recipients, like the people on the public housing waiting list, share with service providers—teachers, social workers—a clear interest in shifting Federal budgetary priorities. Instead of trying to detach military contractors and workers employed on military work from their Department of Defense contracts, the task is to mobilize the discontent of those for whom the warfare state has failed to deliver the good things of daily life. Municipal government can also be seen as a potential participant in this kind of coalition building against the military budget.

On the other hand, the approach lacks the concreteness of the alternative use conversion projects. It is difficult from the local political system to reach out and get a handle on the Federal budget. The Los Angeles Jobs With Peace Campaign in 1984 registered 50,000 voters, 90% of them from low income, Black, and Latino neighbourhoods, and in city after city, non-binding referenda demanding that federal funds be made available for local jobs by significantly reducing military expenditure have passed by large margins. But when the Los Angeles group explored the possibility of actually taxing the military contracts, the lawyers told them it was unconstitutional to do so, and binding referenda can only demand conversion planning of local government. The local triangle coalition is still far away from the Federal budgetary process. One may simply hope that in due course, the mobilization of local constituencies and perhaps their local governments also, will be reflected in Congressional voting at budget time.

5.3 Demilitarization of the economy

A third approach to economic conversion attempts to launch the demilitarization, or partial demilitarization, of the economy as an idea whose time has arrived via the necessities of sensible economic planning.

Thus one paper addressing the question 'Can Business Become a Participant' in the conversion movement opens:

> Economic conversion has long ceased to be a moral good. From the economic point of view, it is a necessity. The arms race and corporate practice have produced such intensive dysfunctions in industrial operations that the whole business process—indeed the very survival of the industrial system and the basic economic and political arrangements that prevail in American society—have been called into question.[13]

Similarly, Seymour Melman's work argues for economic conversion as a way of making the American economy more competitive internationally, pointing to the much smaller proportion of resources going to military use in Japan as one reason for the nation's striking economic success. The Cambridge Peace Commission's report on 'diversification planning' argues for 'a concept of "national security" which includes factors other than an adequate military defense' and argues that 'a narrow view of "national security" has led to an overinvestment of social resources in the military and has sacrificed investment in other elements basic to our nation's future, such as a strong economy, educational system, and social fabric'. The enterprise has as its main goal: 'Through long range planning, to forestall business failures and job losses that would result from sudden reductions in military contracts flowing to Cambridge businesses'.[14]

This approach to peace is not an altogether novel invention. 'As the peace movement of the opening years of the twentieth century began to quicken and expand', a historian tells us,

> it sought desperately to cast off its reputation for utopianism, moral sentimentalism, and impractical idealism. In order to appeal to a wider audience and seize the opportunities of the new century, its leaders concluded, they must prove their movement to be effective and modern. From the beginning of the century, the peace movement's quest for the image of practicality found its major expression in crusades to enlist the support of businessmen.[15] . . . The arguments which were presented to the businessman, both by business spokesmen and others in the peace movement, served to flatter him, to commend his activities, and to encourage him to calculate his economic self-interest in broad terms. Usually it was assumed that only the economic argument would have impact upon the businessman . . .[16] Accepting it as axiomatic that the businessman harbored a very special hatred of waste, speakers at the peace confer-

ences often seemed to assume that proof of the wastefulness of war would be sufficient to convert businessmen to international arbitration.[17]

For what it is worth, the judgement of the historian just quoted is that all this effort to put forward a specifically business-oriented argument for peace was largely wasted. 'Although businessmen joined the peace organizations in increasing numbers, their participation remained largely passive and their commitment superficial. And the *types* of businessmen who joined peace societies suggest that it was the aura of philanthropic respectability and civic responsibility rather than the specific arguments for business support that had attracted them.'[18]

The argument of this historian seems opposite to the present. One might ask: if the prospect of nuclear annihilation does not motivate people to abandon short-term interests and preoccupations for those revealed by a broader and longer-term perspective, why should the prospect of economic decline lead them to do so? But here, too, an organizing perspective suggests some additional considerations. Galbraith is only the most distinguished of economists to call attention to a contrast in the American economy between large, monopolistic (sometimes called central) firms and competitive sector of smaller (sometimes called peripheral) firms.[19] Military spending may be thought of as an issue which splits the interests of capital: advantageous to the big military contractors, and causing economic damage to the rest. So it is perhaps around military spending that the potential conflicts of interest between different parts of the business world could be exploited.

6. Remaking the military-industrial system

Each of the strategies I have sketched seems to be flawed. In each case, the organizing idea runs up against some basic facts. Alternative use planning requires the people most directly benefiting from military production to pass over that immediate connection of material interest in favour of a longer-term interest in economic security. Organizing those most disadvantaged by the economics of the warfare state appeals to direct material interest, but finds it hard to use that interest to exert pressure on military spending. Getting businessmen to demand a less militarized economy requires people to rise above their immediate individual situations into a broader vision of the general welfare, and to work for that.

This is no doubt discouraging, but we should not find it surprising. Nor should it lead us to abandon the problem. If we think of our task as that of remaking the military-industrial system, or the political economy of the warfare state, we should not be surprised that direct interests, institutions, motivations, even the forms of thinking which are current and respectable, all seem to be linked and to stand in our way. It is these links and this consistency which makes it possible for us to speak of a system. This is the environment within which we have to strategize.

I would guess that in remaking the basic institutions of a society, a variety of strategies, simultaneously pursued, are going to be necessary. There has to be a softening of the enforcement institutions at various points to create a space within which changes can work. There has to be a continual process of redefinition which makes it possible for an organizational change here and there to be understood as an example of some more general process and picked up on by others, discussed, and emulated.

This does not mean, however, that all strategies are equally good. We must go on discussing not simply economic conversion as a goal, but the various possible paths for getting there: not simply putting forward one strategy or another, but looking at the particular problems of making each organizing idea a working reality.

In this search for strategies, economic conversion will present all the old problems of coherent programme versus broadbased coalition, with some particularly tough versions of the choice of constituency: is the issue to be presented as a labour issue, as a peace issue, or as an economic planning issue, relevant to a spectrum from community group to business leadership?

7. Between idealism and realism

Organizing around economic conversion also surfaces an even deeper issue which continually recurs within peace work. This is the debate between idealism (pejoratively called utopianism) and realism (pejoratively called economism). How do we move the world? By getting inside the prevailing institutions which manage it, adopting whatever protective colouration is necessary to do so, or by standing at the margin of the institutions and appealing to an alternative vision of possibility?

A moment's reflection will suggest that neither utopianism nor realism can wholly dominate, and that each needs some of the other. Nevertheless, when we look about us, we see that organizers and theoreticians choose to stress one or the other.

The realists have good reasons, often, to blend in and to downplay concern with larger reform. The Jobs With Peace group working in Philadelphia to plan for the shipyard and naval hospital when the Navy pulls out its contracts have found it necessary to talk a tough-minded language and eschew any mention of peace work in order to sit at the table with businessmen, labour leaders, local government, and the Navy. The state legislators in Massachusetts, who introduced legislation to set up a state conversion planning body, let it be known that they did not want to hear from the peace groups until their more conservative support was thoroughly assured.

Nevertheless, in the continuing struggle and debate between realism and utopianism, I know where my sympathies lie. Vision not grounded in constituency lacks an organizing strategy; it is the exercise of isolated intellectuals. Vision which is not represented in specific forms for action, even if grounded in some organizable constituency, is a kind of collective reverie. But we cannot do without vision. The movements which shape the world need to maintain the vision which links participants to each other in a sense of common purpose and makes action make sense as part of some larger enterprise. The vision which is concealed will soon cease to exist, and activity will dissolve into a set of discrete tasks, and collaboration into temporary alliance for particular transitory ends.

Thinking specifically about economic conversion, Michael Closson, executive director of the Center for Economic Conversion in the Bay area, spoke to this issue in a recent interview.

> The conversion of defense plants remains a valid concern. But it is problematic too. Plant level conversion does not capture the public imagination. It tends to lock proponents into stressing the need to preserve the aerospace behemoths which dominate the defense industry. . . . It tends to equate conversion with job insurance. Not to put that down—but we feel it's critical to have a much broader definition of what conversion means and who can benefit. We believe economic conversion must be broadly defined to include not only the conversion of defense plants, but also the diversification of defense-dependent communities, and the transformation of our overall economy . . . Encompassing both of these is the values issue.[20]

Ken Geiser sees conversion as

> . . . a ready candidate for a common metaphor of action. Conversion connotes transcendence and redirection. Modified by the term economic it takes on a special meaning about changing the conditions under which power and wealth are distributed. Applying economic conversion to plant closings, environmental quality or workplace rights suggests changing the way in which industrial production decisions are made . . . economic conversion presents a positive and constructive approach to otherwise defensive and obstructionist struggles.[21]

If economic conversion is necessary—as I believe it is—those of us who care about doing it will have to struggle, then, with the tension between realism and utopianism, and try to find the settings and the organizing ideas which make it possible to respect the necessities of both.

36   *Lisa R. Peattie*

NOTES AND REFERENCES

1. Seymour Melman, 'Economic Alternatives to the Arms Race: Conversion from Military to Civilian Economy'. In *Materials on Conversion and Reindustrialization: Alternatives to Pentagon Industrial Policy*, 1987, Mimeo, p. 13.
2. Seymour Melman, 'A Road Map, Not a STOP Sign: Politics of Peace.' Mimeo, 25 September 1986, p. 5.
3. Seymour Melman, *Pentagon Capitalism*, New York: McGraw-Hill, 1970.
4. Christopher Cerf and Henry Beard, *The Pentagon Catalog: Ordinary Products at Extraordinary Prices*, New York: Workman Publishing Co., 1986.
5. Gordon Adams, *The Iron Triangle*, New York: Council on Economic Priorities, 1981.
6. Marion Anderson, 'The Empty Pork Barrel: Unemployment and the Pentagon Budget', Lansing, Michigan: Employment Research Associates (pamphlet), n.d.
7. Tom Schlesinger, John Gaventa and Juliet Merifield, 'How to Research Your Local Military Contractor', New Market, Tennessee: Highlander Center (pamphlet), n.d.
8. City Hall Annex, Local Elected Officials for Social Responsibility, 57 Inman Street, Cambridge, Massachusetts (flyer).
9. INFACT, Flyer, n.d.
10. Jeb Brugmann et al., *The Cambridge Case for Diversification Planning: Towards Stability in an R&D Economy*. A Report of the Economic Security Committee of the Cambridge Peace Commission (pamphlet), December 1986.
11. Congressional Record H4963, 30 May 1984.
12. Gordon Adams, 'Economic Conversion Misses the Point', *Bulletin of the Atomic Scientists*, February 1986, pp. 24, 27.
13. John E. Ullman, 'Can Business Become a Participant?' in Suzanne Gordon and Dave McFadden, *Economic Conversion: Revitalizing America's Economy*, Cambridge, Massachusetts: Ballinger Publishing Co., 1984, p. 164.
14. Brugmann, op.cit., p. 1.
15. C. Roland Marchand, *The American Peace Movement and Social Reform: 1898-1918*, Princeton, N.J.: Princeton University Press, 1972, p. 74.
16. Ibid., p. 77.
17. Ibid., p. 80.
18. Ibid., p. 85.
19. Robert T. Averitt, *The Dual Economy: The Dynamics of American Industry*, New York: W. Norton, 1968.
20. 'Closson: Conversion to What?' *New Options*, No. 38, 30 April 1987, p. 3.
21. Ken Geiser, 'Converting Economic Conversion,' in Gordon and McFadden, op.cit., p. 189.

Conversion to a Peaceful Economy: Criteria, Objectives, and Constituencies

MICHAEL G. RENNER

1. Meaning of a peaceful economy

Arguments for a conversion of the military economy to civilian use often focus on the adverse impact of military spending and military-led technological innovation on social well-being. Proponents of conversion also raise questions about the riskiness of excessive community dependence on military contracts, and the general effect of high levels of military spending on the productivity and international competitiveness of the civilian economy. There is less discussion, and less conceptual clarity, about the directions a conversion process ought to take. The broadly accepted formula of 'production of socially useful goods' as a central orientation of conversion is too vague and general to serve as a useful guideline. Local conversion efforts have usually offered a catalogue of alternative goods, based primarily on the locally available skills and industrial base at the facility targeted for conversion. This is the path of least resistance in the sense of minimizing the costs and uncertainties of worker retraining. However, the question 'Conversion to what?' is more concerned with an inquiry into the characteristics and structures of a desirable, peaceful economy, in the first instance, than with alternative individual products.

If we want economic conversion to help us move decisively away from the current war system (and its constituent parts—the warfare state and the war-economy), we must ask the question: What drives the arms race and militarization? Part of the explanation no doubt can be found in the momentum that the arms race has gathered for itself, a self-sustained momentum with little real causal relationship to national security. There is also the bureaucratic imperative to enlarge the state's power and its control over ever larger parts of a nation's wealth. Internationally, powerful states engage in geopolitical rivalries to extend their reach and influence. However, economic structures are an important additional factor. It is incumbent on advocates of economic conversion to trace out the particular economic features and mechanisms that are likely to give rise to or exacerbate conflicts—conflicts that governments are predisposed to 'solve' by military means.

37

A peaceful economy is characterized by more than the (momentary) absence of war and war-related production. It can be called peaceful only in the absence of fundamental social, economic, political, and ecological conflicts; that is, if it is not based on or does not lead to (permanent) conflicts between nations, along ethnic, gender, and class lines, and between humans and their natural environment. Conflict per se is not necessarily undesirable. There is a wide range of depth of conflict, from the fundamental to the more or less surface and transitory. It has been argued that some (benign) conflict is desirable, to the extent that it provides a social dynamic moving society ahead. Another, even more crucial differentiation relates to how (and whether) conflict is solved, with the most important distinction being between violent and non-violent means.

Conflict in the context of this paper, then, stands for fundamental inequities and contradictions, for unsolvable conflict, and for violent conflict resolution. A peaceful economy is one that does not, as a matter of its normal functioning: exploit people (create or aggravate conflicts over wealth-distribution); concentrate decision-making powers in a hierarchical fashion; lead to widespread alienation; rely on non-renewable and non-sustainable production and consumption; lead to rapid resource depletion; produce unnecessary waste; or destroy delicate ecological balances. Economic conversion, most immediately, is concerned with the changeover from military to civilian economy. However, in a broader sense, it is also concerned with the kind of civilian economy to emerge. For to prevent a return to using military means to 'settle' conflicts, it is advisable to prevent those conflicts that arise from fundamental inequities. Economic conversion, then, involves more than just a move away from all things military. It is an essential tool to restructure an economy, to create a more just, equitable, and sustainable society.

In this article, the centralized hierarchical industrial system, in both its private and state-controlled variants, is understood as the archetype of the modern conflict-producing economy. It typifies a social production system driven by the central power-oriented development of the forces of production. The incessant growth of production and consumption is its prevailing objective, often at the expense of human equity and ecological concerns. The centralized hierarchical industrial system produces large surpluses at the disposal of corporate and bureaucratic powers. These institutions, largely unaccountable to the public, may take investment, production, and policy decisions without having to consider the needs and preferences of a particular community or even society at large. Indeed, often the vital interests of communities, and the general enhancement of the *quality* of life—as opposed to the *stan-*

dard of living—conflict with the prerogatives of a central power-oriented system.

A basic feature of the industrial system is its expropriation of people's capability to fulfil their needs in a direct and autonomous manner. Individuals are increasingly split into producers of goods which they do not consume, and consumers of products which they have not produced and over whose design, quality and quantity they have no control. This is due to two main features of the centralized hierarchical production system: the control of the means of production and the size of production units. In the private capitalist system, ownership of the means of production is concentrated in the hands of a few: the top 2% of American families, for example, control between 40 and 50% of all privately held US stocks and bonds;[1] in the state-controlled economies, control is vested in the hands of the state bureaucracy (although the Gorbachev inspired reforms in both the Soviet Union and other Eastern European countries point to a reduction in the degree of centralization). The development of highly specialized, often large-scale production units has discouraged more democratic forms of decision-making within the production sphere.

As autonomous ('use value') qualifications decline in significance, people—and their communities—become more dependent on 'exchange value' qualifications, on the (world) market, and on (centralized) bureaucracies for matters of social regulation. The logic of the industrial system forces people to 'adapt to the rhythm and characteristics of machines, rather than machines being designed to adapt to the rhythm and characteristics of people'.[2] In both the military machine and the industrial system a primary aim has been and still is to reduce an autonomous, creative, and spontaneous human being into an obedient part of the system.

Typically, the same human needs are less well satisfied despite an increasing material output. 'Increased amounts of energy, labour, raw materials, and capital are "consumed" without people being significantly better off. Production becomes more and more destructive and wasteful; the destruction and obsolescence is built into the products . . . Endlessly recreating scarcity in order to recreate inequality and hierarchy, capitalist society gives rise to more unfulfilled needs than it satisfies.'[3]

In the industrial system, perhaps especially in free market capitalism, there are no special penalties attached to the profligate use of natural resources, the incessant and largely unnecessary turnover and variation of products, and the polluting of the environment. There are, conversely, no special benefits attached to the production of durable, reliable, and recyclable goods.

The present economy of advanced industrialism can be characterized as a conflict-producing economy. Its characteristics are:

—an immense demand for resources and therefore high levels of conflict over their possession (or access to them) and over the distribution of economic surpluses derived from production;
—an overriding need for outlets for mass-produced goods and therefore rivalry over export markets;
—high concentrations of centralized power and hierarchical decision-making in large production units;
—expropriation of autonomous capabilities and destruction of skills through mass production and standardization;
—alienation and destitution through structural unemployment (automation);
—destruction of diversity in culture and modes of social and economic activity (production and reproduction);
—high levels of waste and pollution in production and consumption and destruction of ecosystems through planned obsolescence and 'externalization' of environmental costs.

Permanent war preparation, as expressed in the arms race and interventionism, is the symptom of a 'society whose economic relationships are fundamentally based on conflict, exploitation, and violence'.[4] The goals of a peaceful economy go therefore far beyond the mere avoidance of war (violence between and within societies) and the preparations for it. They can be broadly stated in their political, social, economic, and ecological dimensions:

—democratic, cooperative decision-making;
—small-scale, decentralized production;
—enhanced local/regional self-reliance;
—reduced claims on the world's resources and fragile ecosystems;
—low or no waste and environmental pollution (durability, recyclability, sustainability of production and reproduction);
—an awareness of the global consequences of economic activity;
—a diversity of modes of economic activity with an emphasis on freedom *at* work rather than *from* work.

2. The industrial system and the military

In assessing the factors which may contribute to or detract from a peaceful economy, it is useful to take a look first at the relationship between the industrial system and the military—to what extent there has been a convergence of features. Various criteria crucial to the development of the industrial system as we know it today—uniformity, repeatability, predictability, mathematical quantifiability, and command and control features—find their origin at least in part in the requirements of the military system. The emergence of centralized nation-states—their growing size, efficiency, and control over society's taxable wealth—went hand in hand with larger armies and frequent warfare. According to Lewis Mumford, the war machine accelerated the speed of standardization and mass production from the sixteenth century on.[5] It contributed to mechanization by requiring from industry a streamlined work organization and a guarantee of uniform results, i.e., interchangeable parts. Munitions factories in France, Russia, and Sweden in the seventeenth century pioneered a new division of labour in serial (weapons) production. Military performance criteria also led to the development of new materials or products, such as quality steels, or to cite a more recent example, the development of computers in the pursuit of missile precision targeting.

Writing about this relationship in the United States, David Noble has argued that the military has been central to industrial development since the dawn of the Industrial Revolution. In the early nineteenth century:

> the [US Army] performance criteria of uniformity necessitated the establishment of *command* over all productive operations, heretofore relatively autonomous. . . . Uniformity of parts was soon followed by uniformity in housing, in working hours, in shop discipline, presaging the scientific management of the next century. . . . Men left the arms business to set up the machine tool industry and went on from there to carry the principle of uniformity into the manufacture of railroad equipment, sewing machines, pocketwatches, typewriters, agricultural implements, bicycles, and so on.[6]

Most of the large-scale technological projects after World War II, such as nuclear power, developed more or less directly out of military technology.[7] Otto Ullrich concludes that 'today, the modern scientific-technical war machine, the political central power with its state bureaucracy, and the industrial system mutually necessitate each other'.[8]

The industrial system, in turn, has left its imprint on the military system and on warfare. Most directly, the impact has been on weapons technology—the lethality, range, speed, and precision of arms. Since 1945 alone, the range of weapons has increased about 260 times, their destructive power 200 times, and their speed 42 times.[9] Today's weaponry is of a distinctly industrial character: arms are highly complex, 'state-of-the-art' systems, which can only be designed and produced by states with a rather advanced industrial base. These weapons are *systems* in the sense that they involve a complex interplay of components, entail a high degree of complicated technical machinery, and require specialists for their maintenance, repair, and use.

To portray a dialectical relationship between the military and industrial systems does not mean that there are no contradictions between the two. Even if a war was 'beneficial' in the past to capitalist industry in the sense of serving as a 'valve' for over-production and overaccumulation, the tremendous and accelerating lethality of today's weaponry had made major war antithetical to capitalism. War between major industrial powers, even in the absence of the use of nuclear arms, may no longer be survivable. This 'unthinkability' may be a significant reason why the wars of the post-World War II era have almost exclusively taken place in the periphery. Proxy wars and the enormous flow of arms to the Third World have lessened the threat of war to the major industrial powers while still allowing them to maintain their war economies.[10]

Secondly, the military claim on society's resources—in terms of capital, innovative capacities, human skills, and raw materials—has, particularly in the case of the superpowers, but also in a country like Britain, become so tremendous as to undermine not only social and economic well-being, but to sap the functioning of capitalism itself (as evidenced in reduced competitiveness and production competence). There is thus a growing cleavage between society at large whose vitality and viability are being drained by the military and those increasingly parasitic state bureaucracies and private corporations which profit from the perpetuation *ad infinitum* of the military machine.

While the military has historically contributed to the development of light and heavy industry, since at least the beginnings of the nuclear era, a growing divide has evolved between the requirements, goals and principles of the military and civilian industry. The military is guided by its pursuit of a margin of strategic advantage over its foreign rival(s)—military superiority. Particularly in the post-World War II superpower arms race, under the conditions of the Cold War, this aim has reigned supreme. Military production is not bound by considerations of cost; rather, a marginal advantage is sought at all costs. Civilian production, meanwhile, has to be much more sensitive to considerations of cost than military production. In market economies, the commercial competition among private enterprises is primarily waged on grounds of cost advantages (although trends towards monopolization and oligopolization may render such competition obsolete). Despite the lack of market competition, producers in state-controlled economies cannot disavow cost entirely. Serving the broad requirements of the population necessitates a certain degree of cost-effectiveness. In the absence of a viable democratic framework in the state-controlled societies, the authorities derive legitimacy from their ability to provide their populations with goods and services at an affordable price. Recent reform measures and proposals in the Soviet Union and various Eastern European countries have the effect of strengthening cost as a factor to be reckoned with.

Military industry does not conform to criteria of civilian production in either the private capitalist or state-controlled industrial systems. Lavish allocations of capital and resources to the military sector have produced the opposite result: military industry has been characterized by cost maximization rather than cost minimization.[11] This has been due to the enormous research intensity in military industry as well as to the system of 'concurrency' (i.e., the parallel conduct of the otherwise consecutive stages of research, design, testing, redesign, and production). Furthermore, the military product specifications have become exceedingly complex, indeed 'baroque', as Mary Kaldor has coined them. These requirements are increasingly dissonant from, and irrelevant to, those of civilian production. 'Spinoffs' are therefore increasingly unlikely.

3. The role of technology

In evaluating the conditions and requirements for achieving the objectives of a more peaceful economy, we need to look at the role played by the forces of production (choice of technology, use of materials, production system, choice of products, input of energy and raw materials) and the social relations of production (decision-making process, ownership and control, scale, degree of centralization and communal self-reliance).

In traditional Marxist critique, undesirable social, economic, and ecological developments are ascribed to the social relations of production, particularly the forms of ownership and decision-making. The mode and forces of production, on the other hand, were and often still are thought of being 'neutral'; i.e., it is assumed that under changed ownership patterns, certain technologies would lose their harmful effects.[12] Certainly, the relations of production are of crucial importance in determining investment and production decisions and the flow and distribution of wealth within society. Yet it is also true that the choice of technology and of other components of the production system is an outcome of the particular socio-economic order of a society, reflecting its norms, goals, and ideology.

Numerous authors have pointed out the myth that technology is neutral. Kirkpatrick Sale, for example, has said that 'political and economic systems select out of the range of current technology those artifacts that will best satisfy their particular ends, with little regard to whether those artifacts are the most efficient or sophisticated in terms of pure technology'.[13] Similarly, Andre Gorz has argued:

Technology is the matrix in which the distribution of power, the social relations of production, and the hierarchical division of labour are embedded. Societal choices are continually being imposed upon us under the guise of technical choices. These technical choices are rarely the only ones possible, nor are they the most efficient ones. An economic system develops only those technologies that correspond to its logic and which are compatible with its continued domination. It eliminates those technologies which do not strengthen prevailing social relations. . . . The struggle for different technologies is essential to the struggle for a different society.[14]

Therefore, a more democratic, ecologically-minded society may not want to adopt unquestioningly technologies designed and developed in a central power-oriented industrial environment. Consideration must be given to the extent to which certain social relations of production (i.e., those characteristic of an exploitative society) are 'built in' to the technology. One crucial distinction is scale and complexity. Many of modern industrial society's technologies, such as nuclear power, are inherently complex *systems* which necessarily bring with them centralized, hierarchical structures. Certain technologies, then, cannot be governed in a democratic, socially useful, and ecologically sound way, no matter what the pattern of ownership and control. They can only be abolished. On the other hand, there are technologies that are no more than components or building blocks (such as microelectronics), which may or may not be built into systems. The less complex a technology, i.e., the less of an integrated machinery it presupposes, of which human beings are only an attachment, the more adequate it is likely to be for a humane and peaceful society.

Harley Shaiken has commented that:

it is ironic that computers and microelectronics should be used to create a more authoritarian workplace. They could just as easily be deployed to make jobs more creative and increase shop-floor decision-making. . . . Automation can amplify rather than eliminate the unique qualities that only humans can bring to production, seeking to increase efficiency by tapping rather than destroying human creativity.[15]

4. Conflict mechanisms

The accompanying table contrasts the parameters of a peace economy with those of a conflict-producing economy. It presents the two 'extremes' of a continuous spectrum, examining the most important determinants of a social production system. It should be noted that this is a schematic presentation—the reality of a particular economy may not converge with either of the ideal cases.

The workings of the centralized hierarchical industrial system give rise to manifold social, economic, and ecological conflicts. The following is a less than exhaustive discussion of a number of 'conflict mechanisms' which conversion advocates may want to keep in mind when designing a comprehensive alternative to the war system.

(1) The scale and organizational form of productive, reproductive, and regulatory units is of great importance to a peaceful economy. The degree of concentration—of investment and production decisions, and of a society's economic surplus—in the hands of central powers (state bureaucracies, private monopolies) is likely to have an important effect on how peaceful a society is, because a lack of accountability combined with large resources at the disposal of a central power can translate into the creation of a (domestically and internationally) powerful and coercive machinery. A society whose social and economic organization is relatively decentralized, non-hierarchical, and small-scale is likely to produce greater checks and balances on the misuse of power. A viable democracy needs such conditions. Workplace democracy (and democratic decision-making in general) is only a meaningful concept within certain limits of size and complexity, because beyond a certain, optimal range, the use and control of technologies, and the administration and implementation of community affairs increasingly requires a bureaucratized and hierarchical machinery. Andre Gorz has pointed out that:

TABLE 1. *Parameters for a peaceful economy*

Conflict economy		Peaceful economy
Profit Orientation	ECONOMIC DEVELOPMENT/	Social & Economic
Capital	RATIONALITY	Well-being
Accumulation		Equality
Exploitation		
←——→		
Quant. Growth	Q) Who controls the flow & distribution of	Qualitative Growth
Uneven Development	wealth? (distributive, redistributive)	Balanced development
	Q) Is the economy based on exploitative	
	relationships?	
Autocratic	PRODUCTION PROCESS/	Workplace Democracy
Decision-Making	WORK ORGANIZATION	Non-Hierarchical
←——→		
Alienation/De-Skilling	Q) Is the decision-making process	Collective Control
Structural	collective and participatory, or	Creativity
Unemployment	hierarchical?	Job Rotation
Monotonous Work		
Monotechnics	CHOICE OF TECHNOLOGY/	Polytechnics
Mass Production	PRODUCT CHOICE	Batch Production
←——→		
Planned Obsolescence	Q) What technology/materials are used?	Durability
	To what extent do they contribute to	Diversity
	pollution, hazardous work conditions,	
	large-scale production units and	
	hierarchical control?	

High Capital Intensity	CAPITAL INTENSITY	High Labour Intensity
←--------	--------	--------→
	Q) To what extent does the choice of technology increase or decrease capital intensity?	
	Q) To what extent does the choice of technology affect an economy's dependence on imported capital equipment?	

Large-Scale	SCALE/COMPLEXITY	Small-Scale
←--------	--------	--------→
Hierarchy Centralization	Q) To what extent does technology 'necessitate', or contribute to, the large-scale & complexity of productive & reproductive units?	Non-hierarchical Decentralization

Reliance Dependence	WORLD MARKET (INTER-) DEPENDENCE	Self-Reliance Autonomy
←--------	--------	--------→
Subject to Instability & Dissociation Overspecialization	Q) To what extent is the local/regional economy being linked to centres of the global economy? How much local control is there over the nature of that link?	Local Equilibrium & Integration
	Q) Is this link of a beneficial nature or is it a burden on the local economy?	

'Exchange Value' Skills Expropriation of Autonomous Capabilities	SEPARATION OF PRODUCTION & CONSUMPTION	'Use Value' Skills Self-Sufficiency
←--------	--------	--------→
Consumerism & Productionism	Q) To what extent are individuals & communities separated into producers & consumers?	Limited Production & Consumption Cycles

Bureaucratization	SOCIAL REGULATION	Self-Regulation
←--------	--------	--------→
Technocratic Elite	Q) Do the economic structures imply the creation of bureaucracies to implement and supervise the use of technologies?	Participation
	Q) To what extent is formal rationality substituted for substantive moral decision-making?	

Non-Renewable Depletion	RESOURCE USE	Renewable Recyclability
←--------	--------	--------→
Non-Sustainable Growth in Production & Consumption	Q) To what extent does the turnover-time of production & consumption of goods & services increase faster than the turnover-time of the relevant ecosystem?	Sustainable Production & Consumption

Pollution/Waste	ECOLOGICAL IMPACT	Conservation
←————————————————————————————————————→		
Permanent Damage	Q) What is the impact on the local regional, & global ecosystem? Q) How are the goals of the production system tied to the ecological system?	Viability

I am grateful to my colleague Greg Bischak for his collaboration in constructing this table.

> local self-management of centrally-regulated units is an absurdity . . . [It is] meaningless in a concentrated and specialized economy. Self-management presupposes tools capable of being self-managed.
> . . . This is not a question of reverting to the Middle Ages, but of subordinating industrial technologies to the continuing extension of individual and collective autonomy instead of subordinating this autonomy to the continuing extension of industrial technologies.[16]

(2) A strong claim and reliance on a steady flow of raw materials may induce a country to adopt coercive (military and non-military) means to maintain either ownership or unimpeded access to foreign resources. Such concerns will mean that the resource-claiming country will seek to wield considerable and continuous influence over the internal affairs of resource-rich countries. Take oil as an example. From the overthrow of Iranian Prime Minister Mossadegh in 1953 to the creation and buildup of interventionary forces in the 1970s and 1980s, the United States, acting for itself and other Western countries, backed up their claim on foreign oil reserves by coercive means.

The way society structures itself to accomplish certain goals—the production system, public infrastructure, and the choice of technology and materials—sets the parameters for the 'need' for resource input. For example, the spatial structure of much of the United States necessitates motorized travel to accomplish such simple tasks as going to work, shopping, or to engage in practically any kind of social or cultural activity. People are thus unnecessarily reliant on transportation, particularly the least efficient modes (automobiles), and thus impose an 'absolute' need for fuel.[17] Similarly, the design of buildings brings with it certain characteristics that have important resource demand implications.[18] Or, to cite still another example, the choice of materials, such as substitution of many traditional materials by plastics (even though the latter have hardly any qualities that could not be satisfied by the former) requires a much higher energy input.[19]

(3) An economy based on industrial mass production, but without a sufficient domestic market, will seek to secure external markets as outlets in order to achieve higher economies of scale. There is strong competition among the leading industrial powers as they mutually penetrate their home markets and Third World markets with exports. During the heyday of colonialism, the attempt to secure export outlets led the

industrializing powers to forcibly 'open up' markets, introduce commodity relationships, and destroy traditional economic structures and
arrangements. Military force no longer plays a prominent role in this
respect, yet the rise of protectionism, leading to trade wars (over steel,
textiles, semiconductors, and agricultural surpluses, to name just a
few) and increasing political friction among countries, underscores the
continued conflict potential of strong reliance on the world market.

To argue for certain constraints in the degree to which an economy
depends on foreign trade—both in the sense of resource imports and
access to export markets—is not to be equated with a call for autarky.
While it is true that trade between countries holds important benefits,
the *nature* of that trade (particularly the question whether the trade
relationship is balanced), and the *extent* of it (i.e., how dependent an
economy is on imports and/or exports) need to be examined. Trade
relations have evolved over the centuries from an exchange of goods not
available locally, often luxury goods, to a situation today where many
goods are shipped across the globe even though they may well be available in sufficient quantity and comparable quality at the point of destination. A reasonably self-reliant economy would try to supply itself with
at least the essential products (especially food items). Certainly it would
not need to forego the benefits of trade, but it could try to avoid the
problems associated with a strong reliance on the (world) market.

(4) The impact of industrial activity on the natural environment is
another cause for conflicts with rising importance. Pollution has become
so widespread that it can no longer solely be considered a local or
national problem. The heavy use of chlorofluorocarbons (CFCs), for
example, has led to a serious assault on the earth's ozone layer. Ozone
loss affects every individual and every nation without exception, while
measures to protect the ozone layer—reducing and halting the production of CFCs—rest with the industrial producers of a few powerful
countries. If these are unwilling to act, future conflicts are inevitable.
An analogous situation exists with respect to the danger posed by the
'greenhouse effect'. Similarly, confrontations may well arise from the
effects of transboundary air and water pollution (such as the severe
damage caused by acid rain), as a result of careless industrialization.

The Chernobyl disaster—the world's worst nuclear accident to date—
has underscored the destructive potential of certain large-scale technologies. Such technologies are under exclusively national (state or corporate) control, but their effect is truly transnational. They have no
respect for political or any other artificial boundaries. The Chernobyl
accident, with the worldwide recriminations against the Soviet Union
for failing to provide an adequate and timely warning of its impact,
has clearly demonstrated the potential of such incidents for raising
international tensions. To summarize, ecological conflicts arising from

exploitative human activities are likely to dominate future international agendas.

5. Constituencies

Economic conversion is a theme around which various movements for social change might coalesce. Conversion can be a powerful tool with which to advance the agendas and goals of such movements. Conversely, conversion can be strengthened by incorporating the principles advanced by these movements. A few illustrations will help make the point.

To begin with, economic conversion and the peace movement can reinforce each other to overcome the problems of militarization. Conversion planning is needed to prevent a disarmament process from leading to widespread social economic dislocation, such as massive unemployment. According to calculations made by Seymour Melman, in the United States there are some 6.5 million people on payrolls directly funded by the Pentagon.[20] Together with their immediate families, some 20 million Americans depend on Pentagon largesse for their livelihoods. Thus, a conversion process, including retraining of military workers and the lending to them of financial support in the transition period, is clearly needed to implement a reversal of the arms race without creating major social and economic havoc. Conversion also addresses the main concerns of the peace and anti-intervention movements by reducing the power of the war-making institutions.

On the other hand, economic conversion depends on a deliberate disarmament process. If conversion is to be more that just a mechanism to adjust for fluctuations and piecemeal reductions in military spending, then there is a need for strong popular pressure for disarmament. A planned disarmament process taking place in successive stages would enable society to anticipate the availability of capital and other resources for alternative civilian uses.

For those concerned about reversing the decay of the civilian economy (what has come to be called 'de-industrialization' in the United States, but is equally apparent in some other market economies and even more so in the Soviet Union), economic conversion is an essential component of a successful strategy. Conversion will help to free the enormous resources (capital, human talent, innovative capacities, raw materials) now being claimed by the military and to rechannel them into economic reconstruction, repairing deteriorating public infrastructure, and improving living standards. Since 1948, roughly $7.6 trillion (expressed in 1982 dollars) have been spent on the US military, surpassing the quantity of capital resources needed to rebuild the entire United States.[21] Incidentally, an estimated two-thirds of the productive plant and physical infrastructure in the United States, or $4.9 trillion, now requires major reconstruction or renewal, as a result of the accumulated effect of years of neglect and diversion of resources to the military.

Similar problems surely exist in the Soviet Union, although comparable data are not available. The central reason for Mikhail Gorbachev's efforts at *perestroika*, or the restructuring of the Soviet economy, and his attempts to end the superpower arms race can be found in the deleterious effects of large-scale military spending and rigid centralized structures on the economy of the USSR.

The parallel objectives of economic conversion and economic reconstruction—namely, to build a non-destructive, non-alienating, democratically-structured, and environmentally benign economy—suggest that there is an opportunity for coordinated action. Merely to 'reindustrialize'—'rationalizing' industries and plunging into 'high-tech' solutions—is unlikely to deal with a host of problems. For example, even industries on which so many hopes were pinned for sustained growth (like semiconductors and computers) are facing global overcapacities. Furthermore, a favourite ingredient in streamlining declining industries—boosting (labour) productivity— would lead to even higher levels of unemployment. Finally, in the quest to reindustrialize, the environment may be assigned an even lower priority than is the case currently.

The environmental movement has an important contribution to make in this respect. It can develop the guidelines for conversion to a production system that does not sacrifice the environment on the altar of unbridled production and consumption. The environmental movement, in turn, needs an economic conversion policy to succeed in its own endeavours. To begin, a changeover away from the military will reduce and halt the production of nuclear bombs (and thus of radioactive wastes)[22] and of other toxic materials (related to the production of chemical and biological weapons). Moreover, conversion will release much needed resources from the military to clean up the environment.

For labour, economic conversion also holds an important promise: the formation of plant-based alternative use committees entails a stepped-up representation of workers in the decision-making process of a state or privately-owned enterprise and therefore a step toward workplace democracy. A less hierarchical workplace, less hazardous and alienating work conditions, and greater job satisfaction and security are important potential benefits flowing from conversion to a more peaceful economy.

Local communities may look toward conversion planning for an escape from the rollercoaster of military pork barrel politics. In making them less dependent on spending priorities in the national capital or in a corporation's boardroom, conversion can also help advance the goal of a more decentralized economy.[23]

6. A powerful instrument of social change

While in theory the interests and goals of various movements find a common denominator in economic conversion, in practice there has been precious little coordination and congruence. Economic conversion remains yet to be accepted, in some cases even to be 'discovered' as a powerful instrument for social change, even though the concept has been well researched and presented for almost three decades.

Instead of focusing on the *institutions* that design, build, deploy, justify, and use weapons, the peace movement remains largely obsessed with military hardware, particularly opposition to certain weapons such as first-strike systems. This attitude can justly be called 'weaponitis'. In some ways, there is an even more restricted focus on nuclear weapons, which may aptly be called 'nuclearism'. The philosophy of arms control in particular has proven to be a powerful delusion, to the detriment of an understanding of the economic aspects of militarization.[24]

The labour movement, far from being able to take up new initiatives such as conversion, has been thrown on the defensive by layoffs and demands for wage givebacks. Moreover, deeply ingrained in the history and tradition of the labour movement (and its erstwhile political ally, the Social Democratic Party) is a *modus operandi* that is oriented toward competing for central power rather than questioning the power structures and the forces of production as they have developed in the capitalist industrial system. Within the history of the labour movement, there have been currents—such as the cooperative movement, the syndicalists, utopian socialists, and anarchists—which were not interested in competing for central power, but which sought instead alternatives to the centralized, hierarchical, and materialistic characteristics of industrial capitalism.[25] Today, as the social, economic and ecological crises of the industrial system have become ever more apparent, the so-called 'new social movements' have renewed the search for meaningful alternatives. They must be seen as a natural ally of any conversion strategy.

There is another constraining factor. Many local conversion efforts have developed out of 'emergency' situations, where the workforce and community were suddenly faced with a factory or military base closure, with very little time left to work up alternatives. Under such circumstances, the organizing and the discussions usually do not focus on such long-term topics as the particulars of a peaceful economy; rather, the immediate, and often sole, concern is with maintaining jobs, with 'full use' of the facility in question. While this is an understandable concern, the *ad hoc* orientation leads to a short-termism that discourages the development of a programme to deal with the problems of jobs, work organization, ownership and control structures, choice of technology, etc., *before* a new crisis emerges in yet another locality.

Environmental organizations for their part, particularly in the United States, have been preoccupied with the politics of compromise, trying to affect the problem of industrial pollution through instalment of control devices and establishment of 'acceptable' pollution levels, rather than confronting the root causes of pollution, namely the character of the production system, as expressed in its products and production technologies now in vogue.[26]

To the extent that the social change movements are preoccupied with a more or less narrow set of goals, they are a sobering, but accurate reflection of the fragmentation and overspecialization reigning supreme in the capitalist industrial system. The alternative is not to seek a centralization of these movements into a formal structure, but to work for a greater tolerance and awareness of common objectives.

NOTES AND REFERENCES

1. AFL-CIO, *The Polarization of America: The Loss of Good Jobs, Falling Incomes and Rising Inequality*, Washington D.C.: AFL-CIO, Industrial Union Department, 1986, p. 46.
2. Lloyd J. Dumas, *The Conservation Response*, Lexington, Massachusetts: D.C. Heath & Co., 1976, p. 24.
3. Andre Gorz, *Ecology As Politics,* Boston: South End Press, 1980, pp. 23 and 8.
4. Tom Woodhouse, 'To Live Our Lives so as to Take Away the Occasion for War: Some Observations on the Peaceful Economy', in Andrew Rigby, ed., *Articles of Peace*, London: Housemans, 1986, p. 70.
5. Lewis Mumford, *Mythos der Maschine,* Frankfurt: Fischer, 1977, pp. 504–506.
6. David Noble, 'Command Performance: A Perspective on the Social and Economic Consequences of Military Enterprise', in Merritt Roe Smith, *Military Enterprise and Technological Change. Perspectives on the American Experience,* Cambridge, Massachusetts: MIT Press, 1985, pp. 336, 337.
7. Otto Ullrich, *Weltniveau,* Berlin: Rotbuch, 1979, p. 76.
8. Ibid., p. 40.
9. Ruth Leger Sivard, *World Military and Social Expenditures 1985,* Washington D.C.: World Priorities, 1985, p. 6.
10. For a discussion of the significance of arms exports to the aerospace industry, see Paul Quigley's contribution to this book.
11. Seymour Melman, *The Permanent War Economy,* New York: Simon & Schuster, revised edition, 1985, p. 51.
12. Francis Sandbach, *Environment, Ideology and Policy,* Montclair, N.J.: Allanheld, Osmun, 1980, p. 142.
13. Kirkpatrick Sale, *Human Scale,* New York: Coward, McCann & Geoghegan, 1980, p. 161.
14. Gorz, op. cit., p. 19.
15. Harley Shaiken, 'A Technology Bill of Rights', in Shaiken, *Work Transformed. Automation and Labour in the Computer Age*, New York: Holt, Rinehart, and Winston, 1984, pp. 267–269.
16. Gorz, op. cit., pp. 39–40.
17. For an extended discussion, see Michael G. Renner, 'Shaping America's Energy Future', *World Policy Journal,* Vol. 4, No. 3 (Summer 1987).
18. Dumas, op. cit., p. 21.

19. Barry Commoner, *The Poverty of Power,* New York: Bantam Books, 1976, pp. 183–197.
20. Seymour Melman, 'An Economic Alternative to the Arms Race: Conversion from Military to Civilian Economy', Paper presented at Rayburn House Office Building, Washington D.C., 18 November 1986, p. 2. There are 1.1 million civilian Pentagon employees, 2.2 million people in the armed forces, and 3.2 million people employed by Pentagon contractors.
21. The money-valued estimate of the fixed-reproducible, tangible wealth in the United States amounts to $7.3 trillion, Ibid., p. 3.
22. For the problems associated with a conversion of the plutonium factories in the United States, see Greg Bischak's contribution to this book.
23. For a discussion of the obstacles to local conversion initiatives, see Jonathan Feldman's contribution to this book.
24. See Robert Krinsky and Michael Renner, 'The Obstacle of Arms Control to Common Security', Paper for 'Conversion and Reindustrialization. Alternatives to Pentagon Industrial Policy' One Day Conference at Columbia University, 13 June 1987 (Corliss Lamont Program in Economic Conversion).
25. Ullrich, op. cit., p. 19.
26. For a recent critique of the politics of compromise, see Barry Commoner, 'A Reporter at Large. The Environment', *The New Yorker*, 15 June 1987, particularly pp. 66–68.

Swords into Ploughshares: The Quest for Peace and Human Development*

MAREK THEE

1. Conversion, the economy and society

The problem of converting military industries and redeploying resources for socially useful purposes touches on two closely inter-related issues of cardinal importance: the quest for peace and disarmament, and the restructuring of society in line with human values and needs. The issues at stake are political, economic and social. Politically, they are tied to the imperative of disarmament as a crucial precondition for peaceful development. Economically, they address a vast complex of questions pertaining to the role of armaments and the arms industry in worsening today's economic crisis. Socially, they bear upon the rational (or irrational) use of human and material resources and the pursuit of the betterment of the human condition. As far as workers and employees are concerned, conversion has implications for job security, work satisfaction and self-realization.

I should like first to consider the significance of conversion for national economies, laying special stress on the interest of working people and trade unions in the redeployment of resources. I shall next briefly discuss problems of converting the arms industry in Western Europe. Finally, I shall turn to the broader aspects of conversion as part of efforts for disarmament and for the transformation of international relations with a view to human development and a more just economic and political order.

1.1. Investment, growth and employment

It is a truism that armaments and the arms race—apart from their inherent political harmfulness as agents of international tension, violence and war—represent a socio-economic burden on society in general, since arms production is by its very nature a socially unproductive pur-

---

* Updated version of a paper which appeared in *International Labour Review*, Vol. 122, No. 5, September-October 1983, pp. 535-548. Reprinted by permission.

suit. Although it is usually included in the national product, it does not provide socially useful goods or services, neither has it any capacity to raise levels of consumption. On the contrary, in countries with a developed arms industry, it absorbs a large proportion of capital, raw materials and highly qualified human resources, all of which are vital to the civilian economy and the satisfaction of social needs. It is thus a drain on the economy, rather than an asset, competing with the civilian sector and interfering with its development. However, since it is crucially located at the power centre of society, the arms industry is a privileged part of the economy. It commands strong political support from governments and is well shielded by vested socio-political interests. As a rule, it enjoys priority treatment by the authorities, both in sustaining production and in the allocation of resources.[1] So it has a profound influence on the state of the market for goods and services.

An important feature of the arms industry is the fact that it is exceptionally capital-intensive. Armaments production relies on the most sophisticated technology, uses expensive equipment and works with lavish administrative overheads and profit margins. It absorbs the lion's share of the research and development budget.[2] When everything is taken into consideration, investment costs per workplace are far higher in the arms industry than in the civilian sector of the economy.

The armaments industry has a critical bearing on employment, inflation, growth and productivity.[3] Concentration of R&D in military production deprives the civilian economy of a vital impetus to development, and this in turn reduces productivity and growth. While military R&D provides the technological momentum for armaments production, the civilian sector of the economy experiences stagnation. The oft-cited 'spin-off' effects to the civilian economy are insignificant in comparison with the magnitude of military R&D investments. The United States Council on Economic Priorities, in a study comparing the performances of 13 major industrialized countries over the past 20 years, found that countries in which the military sector represented a smaller average share of national economic output 'generally experienced faster growth, greater investment, and higher productivity'.[4] Japan and the Federal Republic of Germany are frequently mentioned as examples of this trend.[5] It is certainly true that the higher the investment in armaments, the lower the growth rate and the efficiency of the civilian economy. This is perceptible in both East and West.[6]

The arms industry has a particularly detrimental effect on employment. First, jobs in arms production are the most expensive in the national economy. Second, by absorbing a huge part of the general investment budget—much larger than the GNP percentage of military expenditures—military production preempts a sound employment policy.[7] Third, by constantly introducing a new technology and higher levels of automation, it generates redundancy. A study undertaken by the International Association of Machinists and Aerospace Workers on the employment situation of its members concludes: 'As the military budget goes up, and procurement contracts rise, machinists' jobs in military industry steadily decline . . . Much of this job loss can be attributed to technological development. As military industries become increasingly capital-intensive, jobs decline.'[8]

Similar conclusions emerge from the recent United Nations study on the relationship between disarmament and development, which notes: 'The job-creating differential between spending $1 billion on the military sector and the same amount on public service employment has been estimated to be roughly about 51,000 jobs in a major industrialized country like the United States.'[9] And further: 'On the key issue of employment, there is . . . persuasive evidence that virtually all possible alternatives to military expenditure and production will result in at least as many, and in most cases more, jobs being created.'[10] Other studies corroborate these findings.

These research results contradict the myth that armaments production serves to generate employment. The argument behind this myth is specious. It is true that arms production provides jobs; yet apart from the high political and economic opportunity costs related to the consequences of the arms race, the employment created by the arms industry is far lower than what could be achieved by comparable investments in the civilian branches of industry or in public services. The claim that cuts in the arms industry may cause unemployment is valid only as long as the authorities show no political will to plan for the redeployment of resources.[11]

1.2. The trade unions

In the light of the above, the interest of the trade unions in conversion should be evident. So broad are the issues involved that conversion, closely related to disarmament, economic recovery and the satisfaction of basic human needs, should become a common concern of governments, employers and employees.

Today's acute economic crisis, amplified and aggravated by the arms race, is most strongly felt by the working people. Armaments escalation and its growing drain on the economy tend to clash with the economic interests of workers and consumers, especially as regards employment and unemployment. But a number of other aspects of special interest to the working population are also involved: the quality of life, human values, moral and ethical issues and the very strain imposed by the balance of terror, which overshadows the deep-felt, visionary longings of working men and women everywhere for peace, welfare and a better future.

Conversion policies are in harmony with basic trade union ideals and efforts for social change. They converge with endeavours to mitigate the consequences of workforce reductions due to technological innovation or international economic competition, through redeployment of resources and finding new jobs for redundant workers.[12] They are also in line with the general trend towards humanization of work, not only from the point of view of general well-being and the quality of the working environment, but also as regards job satisfaction, self-realization and the awareness of being engaged in socially useful production.[13] Finally, conversion policies can meet demands for worker participation in the redirection of resources, converging with the general move towards greater involvement of trade unions and works councils in the decision-making process with a view to safeguarding job security and improving the working conditions of employees.[14]

Of course, conversion is a complex issue. It poses dilemmas to the workforce engaged in military production. Faced with unemployment, arms industry workers may find it difficult to reconcile their opposition to the arms race on social grounds with the immediate economic interest of preserving their jobs. They accordingly adopt an ambivalent stance. In self-justification, they tend to acquiesce without demur in establishment rationalizations of the arms industry as being vital to national security, foreign trade and the balance of payments, or simply as a job-creating factor in the economy. Though in the long run conversion may be a better way of meeting the needs of workers, in the short term it often seems impracticable either because no plans have been made for its implementation or because of the resistance of the state administration and vested interests linked to the military economy. What is needed, perhaps, is greater elucidation of the issues involved. But first and foremost, some material reassurance is required; this can be provided by developing—parallel to fundamental long-term conversion planning to follow full-scale disarmament—anticipatory contingency planning focusing on the immediate needs of particular arms plants facing redundancies. The idea of conversion has to leave the realm of Utopia and become a hard-and-fast policy determining a given line of action.

Efforts to achieve this are still in the embryonic stage. The most prominent recent instance was the mid-1970s Alternative Corporate Plan of the British Lucas Aerospace workers, designed to redeploy resources in response to threatened job cutbacks and layoffs.[15] A combine shop stewards' committee was formed representing the entire staff from different plants of the company, including the engineering staff. After 18 months of work, the committee produced proposals for alternative socially useful products to replace military orders. The Alternative Plan included such products as heat pumps, wind generators, a hybrid road/rail vehicle, a series of robot devices, radar appliances for the blind, etc.[16] Other plants, like Vickers, have followed the Lucas example. Yet such redeployment plans have not been fully implemented, even though almost all the ideas in the original plans turned out to be technically feasible and some have been adopted by firms in other sectors. Resistance from the management side has proved too strong. Workers and managements have disagreed on criteria for assessing products. As pointed out by Mary Kaldor: 'For the management, the criterion is profit. For the workers, the criterion is whether the product satisfies a social need and whether it provides employment at nobody else's expense.'[17]

All the same, the Lucas experience served as a valuable lesson to the trade unions, leaving a deep imprint on their activity. It helped to inspire new thinking and broaden trade union interests beyond wages and working conditions to include general employment issues and production profiles of particular plants. In the light of this experience, the expertise of workers and trade unions in production and management matters has come to command greater respect.[18]

As the United Nations Group of Governmental Experts on the Relationship between Disarmament and Development concludes: 'There is an overwhelming consensus, based on solid experience, that the resources employed for military purposes can . . . be adequately "refashioned" to work effectively toward meeting civilian needs.'[19]

2. The case of Western Europe

Problems of converting the arms industry had long been hotly debated in the United States. The new ideas reached Western Europe in the 1970s, as witness the example quoted above. In comparison with that of the United States, the Western European armaments industry is more vulnerable in that it is more exposed to fluctuations caused by international competition for markets, by technological rivalry or by waves of détente. At the same time, Western European arms manufacturers must strive particularly hard for economies of scale to recover the high costs of military R&D and make production profitable, and must fight for export markets to enable their governments to offset foreign trade deficits and ensure oil supplies. For all these reasons, periodical crises involving employment redundancies are increasingly common. The workforce in the United Kingdom defence sector, for instance, decreased from 963,000 in 1963 to 715,000 in 1978.[20]

Keen competition on the international weapons market has developed, especially between East and West, and even between the NATO countries themselves. In 1982-1986 the shares of world exports of major weapons were as follows: United States 34%, USSR 30.5% France 12.1%, United Kingdom 5.5%, Federal Republic of Germany 4.4% and Italy 2.5%. Thus the four major Western European arms exporters accounted for 24.5% of world trade in major weapons.[21] But there have been significant shifts over recent years. While the share of exports of major weapons to Third World countries of the United States and the Soviet Union fell back from 75.4% in 1971-1975 to 59.2% in 1981-1985, the share of the four major Western European arms exporters increased from 18.6% in 1971-1975 to 28.3% in 1981-1985.[22] At the same time there was also a substantial shift in the share of exports of major weapons to the Third World between the four major Western European arms exporters, as follows:

	1971-75	1981-85
France	7.5%	13.9%
UK	8.5%	5.3%
Italy	1.1%	5.0%
FRG	1.2%	4.1%
Total	18.6%	28.3%

Symptomatic of this competition in weapons exports is the rift between the United States and its Western European allies concerning mutual arms purchases. In recent years the imbalance in the United States—Western European arms trade was already 10 to 1 in the former's favour. It was therefore with bitterness that the Western European NATO countries received the December 1982 United States Congress decision to halt arms imports from Europe altogether. This was especially resented in the Federal Republic of Germany, eager to win NATO markets for its weapons production.[23] This episode is but one of several examples showing how volatile the Western European arms industry is.

Estimates vary concerning the number of employees in arms production in Western Europe, both because of the scarcity of available statistical data and because of uncertainty regarding the numbers indirectly employed by subcontractors in services, etc. One assessment of the workforce engaged in arms production in the four major Western European countries mentioned above, was in 1984 as follows: France 330,000, United Kingdom 315,000, Federal Republic of Germany 240,000 and Italy 60,000.[24]

The arms industry in Western Europe is characterized, inter alia, by the following features:

First, high capital- and skill-intensiveness. We have already seen that the same amount of investment creates far fewer jobs in the armaments industry than it does in the civilian sector. As regards skill-intensiveness in France, for instance, the share of engineers in the total industrial labour force in 1973 was 1.4%, but as high as 7.9% in the military aircraft and shipbuilding industries. For technicians, the corresponding ratio was 4.2 as against 19.8%, and for skilled workers 25.6 as against 42.1%. By contrast, the proportion of unskilled workers was 19.3% in the total industrial workforce, but only 13.4% in the arms industry.[25]

Second, heavy dependence on arms exports, which is justified politically on both economic and national security grounds. As one Western European political leader remarked: 'The [national] armed forces would not have such modern equipment if [our] arms industry had to content itself with the domestic market.'[26] Since this holds good for other countries as well, the natural corollary to such a dynamic arms export policy is its contribution to conflict and wars in the Third World. Most of the wars which have taken place there since the Second World War— estimated at over 130—have been fought with weapons supplied by the industrialized countries, including those of Western Europe.[27] The share of national arms production exported by Western European countries is about 70% in the case of Italy, 50% in the case of France, 42% in the case of the United Kingdom, and 20% in the case of the Federal Republic of Germany.[28]

Third, marked direct or indirect control by the State—the lion's share of the arms industry is actually state-owned[29]—and concentration in a few highly specialized branches of industry such as aerospace, electronics, machine-building, shipbuilding and metalworking. It is also dominated by larger companies: the 463 largest industrial groups in Western Europe with a turnover of more than DM 100 million in 1977 included 55% of arms-producing companies in France, 50% in the Federal Republic of Germany and 40% in both the United Kingdom and Italy.[30] The concentration is, however, more pronounced than these figures suggest, since the bulk of arms production is in even fewer hands: the ten largest companies in each of the above four Western European countries command 37-39% of the total arms production turnover.[31]

Finally, most companies in the arms industry have a diversified production mix: in 1977, out of the 18 largest arms producers in France only four, with a combined workforce of fewer than 60,000, worked exclusively on armaments; the corresponding figures for the United Kingdom were four out of the 25 largest arms producers, accounting for fewer than 40,000 employees; for the Federal Republic of Germany four (out of 30) with a workforce of about 4,000; and for Italy two (out of ten) with over 4,000 employees.

The above situation has various implications for the problem of conversion. On the one hand, the fact that the State controls arms production and that the military-industrial complex exerts considerable influence on the economy may stiffen resistance against the redeployment of resources. On the other hand, given a progressive reduction of tensions and an end to the arms race, this same factor of central control and public ownership may facilitate conversion, especially as regards adapting facilities and equipment to civilian production and retraining some of the specialized labour force for civilian jobs.

We must bear in mind, however, that the prospects for conversion are of a long-term nature, stretching over an extended period of stepwise disarmament. Of immediate concern are plants threatened by employment redundancies, which would be natural first candidates for conversion. Such an approach would not neglect legitimate national defence requirements. Seen as part of an effort to restructure society and international relations within the context of disarmament, it might go hand-in-hand with an explicit shift in strategic concepts and thinking. From confrontation to low-profile defensive deterrence.[32] This would be less material-intensive and less costly. In such circumstances, much of the arms industry would become superfluous.

As an integral part of disarmament measures, conversion should have a salutary effect on Europe, both politically and economically. Given sufficient advance planning and political will, it should also be attainable without excessive difficulties. The rebuilding of Europe after the Second World War can serve as an example of what can be achieved by a concerted planned effort. True, circumstances differ today, since there is no war devastation to repair and no deprivation in urgent need of remedy. All the same, the relatively orderly reconversion of the economy after the Second World War provides telling evidence of the feasibility of redeploying resources. In the United Kingdom alone about 7 million people were demobilized within 16 months and reabsorbed in productive work. What has been done on such a large scale before should certainly be possible in relation to the more modest numbers of employees involved in the arms industry today.

3. The wider perspective

Problems of conversion must be seen in the wider perspective of global transformation from a war economy and a conflict-ridden world towards enduring international peace, security, welfare, and human development. Within this context, given its potential for redirecting development in the wake of disarmament, conversion could be a powerful force ment. Within this context, given its potential for redirecting development in the wake of disarmament, conversion could be a powerful force for relieving tension. Disarmament and development, both equally crucial to genuine peace, have been at the centre of international attention since the Second World War. Numerous plans have been conceived and a number of partial agreements concluded to further disarmament and promote development. Yet we have failed in both. The arms race continues unabated, the world is in the midst of a profound economic crisis, and the disparities between the industrialized and the developing countries are steadily growing.

If any lesson can be drawn from the above, it must be that armaments production and development are inherently incompatible. Development is irreconcilable with the annual expenditure on armaments of material resources at present roughly equivalent to the gross national income of the poorer half of the world's population.[33] No upswing in the global economy is possible without channelling at least part of the resources wasted on armaments to productive ends. Disarmament is essential to the social, economic, and political restructuring of international society. In other words, it is a precondition for genuine development. To make disarmament work to the advantage of development must become the concern of mankind as a whole if economic decay and cataclysmic conflict are to be averted and a new, more just international economic and political order established.

Conversion should therefore not be viewed as a measure to shore up the war economy at critical junctures of falling employment or productivity. Although immediate intervention to alleviate crisis symptoms is essential, we must never lose sight of the general social, political and economic context.

How radical are the changes required for economic recovery and the restructuring of society and international relations? Conservative reformist approaches would counsel caution, with a preference for a step-by-step strategy that would not disturb existing socio-political balances and systems. Others may think differently, reasoning that little can be achieved without such fundamental changes as general and complete disarmament under effective international control—proclaimed as the ultimate objective by the United Nations—and a style of development which, 'besides the need for sustained economic growth, would involve the opportunity and responsibility for full participation in the economic and social processes and a universal share in its benefits as a result of profound economic and social changes in society'.[34]

The need for structural reform is confirmed by studies based on the comparison of scenarios computed using a detailed input-output model of the world economy. Even with reduced rates of growth of military spending throughout the world accompanied by increased transfers of economic aid from rich to poor regions, the poorest regions would not make dramatic advances in their standards of living by the year 2000 in the absence of structural changes in their economies.[35]

Whatever the divergence of views on the scope of transformation needed, we must remain aware of the barriers to change. The centre of gravity again lies in the domain of disarmament. Without distinct advances in disarmament and a freezing of resources, conversion must necessarily remain a chimerical goal.

Barriers to disarmament are largely inherent in the current dynamics of the arms race. This is not the place to go into the subject in detail. However, a general indication of the nature of some of the obstacles to disarmament may help to illustrate the magnitude of the problem.

Mention has already been made of the socio-political forces behind the armaments drive. These are generally identified with what former US President Eisenhower termed, in his farewell address, the 'military industrial complex'.[36] Four segments can be distinguished in this 'web of special interests': the armed forces—in Eisenhower's words 'rarely satisfied with the amounts allocated to them',[37] the armaments industry—always pressing 'for even larger munitions expenditures',[38] the state executive bureaucracy, which relies on armaments as an instrument of policy and diplomacy,[39] and, last, but by no means least, the huge technological establishment involved in military R&D. On a global scale this encompasses half a million of the best-qualified scientists and engineers. It is this segment in particular which has developed vested interests against conversion. Public policy, in Eisenhower's words, is in danger of becoming 'the captive of a scientific-technological élite'.[40]

But apart from the 'almost overpowering influence, . . . economic, political, even spiritual'[41] of the military-industrial-bureaucratic-technological complex in the councils of State and government, the arms race is powered by a technological momentum of its own, inherent in the operation of military R&D. Of special importance are the long gestation periods—10 to 15 years—required to invent, test and produce new weapon systems. This factor invests the armaments race with permanency irrespective of outside political processes and negotiations. Then comes the follow-on imperative—the inevitable urge to develop a defensive system to counteract each new offensive weapon, and vice versa. Finally, there comes the competitive thrust, stimulated by the secrecy surrounding armaments production, which leads to constant over-reaction in the arms race, i.e., responses out of proportion to real challenges. A Frankenstein-like spectre of destruction is being set in motion.[42]

If we do not come to grips with this phenomenon, bring the arms race under social and political control and initiate genuine disarmament measures, large-scale conversion may prove unattainable. Increased awareness of the barriers to disarmament and conversion, and of the dangers involved in allowing the arms race to run its course, should invest efforts at disarmament and conversion with determination and persistence. The stake is our future—indeed, with the nuclear cloud over our heads, the very survival of the human race.

4. Challenge and opportunity

To halt and reverse the arms race—the drift towards nuclear catastrophe—is today the greatest challenge facing humanity. For some people it may seem like reaching for the unattainable. Yet in view of the unpredictable consequences of armaments escalation, resignation is no alternative. We must face the challenge with creative policies for change. Inherent in any predicament are both peril and opportunity. Disarmament offers immense opportunities not only for averting war but also for redeployment of resources and the betterment of the human condition. 'We can state with some confidence', the United Nations Study on the Relationship between Disarmament and Development emphasizes, 'that the stock of useful knowledge and technology in the year 2000 will be immeasurably enlarged if we succeed in diverting to civilian ends a considerable fraction of the funds and manpower now programmed to work in the military field'.[43]

In this context, educational efforts to make the arms race and the operation of the arms industry more clearly understood are particularly important. The first step towards change is to develop an understanding of our predicament, of the policies and structures that plunge us still deeper into the quagmire. Out of this understanding, both commitment and alternative policies for change can grow.

Problems of conversion are an intrinsic part of disarmament. They have their specific aspects which can be rationally discussed in economic and developmental terms. They can also be conceptualized on moral and value-based grounds.

Conversion is not a purely technical issue with solutions that lie exclusively in econometrics and organizational measures. Far more decisive is the socio-political context: human versus military needs; socially useful production versus barren waste; science and technology for human development versus their misuse for destructive purposes; and participatory and democratic working conditions versus hierarchical and authoritarian production structures. Like disarmament, and as its corollary, conversion is an existential and spiritual historical necessity for the advancement of the human race. It is the way of the future, and as such needs careful preparation and planning. Inherent in the nature of modern technology is constant adaptation to change, and conversion is but one aspect of this vitally important transformation. However, planning for conversion has to go beyond technicalities, economic feasibility and alternative production. Reaching out for new human relations must be part and parcel of the plan.

Seen from this perspective, conversion research and planning would need to encompass two main areas: economic and technological aspects, and social theory and value-based philosophical aspects.

The first area of research and planning would rely on analysis of past experiences such as demobilization and reconstruction following the Second World War; on actual cost-benefit calculations; on research into the utilization of equipment, redeployment of military R&D and necessary retraining of the workforce; on identifying economic and social destinations for the use of resources now devoted to armaments; on alternative socially useful products; and on concrete projections—local, regional and national—for the redeployment of resources.[44]

The second field of conversion studies would require in-depth consideration of cultural and socio-political structural implications on the one hand and of preferable futures on the other.[45] The military implications involve such matters as security concepts, alternative defence, the role and organization of the armaments industry, arms control and disarmament strategies, and schemes for the abolition of war. Parallel to this, in the realm of development, conversion studies go hand in hand with the search for alternative development models, with the emphasis on basic human needs versus consumerism and inequitable growth, and with development strategies geared to peace. In the socio-cultural sphere, conversion research would encompass value-compatibility studies, ethical approaches, and questions of autonomy, self-realization, life-styles and social responsibility.

Conversion planning is part of our schemes for the future. It has not yet received the attention it deserves in public debate. Scholars, research institutes, trade unions, political parties and governments should be encouraged to take up the issue as a vital part of disarmament efforts: and the quest for equitable human relations. As the United Nations Study on the Relationship between Disarmament and Development recommends:

> Preparation for conversion should be among the first steps on the road to disarmament . . . Governments [should] create the necessary prerequisites, including preparations, and where appropriate, planning, to facilitate the conversion of resources freed by disarmament measures to civilian purposes, especially to meet urgent economic and social needs, in particular, in the developing countries. One might envisage, inter alia, the creation of a core of people within each country with a significant military establishment with knowledge and expertise on conversion issues; the development of contingency conversion plans by plants engaged in specialized military production; the broad involvement of all affected parties in conversion planning, including management, trade unions and national defence research institutes.

Above all, conversion and redeployment of resources must not be perceived as a disagreeable necessity but as a challenging opportunity for beneficial change.

NOTES AND REFERENCES

1. S. Melman, *Barriers to conversion from military to civilian industry—in market, planned and developing economies*, Report prepared for the United Nations Group of Governmental Experts on the Relationship between Disarmament and Development, 1980, New York (mimeographed).
2. Stockholm International Peace Research Institute, *World armaments and disarmament, SIPRI Yearbook 1981*, Stockholm & London: Taylor & Francis, 1981, p. 7.
3. *Economic and social consequences of the arms race and of military expenditures*, Updated report of the Secretary-General (New York, United Nations, 1978), chapters on 'The arms race in terms of resources' and 'The arms race and economic and social development'. See also R. Huisken, 'Armaments and development' in H. Tuomi and R. Väyrynen, *Militarization and arms production*, London: Croom Helm, 1983; and R. L. Sivard, *World Military and social expenditures 1981*, Leesburg, Virginia; World Priorities, 1981, p. 17.
4. R. de Grasse Jr. and D. Gold, 'Military spending's damage to the economy', in *The New York Times*, 29 December 1982, p. A15.
5. During the period 1960-80 military expenditures amounted to approximately 7% of GNP in the United States, nearly 4% in the Federal Republic of Germany and nearly 1% in Japan; the corresponding annual rate of increase in manufacturing productivity was nearly 3% in the United States, about 5% in the Federal Republic of Germany and over 9% in Japan. See R. L. Sivard, *World military and social expenditures 1982*, Leesburg, Virginia: World Priorities, 1982, p. 23.
6. L. J. Dumas, 'Disarmament and economy in advanced industrialized countries—The US and the USSR', in *Bulletin of Peace Proposals*, Vol. 12, No. 1, 1981, pp. 1–10.
7. S. Melman, 'Inflation and unemployment as products of war economy', ibid., Vol. 9, No. 4, 1978; and R.L. Sivard, *World military and social expenditures 1980*, Leesburg, Virginia: World Priorities, 1980, pp. 14-16.
8. International Metalworkers' Federation, *Metalworkers' unions and the armament industry: An enquiry of the impact of armament production on employment*, Geneva, 1979, p. 13.
9. United Nations, *The relationship between disarmament and development*, Study Series 5, New York, 1982, para. 215.
10. Ibid., para. 289.
11. The numbers of jobs directly or indirectly created by the investment of $1,000 million in various sectors of the United States economy, as given in the Bureau of Labor Statistics, *The structure of the US economy in 1980 and 1985*, Washington D.C., not dated, p. 110, are as follows: military production: 76,000; machinery production: 86,000; administration: 87,000; transport: 92,000; construction: 100,000; health: 139,000; education: 187,000.
12. E. Yemin, ed., *Workforce reductions in undertakings: Policies and measures for the protection of redundant workers in seven industrialized market economy countries*, Geneva: ILO, 1982.
13. ILO, *New forms of work organization*, Geneva, 1979, Vols. 1 and 2.
14. See idem, *Workers' participation in decisions within undertakings*, Geneva, 1981.
15. On the Lucas Aerospace initiative and similar action in Great Britain, see M. Kaldor, 'Workers' initiatives for conversion: Reflections on British experiences', in P. Wallensteen, *Experiences in disarmament*, Department of Peace and Conflict Research, Report No. 19, Uppsala University, 1978; also 'Alternatives to military production and to unemployment', in *Development Dialogue*, No. 1, Uppsala, 1977, pp. 31–33.
16. More details in D. Elliot, 'The Lucas Aerospace Alternative Corporate Plan', in D. Smith, ed., *Military spending and arms cuts: Economic and industrial implications, alternative work for military industries*, London: Richardson Institute for Conflict and Peace Research, 1977; see also I. Sachs, M. Rogalski and C. Yakubovich,

Reflexions sur les strategies de reconversion des industries d'armement, Paris: Ecole des etudes en sciences sociales, 1980, Ch. III: 'L'experience Lucas Aerospace'.

17. M. Kaldor, *The role of technology in industrial development*. Report prepared for the United Nations Group of Governmental Experts on the Relationship between Disarmament and Development, Brighton, 1980 (mimeographed), p. 79.

18. The resurgence of interest in conversion has led to the establishment in the United Kingdom of the Centre for Alternative and Industrial Technology Systems (CAITS) at the North East London Polytechnic; and in the Federal Republic of Germany IG Metall, Europe's largest union, has formed a special working party on armaments, technology and employment consisting of works council members from the most important armament companies.

19. United Nations, *The relationship between disarmament and development*, op. cit., para. 301.

20. D. Pelly, 'Arms conversion and disarmament', in *Chronicle*, London: Dag Hammarskjold Foundation, June 1982, p. 33.

21. *World armaments and disarmament, SIPRI Yearbook 1987*, Oxford: Oxford University Press, 1987, p. 183.

22. M. Brzoska and T. Ohlson, *Arms transfers to the Third World 1971-85*, Stockholm International Peace Research Institute (SIPRI), Oxford: Oxford University Press, 1987, p. 4.

23. See 'Ein Job fur uns', in *Der Spiegel*, 24 January 1983, pp. 107-109.

24. *World armaments and disarmament, SIPRI Yearbook 1986*, Oxford: Oxford University Press, 1986, p. 336.

25. Sachs, Rogalski and Yakubovich, op. cit., p. 61.

26. Quoted in J. Klein, 'Arms sales, development, disarmament', in *Bulletin of Peace Proposals*, Vol. 14, No. 2, 1983.

27. I. Kende, 'Kriege nach 1945—eine empirische Untersuchung', in *Militarpolitik Dokumentation*, Heft 27, 6, Jahrgang 1982.

28. *SIPRI Yearbook 1986*, p. 336

29. Tuomi and Väyrynen, op. cit., pp. 300-306.

30. Brzoska, 'Economic problems . . .', op. cit., p. 70.

31. Ibid., p. 75.

32. See B. V. A. Roling, 'Feasibility of inoffensive deterrence' in *Bulletin of Peace Proposals*, Vol. 9, No. 4, 1978.

33. According to *World Development Report*, Washington D.C.: World Bank, 1980, Table 1 the 'low-income countries', with a population of 1,293.9 million had in 1978 an average per capita GNP of $200: in addition, China, with a population of 932.2 million, had an average GNP of $230. Thus the combined GNPs for a population of 2,186.1 million—over half of the world population in 1978—amounted to just under $478,000 million. At the same time world military expenditures were $439,953 million at 1978 prices and exchange trade (*World armaments and disarmament, SIPRI Yearbook 1980*, Stockholm & London: Taylor & Francis, 1980, Table 1A, p. 19). While the average GNP per capita may have risen in the meantime, so have military expenditures.

34. United Nations, *The Relationship between Disarmament and Development*, op. cit., para. 399.

35. See F. Duchin, *How much development can disarmament buy?*, New York University, 1982.

36. See *Department of State Bulletin*, 6 February 1961.

37. D. D. Eisenhower, *Waging peace, 1956-1961*, New York: Doubleday & Co., 1965, p. 615.

38. Ibid.

39. See B. M. Blechman, S. Kaplan et al, *Force without war: U.S. armed forces as a political instrument*, Washington D.C.: Brookings Institution, 1978; and S. Kaplan et al, *Diplomacy of power: Soviet armed forces as a political instrument*, Washington D.C.: Brookings Institution, 1981.

40. Eisenhower, op. cit., pp. 615-616.

41. See M. Thee, 'Military research and development: impact on society', in K. Berg and K. E. Tranoy, eds., *Research ethics*, New York: Allan R. Liss, Inc., 1983.
42. United Nations, *The relationship between disarmament and development*, op. cit., para. 152.
43. See N. P. Gleditsch, O. Bjerkholt, Å. Cappelen and K. Moum, 'The economic effects of conversion: A case study of Norway', in Tuomi and Väyrynen, op. cit., pp. 225-258.
44. See J. Oberg, 'Is the conversion idea to be converted?', ibid., p. 289–299.
45. United Nations, *The relationship between disarmament and development*, op. cit., recommendation 5, p. 168.

II. Economic Conversion in the United States

Arms Exports: The Stop-gap Alternative to Pentagon Contracts?

PAUL QUIGLEY

1. Excess production and weapon exports

The parallel discussions of economic conversion and international arms transfers have to date been unnecessarily narrow in their focus. In the case of the conversion literature, much attention has been paid to the national budget priorities of the country in which conversion is being considered without sufficient regard for the fact that modern military contractors generally do not exclusively supply the host government. For example, in 1984, corporations such as McDonnell Douglas, General Dynamics and Boeing were all exporting over 10% of their military production from the United States.[1] In the case of European military industry, this proportion is generally higher. Alternatively, in much of the literature on the causes and effects of international arms transfers, explanations are generally cast in terms of strategic and political motives while little or no reference is made to the internal economic dynamics of the supplying industry. This is an attempt to broaden both analyzes and explore the links between these two areas of concern.

A number of writers have referred to the propensity of military industry in the United States to use export sales contracts as a way of providing a 'stop-gap' solution to problems created by reduced Pentagon procurement.[2] While this is generally cited as being one of the motives behind the increase in military exports from the US in the mid-1970s, little has been written on how concretely excess capacity might translate into export orders and the implications of this for future levels of military production and weapons exports.[3]

To the extent that US military-industrial corporations are able to manipulate the demand for weapons imports for foreign governments and use this demand to fill excess production capacity generated by short-falls in domestic demand, then any attempt at conversion in the US requires attention to simultaneous restraint of weapons exports. Aside from a general unwillingness on the part of the managers of military industry to explore unfamiliar civilian markets, if they can argue that the inherent insecurity of reliance on domestic military orders can be compensated by an access to a complementary foreign market, then that intransigence is reinforced.

This discussion is an attempt to explore these two assertions—that vacant capacity leads to arms exports and that this phenomenon forms an obstacle to conversion—as they apply to the aircraft industry in the United States.

In formulating what might be a successful strategy to facilitate the movement away from military production in the US, an important component must be a close examination of what has been and what is at present the response of the controllers of military industry to declining military budgets. For the purposes of analyzing possible responses, it is beneficial to view military industry as a system of production units rather than what might be thought of as 'paper corporations'. Some of these production units will be nominally autonomous, while others will form one part of a larger corporation. The reason for making this distinction is that it prevents misleading references to conglomerates as being 'diversified' when within these corporations the individual (and usually spacially separated) production units are ordinarily oriented to either military or civilian markets. In this context, there are three main domestic options facing military-industrial managers upon learning that weapons contracts to a particular production unit will terminate or decline:

  (i) A mobilization of political support (representatives in Congress, trade unions, employer associations, etc.) for continued funding of military contracts to a particular production unit.

  (ii) An effort to diversify and/or convert production within the unit under consideration towards serving civilian markets.

  (iii) Contraction or complete closure of a unit, with the associated disposal of assets and lay-offs of employees.

The possibility of exporting the products of a particular military production unit thus opens up a fourth alternative path that further distracts attention from planning for conversion. Furthermore, if the pattern of substitution of export for domestic orders has had any substance in past reality, then it obviously has implications for the present day. The unbridled expansion in US military production initiated under the Carter Administration is now anticipated to level off and perhaps even decline towards the end of the decade, due partly to the restrictions imposed by Gramm-Rudman-Hollings budget-balancing legislation. Although it is unlikely that this will result in a repetition of the drastic across-the-board reductions experienced after World War II or the Vietnam War, it will nevertheless cause some contractors to experience a loss of demand.

In exploring the activities of military-supplying corporations with respect to not only the US Government but also other national governments, the discussion here will inevitably have some bearing on the debate concerning the relative autonomy of these corporations. In practice, whether the military-industrial-complex model or alternatively the state-managed military bureaucracy model reflects the American situation more accurately, this relatively new international dimension must be taken into account.

First, the evidence that military experts from the US in the 1970s were in part a response to the decline in the level of Pentagon contracts will be examined. This discussion is supported by analysis of production figures for the aircraft industry in numbers of units. Using numbers of units in place of dollar values in the analysis yields greater comparability between acceptances to US forces and deliveries to foreign governments. The latter part of the analysis will outline three case studies from the recent past in order to reveal some of the mechanisms which might relate the level of domestic demand for weapons to the level of military exports.

2. US military aircraft production and exports since 1944

The first major decline in military procurement of aircraft which took place in the United States was in the two years after the peak of wartime production in 1944. In the calendar year of 1944 over 95,000 units were delivered to US forces, while just two years later, military production had fallen by 95% to just 2,000 units. During the same period, however, production for civilian markets had increased from zero to an annual figure of some 37,000 units.[4]

While these statistics are of little direct relevance as a scenario for conversion of the aircraft industry of the 1980s, they serve to illustrate the magnitude of change that once occurred. It is quite clear that while a large portion of the production capacity available in 1944 was disposed of at the end of hostilities, a substantial portion of capacity was simultaneously converted or reconverted to serve new civilian markets. At this time arms transfers had a very marginal industrial impact. In the period between the end of World War II and the outbreak of war in Korea (a period which saw the establishment of NATO, and the passage of the Mutual Defense Assistance Act), arms transfers remained at a low level. It seems that the options (ii) and (iii) outlined above were those generally taken by military industry in 1945.

The decade of the 1950s marked the beginning of the Cold War and high levels of 'peacetime' military spending in the US. During this period the international transfer of military equipment, which took place predominantly through the Military Assistance Program, was at a generally higher level than previously. The principal recipients of

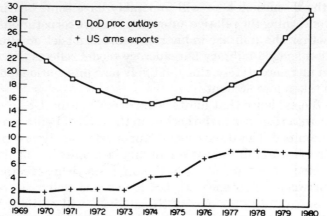

FIGURE 1. Comparison between DoD procurement outlays and US arms exports.

Horizontal axis: US Federal Government fiscal years, 1969-1980.
Vertical axis: Billions of current US dollars, 0-30.
Sources: DoD Procurement Outlays:
US Department of Defense Office of the Assistant Secretary of Defense (Comptroller), *National Defense Budget Estimates for FY 1988/1989,* May 1987, pp. 102-103.

Value of US Arms Exports:
US Department of Defense Security Assistance Agency, *Fiscal Year Series,* Data Management Division, Comptroller, DSAA, As of 30 September 1986, pp. 2-3. (N.B. Data shown include deliveries through the Foreign Military Sales, and Military Assistance Programs (including sales under section 506 of the Foreign Assistance Act) and commercial export deliveries. FY76 includes transitional quarter (FY77).)

US military exports during this early period of 'containment' were the countries of Western Europe.

In the early 1960s a military sales agency was established in the Department of Defense (DoD) which assisted in marketing US weapons overseas. The establishment of this institution accompanied a shift away from viewing arms transfers as military assistance, towards an emphasis on their commercial benefits to the supplier. The increases which resulted, however, were derived from a greater level of military exports to industrialized rather than underdeveloped countries.

While some industrial demobilization had taken place after the Korean War, the only sustained decrease in US military spending after 1945 occurred in the period between the peak created by US involvement in Indochina in 1969 and the low in federal expenditure for military purposes in the mid-1970s. This reduction was only a fraction of that experienced in 1945, but, over a period of seven years, nevertheless removed $92 billion (in 1988 dollars) from the Department of Defense budget authority of 1968, a figure which represented one-third of the budget at that time.[5]

What then was the apparent effect of this decline in weapons procurement by the Federal Government on the flow of military export deliver-

FIGURE 2. US military aircraft production (number of aircraft).

Horizontal axis: Calendar years, 1968-1983.
Vertical axis: Deliveries in thousands of aircraft, 0-2.6.

Source: *Aerospace Facts and Figures* (Washington, D.C.: Aerospace Industries Association of America, 1986/87), p. 31. (1968 figures taken from 1982/83 edition, p. 34.)

ies from the US? Figure 1 compares the level of DoD procurement outlays with that of the value of Foreign Military Sales (FMS) and Military Assistance Program (MAP) deliveries for the decade of the 1970s. This period includes the post-Vietnam decline in domestic procurement and the start of the present build-up. It appears from these data that the value of FMS/MAP deliveries remained more or less constant during the decline in procurement which took place between 1969 and 1972, then export deliveries increased concurrently with domestic procurement from 1974 to 1978. These data then suggest that changes in the level of arms exports either continued independently of the level of domestic military production or that the two variables have a positive relationship. But this is less than conclusive: firstly no allowance is made for any lead or lag effect, and secondly, the general trends indicated here may conceal more specific, while still substantial, contradictory trends. Hence it is necessary to analyze this relationship at a more disaggregated level.

The aircraft industry is at the centre of the war economy of the United States. It has, in the last decade, consistently been the recipient of more than 30% of the value of DoD prime contract awards to business in the US for major hard goods. Furthermore, in the years since 1980 it has taken an increasingly large portion of this category of expenditure.[6] At least for the Third World, aircraft are one of the more widely imported types of military equipment. This industry therefore forms the logical point of disaggregation in attempting to explore the nature of the relationship between military production for domestic and foreign markets.

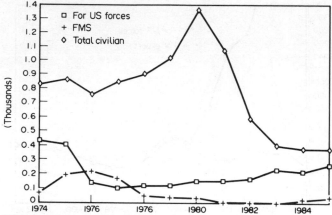

FIGURE 3. US helicopter production.

Horizontal axis: Calendar years, 1974-1985.
Vertical axis: Number of aircraft delivered in thousands, 0-1.4.

(N.B. Only sales through the US Foreign Military Sales Program are included. Exports made through other channels are not included.)

Source: Compiled from AIA data. See *Aerospace Facts and Figures* (Washington D.C.: Aerospace Industries Association). Annual.

Figure 2 shows the extent of production of military aircraft in the US for both markets during the period 1968-1983. Again, while the reduction in the domestic market in terms of units produced is over-shadowed by what took place in 1944-46, in absolute terms the cutback was substantial. At the peak of production in 1968, an annual figure of 4,440 military aircraft were produced for US forces while nine years later in 1977, only 454 were produced. This evidence does point to a slight compensatory effect in the relationship between the two trends. Figures 3 and 4 also indicate the same effect in the disaggregated production figures for domestic and foreign military sales programmes in the fighter aircraft and helicopter sectors respectively.

It might be argued that a representative picture of what took place in the industry cannot be achieved without some illustration of the concurrent levels of production for civilian markets. In the case of fighter aircraft, however, production can be viewed as largely continuing independently of the civilian sector. In other words, unlike the transition which took place in 1945, the divergent course of military and civilian industrial sectors had, by the 1970s, prohibited any easy transfer between markets.

It might also be argued that these figures tell us little about the actual amount of vacant production capacity in the aircraft industry, and in that respect reveal little about the relationship between vacant capacity and the pressure for exports. While there is little doubt that most of the capacity used to service the needs of the Vietnam War was in some way

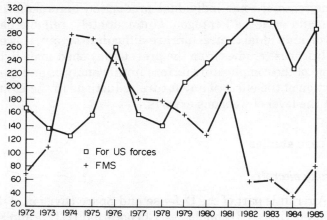

FIGURE 4. US fighter aircraft production.
Horizontal axis: Calendar years, 1972-1985.
Vertical axis: Number of aircraft delivered, 20-320.

(N.B. Only sales through the US Foreign Military Sales Program are included. Exports made through other channels are not included. Fighter is defined here as any military aircraft given the designation 'F' by US forces.)

Source: Compiled from AIA data. See *Aerospace Facts and Figures* (Washington D.C.: Aerospace Industries Association). Annual.

disposed of, the thesis here is that, at a time of declining domestic demand, exporting military aircraft was preferable from the point of view of military and industrial managers to closing or converting a facility.

While the data in Figures 1 to 4 reveal to some extent the domestic context in which production for export took place, any explanation of the increase in weapons transfers must of course take into account external factors. One such effect was the US defeat in Vietnam which precipitated a change of policy under the Nixon Administration towards the replacement of US troops based abroad by arms sales as a mechanism for enforcing US hegemony. A further important external effect was the oil boom of the mid-1970s which increased the demand for imports, especially among Middle Eastern states.

While we were able to draw preliminary, tentative conclusions from the data in Figures 1 to 4, this investigation leaves some important questions unanswered. For example, were the production units which suffered from a loss of demand from the US forces the same ones which benefited from receipt of export orders? If so, was it coincidental that the demand for weapons overseas increased as domestic demand fell away, or did the corporations involved and government agencies play some part in influencing the timing, nature and scale of purchases by foreign governments?

We might answer some of these questions through the examination of the experience of some individual production units suffering from loss of demand from the Pentagon. Unfortunately, reliable data from the 1970s on individual contractors are difficult to obtain. However, the following brief case studies from the present day shed some light. They reveal some of the complicating factors in this analysis and may assist the prediction of the effect of any future reductions in the US military budget on the level of weapons exports.

3. Some case studies

3.1 Sikorsky aircraft

Sikorsky Aircraft is part of the Defense and Space Division of the massive US-based United Technologies Corporation (UTC) and employs approximately 12,000 people at two plants in Stratford and Bridgeport in southwest Connecticut.[7] In 1986, Sikorsky sales totalled $1.6 billion and this accounted for 10% of total UTC sales for that period.[8] Sales to the US government, considered here to be essentially military, generally account for around 30% of UTC sales.[9]

The Black Hawk combat assault transport helicopter and derivatives of it, such as the Sea Hawk naval helicopter, have been Sikorsky's main product line over the last few years. However, procurement of the Black Hawk reached a peak in 1982 when $638 million was authorized in the annual Department of Defense budget for the purchase of 97 such helicopters and has since been in decline.[10] For the six years 1980 to 1985 Congress authorized the procurement of an average of 89 Black Hawks per year while for the period 1986 to 1989 this figure is expected to be only 73.[11]

There is no doubt that at an early stage the corporate managers of UTC and Sikorsky were aware of this imminent decline and were formulating strategies to maintain revenues and profits. There is also little doubt that an expansion into foreign markets was one of the strategies under consideration. Soon after appropriations for the Black Hawk started to decline, the corporation's annual report revealed the success of this strategy by commenting: 'In 1983 effective overseas marketing efforts resulted in Sikorsky's first foreign orders for Black Hawks and the militarized version of the commercial S-76.' Robert Zircone, President of Sikorsky, is quoted in 1985 as commenting: 'We expect to expand our international sales significantly in the years ahead . . . We plan to expand our presence internationally through joint ventures, or in some cases by the creation of new companies'.[12]

It appears that this plan was fulfilled in several ways. As early as 1984, United Technologies had been accused of using the influence of former Secretary of State Alexander Haig, who was then consultant to the corporation, to sell helicopters, including Black Hawks, to the governments of the Philippines and Taiwan. Whatever Haig's role in the sales, UTC was successful in concluding an agreement to sell Black Hawks to the government of the Philippines.[13] Similarly the European market has been the target for Sikorsky sales through the newly established minority share in Westland, the British helicopter manufacturer and military contractor.

However, this particular strategy appears until now to have been less successful in terms of gaining work for either Westland or Sikorsky's operations in Connecticut. Nevertheless, since US procurement of Black Hawks started to decline in 1982, Sikorsky has received orders for 42 such helicopters from seven countries.[14] The ability of UTC to actively create the demand for these products is unclear from this evidence, but one indication of the importance in which the international promotion of UTC products is regarded might be the election in 1984 of Rupert Murdoch, the Chief Executive of the News Corporation media conglomerate, onto the board of UTC.

3.2. McDonnell Douglas helicopters

The McDonnell Douglas Helicopter Company forms one part of the combat aircraft operations of McDonnell Douglas Corporation, the largest military contractor in the US. Sales for this category amounted to $6 billion in 1986, 47% of total McDonnell Douglas sales.[15] In 1982, McDonnell Douglas shifted a large part of its helicopter production facilities, which were formerly owned by Hughes, from Culver City in California to a newly constructed plant in Mesa, Arizona. This move was undertaken to accommodate the expanding production of the AH-64 Apache attack helicopter for the US Army. At the beginning of 1987 around 7,000 people were employed at these two plants with 5,000 at the new facility at Mesa.

In the 1970s, development of the AH-64 took place in the light of an anticipated purchase by the Army of over 1,200 Apaches. By 1978, however, this figure had been reduced to less than 600. At the end of fiscal year 1986 the US Administration announced unexpectedly that budget restrictions meant that there would be no new orders for Apaches after 1988 and that the final number purchased would be 593.

This left the management of McDonnell Douglas Helicopters and the Army with a problem. The company had invested $328 million in the new factory, including the construction of a 570,000 square foot assembly and test centre for the Apache. Although helicopter production other than the Apache programme might continue, about 3,000 of the 5,000 employees at the Arizona facility were engaged in building 12 Apaches a month and an estimated five to seven year gap would be left between the last Apache delivery and the start of the next substantial military production programme, the Light Helicopter Experimental (LHX).

McDonnell Douglas commented in its 1986 annual report: 'MDC believes that there is a strong case for continued Apache production and is presenting that case to the appropriate decision-makers while also pursuing export opportunities'. The second of these strategies was also at the forefront of comments by the company in the local press: 'We are pushing the Army to help us sell overseas . . . and they could be tremendously helpful there'.[16] At this writing the Israeli and Dutch Governments had already been identified as potential customers for the Apache abroad.[17]

3.3. Fairchild Republic

The Fairchild Republic Company, located at Farmingdale on Long Island, New York, is a subsidiary of Fairchild Industries, a multi-divisional corporation operating primarily in the aerospace, communications and electronics industries. Fairchild Industries sales totalled $643 million in 1986 and it employed a total workforce of 11,230.[18] In 1986 Fairchild Republic accounted for over 30% of this workforce with 3,500 employees.[19]

In July 1982 Fairchild Republic was awarded a contract by the Air Force for the development and production of two T.46A jet trainer aircraft. The contract included options for a further purchase of up to 65 aircraft.[20] However, less than a year after the first complete T.46A was unveiled on Long Island in February 1985, the US Administration announced that due to 'numerous management and production deficiencies' and the prevailing budget restrictions the programme would be discontinued. The programme was described in the press as 'the Pentagon's first victim of the Gramm-Rudman-Hollings deficit-reduction law'.[21]

Again, as in the case of Sikorsky and McDonnell Douglas, the Fairchild Republic plant had neglected to maintain a diversity in operations which might have provided more security under these conditions. While the plant had been engaged in a number of product lines within the aircraft industry, including major subcontracts for Boeing, Lockheed and the Swedish aircraft manufacturer Saab, in 1986 1,400 of the 3,500 jobs at the plant were directly related to research and production on the T.46A.[22]

The first reaction of the company to the imminent discontinuation of funding for T.46A production appears to have been to seek political support for continuation of the contract amongst the local delegation to Congress together with potential allies in the 31 states which were the locations for 280 subcontractors to Fairchild Republic. Perhaps as a political lever in this struggle, the company was frequently quoted as anticipating receiving several billion dollars in revenues if the T.46A programme were to continue, the major part of which was expected to come from foreign sales. However, a number of factors, including the opposition of the influential Republican Senator Robert Dole from Kansas (which is the location of Cessna, a competing trainer manufacturer) and the lack of commitment from Fairchild Industries corporate headquarters to continued production on Long Island, combined in 1987 to ensure that funding from the Air Force for the T.46A was indeed terminated. Fairchild Republic was closed as a result. This meant that not only did the revenues to Fairchild from domestic and foreign sales of the T.46A fail to materialize, but with the exception of a few hundred, all of the 3,500 employees at the plant were expected to be made redundant.

4. Conclusion

It seems that in some cases the decline in demand from the Pentagon may precipitate a higher level of exports of particular weapons systems through increased corporate marketing efforts, sanctioned if not supported by the Federal Government. However, the exceptions to this, such as the case of Fairchild Republic, require that a more complex explanation is constructed. Some of the factors which might contribute to this explanation are:

(i) *Prenotification.* As in the case of conversion to civilian production, the ability to conclude export sales will depend on the length of the period of prenotification. Thus while Sikorsky was able to plan and organize over a period of years, McDonnell Douglas and Fairchild were not given the advantage of the same time period in order to mount their sales effort.

(ii) *Use of Product by US Forces.* If a product which is offered to foreign governments is already in service with the US military it is more likely to be sold abroad, since the provision of spare parts and services are then guaranteed. An illustration of this might be the inability of Fairchild to market the T.46A abroad without the patronage of the US Air Force.

(iii) *Nature of Product.* Especially expensive or sophisticated weapons systems such as the Apache helicopter will generally have relatively smaller overseas markets.

(iv) *International Influence of Corporation.* The ability of a corporation to market its product abroad will depend to some extent on the previous level of its exports and its influence in foreign markets. Thus United Technologies and McDonnell Douglas, corporations with considerable experience in and familiarity with markets outside the US, would be expected to experience less difficulty selling military equipment abroad than a corporation such as Fairchild.

(v) *Government Support for Export.* Export of a weapon system will generally not be possible without government sanction. This in turn might be motivated by political factors as well as economic/ strategic considerations such as the desire to keep production lines open and maintain a 'warm' military-industrial base.

(vi) *Demand for Import.* Variations in the ability of importing countries to finance weapons purchases will necessarily influence the ability to export. In this regard the increasing indebtedness of the developing countries may serve to inhibit a large expansion of the international market such as that which took place in the 1970s.

(vii) *International Competition.* The increasing number of countries able to supply arms will generally reduce market shares. The US has however so far been able to maintain its market shares in the face of this new competition.[23]

(viii) *Influence in Congress.* Congressional support for a weapons programme may prevent its purchase being discontinued and thus reduce the likelihood of aggressive marketing abroad.

In the context of declining domestic US orders of military equipment, if we consider there to be some level of trade-off between the amount of conversion which takes place and the level of arms exports, there may be additional influences on the level of weapons transfers. Generally these might be conceived as comprising an index of 'convertibility'. Specifically, while in 1945 a large measure of conversion was possible within the aircraft industry, the skills and resources required for military production have become increasingly divergent and irrelevant to what is required for civilian manufacturing. This point might be emphasized in the minds of the corporate managers of the military aircraft industry by the failure of 'diversification' efforts which were formulated to address the post-Vietnam decline. Lockheed, Rockwell, Northrop and Boeing were some of the contractors involved in this experience.[24] Secondly, de-industrialization and the flight of production from the US must have serious negative effects on the ability to facilitate conversion, as without a civilian manufacturing skill and resource base, conversion will have less to build on. These factors lead to the conclusion that, since conversion is becoming more difficult, military exports will be more likely in times of reducing domestic military procurement.

Smith et al. have suggested that in general the relationship between domestic military procurement and exports may be contradictory and they later conclude that for the US, domestic military expenditure depresses arms exports.[25] To the extent that the analysis here reinforces the idea that the decline in US procurement expenditure in the early 1970s contributed to the increase in military exports, it concurs with the conclusion that the two variables had a negative relationship at that time. With regard to the discussion of possible ways of controlling the level of international arms transfers, this analysis supports the view of Brzoska and Ohlson that it is the primary task of supplying countries to facilitate reductions in arms production.[26] This must be taken to mean not simply reductions in procurement, which leave production capacity intact, but also an effort to attend to the transitional problems in the move from military to civilian production.

As we have seen, reductions in procurement may contribute to increases in arms exports. Yet, export production, in so far as it is a solution from the point of view of military industry, is unreliable. Military orders from foreign governments are ultimately as insecure, if not more so, than those from the host. Thus if economic security is to be achieved in US industry, a long-term focus on preparing to serve civilian markets seems a far more reliable strategy.

NOTES AND REFERENCES

1. See *Aviation Week and Space Technology*, 13 May 1985, p. 67; Paul L. Ferrari et al., *US Arms Exports*, Washington D.C.: Investor Responsibility Research Center, 1987, pp. 302-303.
2. See Michael Klare, *American Arms Supermarket*, Austin, Texas: University of Texas Press, 1984, p. 33; Seymour Melman, *The Permanent War Economy*, New York: Simon & Schuster, 1974, p. 269; Roger Labrie et al., *US Arms Sales and Policy*, Washington D.C.: American Enterprise Institute, 1982, p. 72; Jacques Gansler, *The Defense Industry*, Cambridge, Massachusetts: MIT Press, 1980, p. 171.
3. A notable exception to this is the analysis of the relationship between arms exports and military expenditure in supplier countries which appears in Ron Smith, Anthony Humm and Jacques Fontanel, 'The Economics of Exporting Arms', *Journal of Peace Research*, Vol. 2, No. 3, 1985.
4. See *Aerospace Facts and Figures*, Washington D.C.: Aerospace Industries Association of America, 1964, p. 25.
5. See US Department of Defense, *National Defense Budget Estimates for FY1988-1989*, May 1987, p. 98. 'Billion' in this context is taken to be one thousand million.
6. See US Department of Defense, *Prime Contract Awards*, Fiscal Year 1985, pp. 25-28. For FY1985, Electronics and Communications Equipment forms the next largest category after Aircraft, followed by Missiles and Space Systems.
7. See Robert Waters, 'Cutback Plan Worries Sikorsky', *Hartfort Courant*, 28 August 1985, p. A15.
8. See United Technologies Corporation, *Annual Report*, 1986.
9. Ibid.
10. See Defense Budget Project, *Defense Spending in the 1980s: Analytical Tables and Graphs*, Washington D.C.: Center on Budget and Policy Priorities, 31 March 1986.
11. See US Secretary of Defense Annual Reports to Congress.
12. See United Technologies Corporation, *Annual Report*, 1985.
13. See Howard Kurtz, 'Critics Claim Haig's Influence Boosted Copter Maker Unfairly', *Washington Post*, 12 February 1984.

14. See Paul Ferrari, op.cit.
15. See McDonnell Douglas Corporation, *Annual Report*, 1986.
16. See 'McDonnell Douglas Fighting to Save Helicopter Project', *Arizona Business Gazette*, Vol. 87, No. 25, Section 1, P. 1a, 16 February 1987.
17. Ibid. See also Len Farmiglietti, 'McDonnell Douglas Hoping for Dutch Apache Buy,' *Janes Defence Weekly*, 25 April 1987.
18. See Fairchild Industries, *Annual Report*, 1986.
19. See Elizabeth Tucker, 'Fairchild Threatens to Close Unit if Trainer Isn't Funded,' *Washington Post*, 4 March 1986.
20. US General Accounting Office, *Aircraft Procurement: Development and Production Issues Concerning the T-46A Aircraft*, May 1986.
21. See Michael Weisskopf, 'Flak Follows Air Force Trainer Project', *Washington Post*, 4 March 1986.
22. See Elizabeth Tucker, op.cit.
23. See Michael Brzoska and Thomas Ohlson, 'The Future of Arms Transfers: The Changing Pattern', *Bulletin of Peace Proposals*, Vol. 16, No. 2, 1985, p. 131.
24. See Mark Clayton, 'For Contractors, a Retreat but not a Rout in Pentagon Spending', *Christian Science Monitor*, 12 January 1987.
25. See Ron Smith et al., op.cit.
26. See Michael Brzoska and Thomas Ohlson, op.cit.

Swords and Sheepskins: Militarization of Higher Education in the United States and Prospects of its Conversion

ROBERT KRINSKY

1. Introduction: the military and academia

Colleges and universities in America are the central institutions for organizing, evaluating, and transmitting knowledge. The principal bases for the academy's legitimation in society and its claim to a significant portion of public resources can be ascribed to the following tenets: (1) access to knowledge is a foundation of democracy, (2) education is essential for sharing in the economic benefits of the society, (3) academic institutions are vital contributors to the development of technologies and methods for improving the material welfare of the community, and (4) the academy is an institutional space for unfettered inquiry of fundamental aspects of the structure and operation of society. Regarding the latter point, Noam Chomsky has observed that, 'the university will be able to make its contribution to a free society only to the extent that it overcomes the temptation to conform unthinkingly to the prevailing ideology and the existing patterns of power and privilege'.[1]

The tacit social contract between academia and society which encompasses the aforementioned tenets is not being honoured in full measure either by the federal government, academic administrators, or the corporate partners of academia. The following conditions are indicative of the crisis in the American academy: dramatic re-allocation of federal funds from civilian to military-oriented research and development projects, broad acceptance of this situation by university administrators, arrangements between university administrators and corporations which cede to the latter party an unprecedented degree of exclusive access to university resources, and the increase in litigation brought by professors contending that they were punished with the denial of tenure because of their pursuit of critical inquiry in their scholarship.

This paper considers breaches in the social contract between academia and society. Particular focus is given to the militarization of higher education. Three central questions are addressed: To what extent have

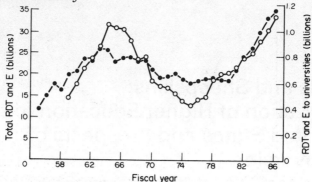

FIGURE 1. Historical trend in total RDT&E funding (dark point, left-hand vertical) for FY55-86 and in RDT&E funding at universities (open points, right-hand vertical scale) for FY59-86. Both shown in constant FY87 dollars.

colleges and universities been militarized? What are the effects on the process and direction of inquiry? What are the points of leverage both inside and outside academic institutions for accomplishing the reconstruction of academia in a manner that will foster thought, debate and action towards development of more equitable social relations of power in society?

The emergence of sustained close relations between the military and academia occurred concomitantly with the rise of the United States as the dominant economic, political and military power in the aftermath of World War II. In 1946, General Dwight Eisenhower, Army Chief of Staff, sent a memorandum to senior officials of the War Department on the subject of 'Scientific and Technical Resources as Military Assets' in which he stated:

> The lessons of the last war are clear. The military efforts required for victory threw upon the Army an unprecedented range of responsibilities, many of which were effectively discharged only through the invaluable assistance supplied by our cumulative resources in the natural and social sciences . . . Their understanding of the Army's needs made possible the highest degree of cooperation. This pattern of integration must be translated into a peacetime counterpart . . .[2]

In that same year the Office of Naval Research (ONR) was established by the US Congress as the first federal agency to contract for basic research. ONR immediately received $40 million in unspent wartime project money.[3] Shortly thereafter came the establishment of the Army Research Office (ARO) in 1951, the Air Force Office of Scientific Research (AFOSR) in 1952, and the Defense Advanced Research Projects Agency (DARPA) in 1958.[4]

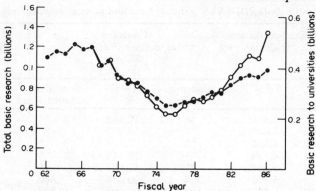

FIGURE 2. Historical trend in total basic research (6.1) funding (dark points, left-hand vertical scale) for FY62-86 and in basic research funding at universities (open points, right-hand vertical scale). Both shown in constant FY87 dollars.

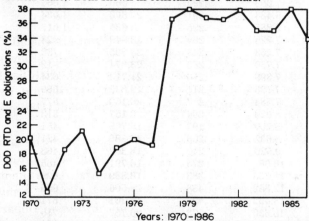

FIGURE 3. The growth in advanced applied R&D at US universities and colleges.

Source: Derived from data presented in US DoD, *The Department of Defense Report on the University Role in Defense Research and Development* (Washington D.C.: The Pentagon), April 1987.

2. The case of the natural and physical sciences

Over the 26 year period from 1960 to 1986, Department of Defense (DoD) obligations to academic institutions for research, development, testing and evaluation (RDT&E) totalled $20 billion (constant 1987 dollars). In 1986, funding levels reached their zenith at the $1.11 billion level (see Figure 1 and Table 1).

The DoD RDT&E budget category is comprised of six sequenced components: 6.1 activity supports investigations in the nature of basic processes and phenomena, 6.2 is exploratory development, 6.3 concerns advanced development, 6.4 addresses engineering development, and 6.5 includes management and support of R&D activities. The balance of R&D programmes is allocated to operational systems development.[5]

TABLE 1. *DoD RDT&E obligations: total and to academic institutions*

Fiscal year	Current dollars (billions)		Constant dollars (FY87 billions)		Percent of RDT&E to academic institutions
	Total	to academic institutions	Total	to academic institutions	
1955	2.621	**	12.142	**	
1956	3.539	**	15.029	**	
1957	4.381	**	17.524	**	
1958	4.159	**	16.311	**	
1959	5.144	**	19.639	**	
1960	5.476	.154	20.636	.580	2.8%
1961	6.366	.191	23.593	.708	3.0%
1962	6.269	.208	23.279	.772	3.3%
1963	7.028	.237	25.848	.872	3.4%
1964	7.053	.292	25.666	1.063	4.1%
1965	6.433	.291	22.866	1.034	4.5%
1966	6.885	.295	23.635	1.013	4.3%
1967	7.225	.280	23.949	.928	3.9%
1968	7.263	.244	23.305	.783	3.4%
1969	7.730	.263	23.874	.812	3.4%
1970	7.399	.216	21.710	.634	2.9%
1971	7.123	.211	19.895	.589	3.0%
1972	7.584	.217	20.160	.577	2.9%
1973	8.020	.204	20.157	.513	2.5%
1974	8.200	.197	18.768	.451	2.4%
1975	8.632	.203	17.888	.421	2.4%
1976	9.520	.240	18.362	.463	2.5%
1977	10.585	.273	18.791	.485	2.6%
1978	11.503	.383	18.889	.629	3.3%
1979	12.362	.438	18.506	.656	3.5%
1980	13.492	.495	18.301	.671	3.7%
1981	16.630	.573	20.757	.715	3.4%
1982	20.070	.664	23.674	.783	3.3%
1983	22.829	.724	25.966	.823	3.2%
1984	26.862	.830	29.474	.911	3.1%
1985	30.571	.940	32.489	.999	3.1%
1986	33.676	1.074	34.803	1.110	3.2%

Source: US DoD, *The Department of Defense Report on the University Role in Defense Research and Development for the Committees on Appropriations United States Congress* (Washington D.C.: The Pentagon), April 1987.

** Reliable data for these years not available.

Categories 6.1 and 6.2 taken together are regarded by the DoD as the 'technology base'.[6] Historically, this has been the predominant area of academia's involvement in military R&D. Though 6.1 funding is regarded as basic research it is noted by Dr. Jimmie Suttle, formerly DoD Assistant Director for Research and Advanced Technology in the first Reagan Administration, that such projects are selected in view of their 'potential relationship to the DoD mission'.[7] Suttle explains, 'When a 6.1 program is successfully completed the results often lead to a 6.2 program to explore the use of the proven concept in a device for military use'.[8]

TABLE 2. *DoD basic research (6.1) obligations: total and to academic institutions*

Fiscal year	Current dollars (billions)		Constant dollars (FY87 billions)		Percent of 6.1 to academic institutions
	Total	to academic institutions	Total	to academic institutions	
1962	.292	**	1.083	**	
1963	.313	**	1.150	**	
1964	.310	**	1.129	**	
1965	.347	**	1.234	**	
1966	.341	**	1.171	**	
1967	.362	**	1.201	**	
1968	.318	**	1.021	**	
1969	.353	**	1.091	**	
1970	.323	.127	.948	.373	39.3%
1971	.318	.130	.889	.363	40.8%
1972	.328	.130	.872	.346	39.7%
1973	.304	.115	.764	.288	37.7%
1974	.303	.106	.693	.243	35.1%
1975	.305	.106	.633	.219	34.6%
1976	.328	.112	.632	.216	34.2%
1977	.373	.142	.662	.252	38.0%
1978	.413	.168	.678	.276	40.7%
1979	.475	.179	.711	.268	37.7%
1980	.553	.208	.750	.283	37.7%
1981	.615	.244	.767	.305	39.8%
1982	.697	.305	.822	.360	43.8%
1983	.786	.360	.894	.410	45.8%
1984	.842	.405	.924	.445	48.1%
1985	.852	.409	.902	.434	48.0%
1986	.954	.520	.986	.537	54.5%

Source: US DoD, *The Department of Defense Report on the University Role in Defense Research and Development for the Committees on Appropriations United States Congress* (Washington D.C.: The Pentagon), April 1987.

** Reliable data for these years not available.

The DoD nearly doubled the level of technology base R&D obligations in real terms to academia between 1976 and 1986. In 1980, academia's share of total obligations for 6.1 began a steep increase from 39.8% to 54.5% in 1986 (see Figure 2 and Table 2).[9] Fluctuations in the percentage of total 6.2 obligations to academic institutions have been less dramatic over this period, but in real terms the amount of money has increased by a considerable 40% above the 1980 level to $198 million in 1986.[10]

TABLE 3. *The growth in DoD advanced applied R&D at US universities &*
colleges 1970-1986

Year	Share of DoD R&D to universities & colleges
1970	20.2%
1971	12.7%
1972	18.5%
1973	21.2%
1974	15.3%
1975	18.8%
1976	20.0%
1977	19.2%
1978	36.6%
1979	38.0%
1980	36.8%
1981	36.6%
1982	37.8%
1983	35.0%
1984	35.0%
1985	38.0%
1986	33.8%

Source: Computed from data provided in
US DoD *The Department of Defense Report
on the University Role in Defense Research
and Development* (Washington D.C.: The
Pentagon), April 1987, pp. 7, 10.

In order to fully understand the pattern of increasing academic involvement with DoD research and the extent to which this is dramatically influencing the character of the R&D agenda at colleges and universities, it is essential to consider the changing composition of DoD RDT&E obligations. While 6.1 and 6.2 funds collectively compromise more than 60% of RDT&E funds obligated to colleges and universities on an annual basis throughout the period 1978-1986, this is a sharp decline from the levels ranging between 78% to 88% annually from 1970 to 1977.[11] The converse of this decline is the dramatic increase in the percentage of advanced applied research (see Figure 3). This pattern is likely to persist due to such programmes as the Strategic Defense Initiative (SDI). All funding to academia from the SDI Innovative Science and Technology Office (ISTO) is categorized as 6.3 funding.[12] SDI funding to academic institutions grew more than five-fold in real terms from $24.7 million in 1985 to $133.4 million in 1986 and has maintained its high level in 1987 at $101.3 million (all figures expressed in constant 1982 dollars).[13]

Though it is beyond the scope of this paper to delve deeply into the composition of military-related R&D funding to academic institutions from the Department of Energy (DoE) and the National Aeronautics and Space Administration (NASA) it is noted that these are significant funding sources servicing the military. Aggregate DoE appropriations for weapons spending more than doubled from $3.6 billion when President Reagan assumed office in 1981 to $7.6 billion in 1987. Over this period weapons programmes accelerated from 38% of the DoE budget to 65% with the 1988 budget request of $8.1 billion. Meanwhile, requested appropriations for energy conservation (including weatherization for low-income households, schools and hospitals) in 1988 are 89% lower than 1981. Appropriation requests for solar energy and other renewable fuels are 88% lower than appropriations granted in 1981.[14]

Similarly, estimates of the level of militarization at NASA during the Reagan Administration range from 50% to 90%.[15] 'Events make it plain that military men . . . are increasingly calling the shots in the U.S. space program', reports the *Wall Street Journal*.[16] Reagan's National Space Policy gives the DoD priority access to the shuttle—the design of which was heavily influenced by military requirements. Prior to the space shuttle accident, 34% of shuttle payloads through 1994 were scheduled for military commitments.[17] The consequent backlog due to the shuttle crash is likely to cause a dramatic increase in this commitment if and when the shuttle ascends again.

Finally, the National Science Foundation (NSF) is increasingly being leveraged for military purposes through such joint efforts as the NSF-DARPA-ONR support for advanced computer architectures at Princeton University. In what seems to be a bid to ensure significant NSF funding, Eric Bloch, director of NSF, recently asserted to Congress, 'We should have joint support of some of the new science and technology centers in the president's competitiveness initiative. NSF has taken the lead, but other agencies, especially in Defense, should be involved'.[18]

The pattern of DoD RTD&E funding to academic institutions traces significant political acts by both the executive office of the president and executives of academic institutions. Funding obligations rose and were sustained at relatively high levels through the massive missile build-up and the escalation of the US Government's aggression against Vietnam during the administrations of presidents John Kennedy and Lyndon Johnson. When President Nixon further escalated the US war on Vietnam, a crescendo of opposition on college campuses across the country caused the contraction of university-military funding. Academic senates adopted policies prohibiting secret research. In 1970, the US Congress enacted the 'Mansfield Amendment' (Section 203 of the 1970 DoD Authorization Act), which further curtailed relations by restricting R&D to 'a specific military function or operation'.[19] DoD obligations to academic institutions dropped 22% (constant 1987 dollars) in 1970 from the previous year, and by 1975 obligations had plummeted by 48% below the 1969 level.[20]

The nadir in DoD-academia relations lasted through the middle of

President Carter's Administration. At that time Carter began to accelerate a wide variety of military programmes. In 1978, Carter directed the formation of a special working group to review the policies and practices of the DoD research policy. The so-called Galt Committee cited the importance of access to university resources in a manner echoing the observations of Eisenhower in 1946:

> The DoD has supported basic research for decades, and it must continue to do so if it is to pursue its overall national defense objectives at the highest possible level of effectiveness, and insight. There are three fundamental reasons. Many of the known technological problems stem from gaps in knowledge which only basic research can fill. Basic research is a source of new concepts which introduce major changes in technological and operational capability. And finally, it is a source of insight for DoD-policymakers and others in evaluating and reacting to the possibilities inherent in technical proposals and in technological developments anywhere in the world.[21]

Immediately acting on the Galt Committee recommendations, Carter in 1978 increased RDT&E allocations to colleges and universities by 30% above 1977 obligations. In 1979, Carter rendered a broad interpretation of the 'Mansfield Amendment' so that virtually no research funding would be excluded from academia.[22] Additionally, a new position of Director of Research was installed; and in 1980 the DoD reconstituted its office of university affairs.[23]

The Carter-Reagan military build-up in academia had by 1986 brought RDT&E obligations to a level 126% higher in real terms than they were in 1977, a year before the acceleration began in earnest.[24] New institutional structures emerged during the Reagan Administration to cement enduring close ties between the military and academia. Formation of the DoD-University Forum (hereafter, Forum) is the centrepiece. The Forum is a policy advisory group consisting of senior level DoD and university administrators. It is jointly sponsored by the DoD and the three most prominent higher education associations collectively representing all such institutions in the United States: the Association of American Universities (AAU), the National Association of State Universities and Land Grant Colleges (NASULGC), and the American Council on Education (ACE). The official function of the Forum is to 'advise the Department of Defense on the full range of research-related needs and issues that affect the Department's ties with universities'.[25]

It is noteworthy that the idea for the Forum was initiated by the AAU and adopted as part of *The Defense Science Board Task Force Report on University Responsiveness to National Security Requirements* issued in 1982.[26] University administrators have not been passive agents in the resurgent militarization of academia. The AAU, representing 54 of the largest public and private research universities, has been extremely effective in securing institutional access to public coffers. AAU also spearheaded the political action that resulted in the inclusion of the

Office of Energy Research in legislation establishing the Department of Energy.[27]

Though the Forum is co-sponsored, one indication that the DoD ultimately has the upper hand is that nominations to the Forum by the sponsoring education associations must meet the approval of the Secretary of Defense.[28] In a short time, the Forum has significantly influenced the magnitude, direction and character of DoD research at universities through its working groups on science and engineering, foreign language and area studies, and export controls. Examination of these activities reveals the many ways in which militarization of higher education is limiting the range of free thought; channelling the militarization of science and engineering research and education (thereby diverting crucial resources from civilian needs); and influencing the direction of international affairs education in its prevailing direction of training and theorizing for the threat and use of force. (The work of the latter is considered in a subsequent section of this paper.)

DoD decided to take the advice of the Forum's Engineering and Science Education Working Group in implementing the University Research Initiative (URI), which was funded by Congress at $90 million in 1986 and an additional $35 million in 1987.[29] The URI is a multidisciplinary research programme focusing on a number of priority military technologies (involving both the natural and physical sciences): (1) technologies for automation; (2) biotechnology; (3) electro-optical systems and signal analysis; (4) high performance materials for a broad spectrum of defence applications; (5) fluid dynamics systems; (6) human performance factors for guiding design of machines; (7) submicron structures, in order to meet the military's need to increase electronic information processing five orders of magnitude by the 1990s; (8) environmental science and technology, in order to understand the conditions in which the weapons systems will have to operate; (9) and propulsion technology, including plasma propulsion systems for use on future space missions.

The formulation of the URI is indicative of the increased emphasis upon advanced applied research in universities. Ronald Kerber, Deputy Under Secretary of Defense for Research and Advanced Technology, states that the purpose of the URI is to 'accelerate the process by which scientific discoveries are translated into practical applications for advanced defense systems'.[30] The URI effort, which is currently slated for a three to five year duration, will facilitate contacts among university, industry, and DoD labs, as well as increase the number of science and engineering students working in areas of concern to the military.

In announcing the URI, DoD stated that it 'has an important stake in both the research produced by universities and the quality of the scientific personnel being educated in defense related disciplines'.[31]

Approximately 85% of the URI funds are allocated to the multidisciplinary research programmes, with the balance financing graduate fellowships, young investigator awards to starting faculty, and scientific
personnel exchanges between DoD labs and universities.[32] These
arrangements are financially lucrative to the researcher and university
alike. The Air Force's Laboratory Graduate Fellowship Program provided 45 three-year fellowships to doctoral students in 1986. All tuition
and fees are paid and the fellow's department receives $2,000 per year.
The fellow receives an increasing annual stipend of $13,000, $14,000,
and $15,000.[33]

The ONR's Young Investigator Program provides a base funding of
$50,000 annually for three years to academic faculty who received a
PhD or equivalent within five years of the award date. Further incentive
is provided by the ONR's offer to match on a two-for-one basis support
gained by the investigator from Navy labs and/or the Navy Systems
Commands. Though ONR has a $80,000 cap on this lucrative deal,
there is no limit on the amount of funds obtainable from these other
Navy sources. ONR's goal is to 'establish strong long term ties between
DoD and outstanding academics'.[34]

The cost of these programmes is very high because of the damage
done by diverting precious highly skilled human and financial resources
from the civilian economy. The 'spinoff' argument which peppers nearly
every public DoD document is an oversold strategem to fend off resistance to their accumulation of research dollars. A retrospective study
conducted by the National Academy of Engineering (NAE) in 1974 concludes:

> With a few exceptions, the vast technology developed by Federally funded programs
> since World War II has not resulted in widespread 'spinoffs' of secondary or additional
> applications of practical products, processes and services that have made an impact
> on the nation's economic growth, industrial productivity, employment gains, and
> foreign trade.[35]

The intensified shift towards 'mission oriented' advanced applied
research since this evaluation, assures that the opportunities for spin-
offs will fall off to zero. Seymour Melman, Professor of Industrial Economics at Columbia University, and others have documented in
numerous instances that the characteristics of the design criteria and
production practices in the military are inimical to competence in the
civilian sector.[36] The military practices the art of 'anti-engineering'
according to James Melcher, Professor of Electrical Engineering at the
Massachusetts Institute of Technology (MIT) and Director of the MIT
Laboratory for Electromagnetic and Electronic Systems.[37] Regarding
DoD's civilian spinoff claim, Melcher asserts, 'If you're going to run

business in this country that way we now know that it is not competitive'.[38]

The drain on the civilian economy is further exacerbated through the Independent Research and Development (IR&D) programme, an effort which both encompasses and complements the achievement of DoD's URI goals in other projects. The IR&D programme which was developed during the Reagan Administration provides incentives to military contractors in industry for subcontracting their R&D work to universities. As far as the military's agenda is concerned, the DoD concludes that 'while it is difficult to quantify the additional support for university R&D due to these incentives because the support includes exchanges of engineers, the IR&D incentives are considered effective . . .'[39]

Engineering and the physical sciences have historically been the recipients of the greatest share of DoD largesse and currently these academic departments remain heavily reliant on DoD funds as Table 4 indicates.[40]

In an historical account of electrical engineering development, Carl Barus, Professor Emeritus of Electrical Engineering at Swarthmore College, concludes that military perspectives have dominated the electrical engineering undergraduate curriculum since World War II:

> As early as 1944, a committee of the then Society for Promotion of Engineering Education (SPEE)—later renamed American Society for Engineering Education (ASEE)—produced a report urging more scientific content in the undergraduate program. The better known ASEE Grinter report of 1955 introduced the term 'engineering science' . . . Although the Grinter report caused much controversy at the time, it succeeded in establishing the engineering sciences—discovered, as it was in World War II—as part of the curriculum . . .
> In 1968 another committee of ASEE published its final report on the *Goals of Engineering Education* . . . Part B, The Engineer in Future Society, begins by summarizing 1964 RAND Corporation forecasts of the world in 1984 and in 2000. Both forecasts give strong emphasis to military technology . . . The report then claims that 'within this context' *Goals* 'has attempted to point the way toward the development of engineering education in the decades ahead'. Thus forecasts by an essentially military organization (RAND) . . . were used to tell us where we should be going, a classic case of self-fulfilling prophecy.[41]

In addition to DoD's historically heavy presence in the physical sciences, it is now the most active federal agency in biological science. Funding for biological weapons has increased 400% to 500% in the last few years, according to Jonathan King, Chair of the MIT Department of Molecular Biology. 'For the first time in my memory the Department of Defense is directly approaching academics in departments like this [one] for requests for proposals for general support—including graduate students—in biotechnology'.[42] By comparison, King notes, 'The NIH [National Institutes of Health] budget in an explosive period of biological science is flat. The NIH biomedical funding is not keeping pace with the growth of the opportunities . . . New developments continually emerge so people are drawn into the military'.[43]

TABLE 4. *DoD support for university R&D in selected fields*

	Support for R&D Million 1985 $ FY 1986	Share of all Federal Support FY 1986
Physics	59.0	14.0%
Mathematics	34.5	35.3%
Computer Sciences	59.6	53.9%
Materials Sciences	49.7	48.4%
Aeronautics/Astronautics	36.7	56.0%
Electrical Engineering	83.5	59.8%
Mechanical Engineering	38.4	48.1%

Source: Federation of American Scientists, *Public Interest Report*, September 1986, Vol. 39, No. 7.

TABLE 5. *Grants to universities for arms control activities from Ford, Rockefeller, Carnegie, and MacArthur foundations, 1983-1986 (in millions of current $)*

	1983	1984	1985	1986
Ford	.40	1.5	.30	1.52
Rockefeller	.015	1.4	.048	.72
Carnegie	.49	3.5	2.45	2.5
MacArthur	.025	.01	6.5	1.62

Source: Data compiled from *Grants Index Guide*, selected years and bi-monthly supplements (New York: The Foundation Center).

Because the DoD is such a significant source of funding in science and engineering it is able to leverage the thoughts of a great many more capable minds than even it is able to fund. These are minds that are not thinking about problem-solving in the civilian sphere. More than 170 academic institutions submitted a total of 965 proposals requesting more than $6 billion in the URI competition. DoD judged 165 to be 'of greatest scientific merit and importance to national defense'.[44] In a recent evaluation, the DoD estimates that between one-third and one-tenth of the proposals submitted by university researchers are funded, but twice as many are worth funding.[45].

When evaluating proposals from university researchers the DoD substitutes its own evaluative regime for the traditional peer review process of the academic community. The peer review process is designed to ensure scientific merit. Though it may be an imperfect system worthy of change, for an external institution to do so by fiat according to its own distinct agenda hardly seems an improvement in academic freedom and accountability to broader segments of society.

ELON COLLEGE LIBRARY

Nevertheless, the DoD has done so, and academia has largely complied. DoD's rationale for substituting its 'merit review' procedure is further evidence of the applied nature of all R&D; dismantling the shibboleth that science is not political:

> While external peers can help to judge the merit of the science, they are often not aware of the many facets of projects already supported by a particular agency, or how a proposed research project might fulfill a specific mission requirement. As a result, the Services and Defense Agencies rely heavily on the recommendations of their scientific program managers who are credentialed experts themselves in scientific or technical disciplines, and who also must be knowledgeable of relevant areas of military systems and operations.[46]

The pursuit of knowledge as defined by the military and for the military is the consequence of DoD's merit review process.

3. The case of international affairs studies

The physical and natural sciences are not the only academic sectors undergoing resurgent militarization. Under the auspices of the DoD-University Forum's Working Group on Foreign Language and Area Studies an ambitious effort is being pursued in international affairs studies. In 1984, the Working Group proposed the creation of a National Foundation for Foreign Languages and Area Studies (NFFLAS) modelled on the NSF. The report entitled *Beyond Growth: The Next Stage in Foreign Area and Language Studies*, was prepared by the AAU under contract from the DoD and the National Endowment for the Humanities.[47]

'For the first time since colonial days', declares the preamble, 'we have a durable adversary in the Soviet Union, which acts as a lodestone for all our foreign policies'.[48] The ominous Cold War tone is matched by the recommendation that the NFFAS be supported by a 'share of monies flowing back into the US Treasury from foreign loan repayments or from sales of military and other equipment abroad. In the private sector, the body should be eligible to receive some of the non-repatriatable profits held overseas by American business'.[49] This is a formula for deepening US military intervention and economic exploitation by US corporations abroad, as well as perpetuation of bellicose relations with the Soviet Union. These phenomena clearly point to increasing military influence in civilian society. The end to intervention abroad is essential to redistributing decison-making power away from the war-making institutions domestically. Efforts at reconciliation and cooperation in foreign affairs is not to be on the agenda of the proposed NFFLAS.

Completion of *Beyond Growth* was followed by the commissioning of *Points of Leverage: An Agenda for a National Foundation for Inter-*

national Studies by five private foundations: The Exxon Foundation, the Andrew W. Mellon Foundation, the Ford Foundation, the Rockefeller Foundation, and the Carnegie Corporation of New York.[50] *Points of Leverage*—authored by Richard Lambert, a member of the Forum's Working Group—is 'self-consciously modeled on *Science: The Endless Frontier'*—the 1946 document written by Vannevar Bush, Director of the World War II US Office of Scientific Research and Development, leading to the development of the NSF.[51]

Foundation involvement in international affairs curriculum is not at all unusual. Since World War II, the large private philanthropic foundations in the United States have been the financial architects of international relations studies. These establishment-based foundations have used the university as an instrumentality for developing and disseminating theories for the conduct of international relations through the threat and use of force. Their efforts have been essential complements to the DoD's direct efforts in science and engineering.

The Carnegie, Ford, and Rockefeller Foundations were the leading underwriters of this new academic field.[52] The programmes at Harvard University have yielded the greatest impact from the foundation's investment. Harvard's first programme was a graduate seminar in 'Defense Policy and Administration' offered in 1954. The course objective was to provide training for civilians who might later be involved in the formation of military policy. This effort caught the attention of the Ford Foundation which a year later provided a three-year grant for the establishment of the Defense Studies Program. Harvard would become a national centre for military policy studies. The Program had three purposes: (1) to carry out experimentation in courses dealing with defence policy as a problem in public administration; (2) to prepare teaching materials and guidance for other universities; and (3) to make a programme available to those interested in entering government agencies dealing with these issues.[53] Just one year after the Ford funds expired the Carnegie Corporation supplied another three-year grant in 1960. By 1959, the Defense Policy Seminar was under the direction of Henry Kissinger. During the period of Ford Foundation support Kissinger wrote the book, *Nuclear Weapons and Foreign Policy* (1957) which gave the first articulation of the doctrine of so-called 'limited war' (also known as 'escalation dominance'): In a limited war the problem is to apply graduated amounts of destruction for limited objectives and also to permit the necessary breathing space for political contacts.[54]

This infamous strategy was wielded by Presidents Kennedy, Johnson, and Nixon (with Kissinger at his side) in their destruction of Vietnam. However, no 'breathing space' was allowed in this particular application.

In 1958, the Defense Studies Program was accompanied by the Harvard Center for International Affairs initiated with a $500,000 grant from the Ford Foundation.[55] The Rockefeller Foundation provided funds for the establishment of Harvard's Science and Public Policy programme in the following year.[56]

By the beginning of the 1960s foundations had built the academic infrastructure for 'defence policy' studies premised on maintaining US military, economic and political dominion in the world through the threat and use of force. Harvard was the flagship academic institution for this work: the Defense Policy Program focused on training; the Center for International Affairs focused on policy design; and the Science and Public Policy programme attended to the role of scientists in the formulation of military policy.[57]

Arms control theory emerged from a 1960 seminar funded by the Rockefeller Foundation and co-sponsored by the Center for International Affairs and MIT's Center for International Studies (established in 1951 and sustained in part with $2.25 million from the Ford Foundation between 1953-1959).[58] Arms control is a theory of joint steering and managed escalation of the arms race, and is grounded in the deterrence principle of the threat and use of force as the basis for conducting foreign policy. Reversal of the arms race was not the intent of arms control formulators. In fact, the intent seems to have been to divert public attention and scholarship away from consideration of the institutional forms of power which perpetuate the arms race.[59] Thomas Schelling, Professor of Political Economy at Harvard's John F. Kennedy School of Government and a principal architect of arms control doctrine, recently stated in the journal *Foreign Affairs*, 'If people really believed that zero is the ultimate goal it is easy to see that downward is the direction they should go. But hardly anyone who takes arms control seriously believes that zero is the goal'.[60]

The papers of the 1960 conference were mass marketed in a volume entitled, *Arms Control, Disarmament, and National Security* (1961) which became a Book-of-the Month Club selection and a basic reader in foreign policy courses.[61] For a quarter of a century arms control doctrine has delimited the bounds of public discourse on foreign policy. Uncritical acceptance—except for those, such as members of the Reagan Administration who dispensed with this pretence—garners a theological status for arms control dogma. The equivocal term 'arms control' even leaves honest supporters of reversal of the arms race confounded. 'Control' can mean upward, downward, or constant. Thus far it has been upward.[62]

In 1983 the Carnegie, Ford, and Rockefeller foundations were joined by the John D. and Catherine T. MacArthur Foundation in a redoubled effort to fund the elaboration and dissemination of arms control theology in order to beat back the heightened public concern in Europe and the United States for a reversal of the arms race.

The Carnegie and MacArthur foundations have provided the prime financial stimulus through deliberate coordination of their efforts.[63] In 1983, Carnegie announced a $11 million programme to fund arms control projects over a three-year period. The MacArthur Foundation announced a $25 million programme also over a three-year span for arms control activities.[64] Once again, Harvard is the flagship school. Harvard's 'Avoiding Nuclear War' (ANW) project established in 1983 with a grant from the Carnegie Corporation is committed to the 'long term future of nuclear deterrence', and they have been teaching their students and the public about 'living with nuclear weapons'.[65]

Living with Nuclear Weapons is the title of a book aimed at the American lay public. The authors are members of the Harvard Nuclear Study Group (among them are two of the three joint directors of the ANW project), and the document is introduced with an endorsement by Derek Bok, President of Harvard. The Harvard Nuclear Study Group instructs people to abandon ideas of a world without nuclear weapons:

> Complete disarmament would require some form of world government to deter actions of one nation against another. In a disarmed world, without such a government armed with sufficient force to prevent conflict between or among nations, differences in beliefs and interests might easily lead to a renewal of war. But any world government capable of preventing world conflict could also become a world dictatorship. And given the differences in ideology, wealth, and nationalism that now exist in the world, most nations are not likely to accept a centralized government unless they feel sure of controlling it or minimizing its intrusiveness . . .
>
> Ironically, while complete disarmament may be a worthy long term goal, trying to achieve it before the requisite political conditions exist could actually increase the prospects of war.[66]

Harvard is silent about how a reduction in the decision-making power of the war-making institutions in the United States would reduce their own power and privilege which they have built as acolytes to these institutions of government. The claim that central authority is the only way to accomplish reversal of the arms race is a politically self-serving Orwellian scare tactic. Indeed, it is the greater decentralization of decision-making power within and among societies that is crucial.

Nuclear weapons have been deliberately used by presidents to accrue an unprecedented level of decision-making power at the expense of the legislative branch of the federal government. Indeed, the Congress (with occasional dissenters) has acquiesced in this transfer of power. Congress is today little more than a spectator with *ex post facto* comments and insignificant will to reclaim its constitutionally endowed powers. Senator Albert Gore (Democrat, Tennessee) recently stated, '[Nuclear] technology has changed the way the Constitution balances the relative power of the President and the Congress with respect to the use of weapons . . .'[67] Of course, the Constitution itself doesn't do anything. The document is interpreted, amended and/or ignored only through human agency.

Explicitly and implicitly the Congress accepts the rationale that nuclear technology forces the abridgement of its war-making powers. The recent remarks of Representative Henry Hyde (Republican, Illinois) are closer to the point:

> I think that the power to declare war is almost an anachronism because these days nobody declares war. The last two confrontations we've had in Korea and Vietnam were wars in the sense that people were shooting and getting killed, but a declaration of war kicks in trading with the enemy, treason, censorship . . . So, you call it something else—a police action, but it is still a shooting war. So I think our Constitution in that sense is not too useful.[68]

Congress has accepted a technologically deterministic rationale which at its core is a political strategem by the president. The rational posits that because of both the terrific danger of nuclear weapons and the speed with which a decision to use them is required there is no time for congressional consultation—let alone convening the entire Congress for a vote to declare war. Furthermore, since the potential for nuclear hostility is constant, the president must have an unusually free hand in the use of military power (including covert actions). Since financial resources are essential, the effect is the concentration of military, economic and political power in the hands of the president in both the domestic and foreign affairs of state. The study of this problem is not of concern to Harvard or the many other university-based arms control programmes.

4. Strategies for conversion

Conversion of academic institutions can only be leveraged by mobilizing new coalitions of groups that are negatively impacted by the diversion of federal resources to the military and the concentration of political, military and economic power in the White House. Increasingly these groups have come to include a broad array of middle-class professionals, in addition to the historically disenfranchised groups in society and academia,—in particular, people of colour, rank-and-file labour, and environmental organizations.

Campuses have recently been the site of campaigns against university complicity with apartheid in South Africa, US government military intervention in Central America, and resistance to Star Wars—highlighted by a pledge by nearly 7,000 university scientists (including a majority of the physics professors at the top twenty university departments and fifteen Nobel laureates) not to solicit nor receive SDI funds.[69] Nevertheless, effectiveness of these efforts is limited by a single-issue, ad-hoc approach addressing only the symptoms of a fundamentally institutional problem of the distribution of decision-making power in society. The university is increasingly the exclusive preserve of ideas and knowledge that sustain and increase the power of the militarized state-capitalist government.[70] The trustees, administrators and many of the students are in violation of the social contract of university with society.

If academic institutions are to be responsible to a broader spectrum of society, new institutional forms must be developed within and outside academia to ensure accountability and access. This is the task of the new coalitions. Groups within and outside the university must recognize that the institutional source of their problem is the same, and mobilize in collective effort.

A critical point of leverage is recognition that both public *and* private colleges and universities rely on a substantial amount of funding from the government through direct monies and in-kind subsidy through tax free status. In a 1984 survey of a cross-section of academic institutions, the US General Accounting Office found that 32% of total educational and general operating revenues for private institutions were derived from the federal government. For state colleges and universities a total of 20% of educational and general operating revenues were obtained from federal government sources. State government funds provided an additional 2% to the coffers of private institutions and 49% to public institutions. Tuition and fees account for 43% of educational and general operating revenues in private institutions and 17% in public institutions. The federal government is by far the largest funder of research in both public and private academic institutions, comprising 57% and 81% of research revenues, respectively.[71]

While public monies underwrite a substantial amount of university operations, public input regarding the disposition of these funds and access to university resources is narrow by comparison. As an illustration, while David Noble, Professor of History at Drexel University, was teaching at MIT in the mid-1970s and early 1980s he tried for several years to negotiate the development of a labour branch in the long-established MIT Industrial Liaison Office which facilitates links by professors and students with industry. Noble was trespassing on a privileged preserve and was rebuffed.[72]

University administrators and professors soliciting federal funds and entering proprietary arrangements with corporations complain that restrictions on these activities would abridge their academic freedom. A constant refrain by these people is that scientific inquiry is not political. These beneficiaries of the public largesse corrupt the essence of academic freedom in order to dodge public accountability. Research is a social process with social impacts and is informed by political and economic agendas. At the Massachusetts Institute of Technology (M.I.T.), where the biology department voted not to accept funds from the DoD because of its focus on biological warfare, the M.I.T. administration threatened to withhold all inhouse funding to the biology department.[73] The department reversed its decision after this coercive action. The university administration was anxious for the Pentagon revenue which significantly contributes to overhead costs at the university. The denial that politics and economics do not play a significant part in academia's agenda for inquiry is disingenuous and a disservice to the public.

The National Coalition for Universities in the Public Interest was formed in 1984 to redress the narrowing intellectual spectrum within universities. The Coalition is based in Washington D.C. and has a growing number of chapters throughout the nation. 'It is not surprising that the people who founded it were Ralph Nader (noted consumer advocate), Albert Meyerhoff (Counsel, National Resources Defense Council) and me', observes Noble who was then with the Smithsonian Institution.[74] Noble describes the task of the Coalition:

> What is going on now in the universities is (that) there is such a chilled atmosphere . . . that there is no hope whatsoever of generating this type of social awareness and concern among faculty . . . The key is to link up people in the university who might be disposed (to this) . . . with people outside.[75]

Thus far, the Coalition is pursuing this by litigating against universities that the Coalition believes have fired professors for their political viewpoints. According to Noble, this is done to 'clean up' the image of the university in order to attract funds.[76] More is at stake than the professor's job. Intellectual access to the university is denied to entire ranges of the public. The spectrum of ideas about what is asked, what is known, and what is conceivable contracts.

Charles Schwartz, Professor of Physics at University of California, Berkeley, is among those within the university community who believe that academic accountability will only come from the linkages that the Coalition is working to forge together. Without pressure through such linkages faculty and administrators will continue to hide behind their 'pet rationales'. 'There are quite a variety of them', Schwartz adds, 'but it all means, don't rock the boat'.[77] Indeed, Schwartz could not get a single faculty member in his department to discuss the issue of the militarization of science:

> When I attempted to discuss it privately with one or two, they can't comprehend it, they can't understand it. That's because it clearly implies difficult choices for them which they prefer to ignore or to define away by simplistic rationalizing . . .
> Many students, I think, are concerned about this question of the military uses of

science. But others manage to keep their minds closed to it. I don't want to say they are apathetic. I would say they are in a condition of encouraged ignorance. And the silence of teachers helps to protect and maintain that passive ignorance.[78]

Schwartz is now teaching physics to non-majors and is focusing his attention on getting physics teachers and the American Physical Society to acknowledge a responsibility to tell students about the militarization of the job market for physicists. 'I've noted . . . the increasing number of reports from physics students leaving the university who say it seems extremely difficult, if not impossible, to find jobs that are not related to weapons programs in one way or another'. While acknowledging that this is not new, Schwartz maintains that there has been a 'sharp shift' from physics jobs to weapons programmes during the Reagan Administration.[79] To date, Schwartz's colleagues have not cooperated in his attempt to inform students whether their sub-speciality is likely to lock them into a military job. Student pressure on the faculty and the job placement office for an employment 'right to know' provision is an important step.

A critical evaluation of arms control is desperately needed within the academic community. Once again, the best possibility comes from beyond the academic groves. Since 1986, Marcus Raskin, Senior Fellow at the Institute for Policy Studies, has been speaking before audiences inside and outside of academia about his *Draft Treaty for a Comprehensive Program for Common Security and General Disarmament*.[80] This is a fifteen-year programme for security through global disarmament incorporating conversion of the economic and political war-making institutions of government. Raskin was a principle author of President Kennedy's *Outline of Basic Provisions of a Treaty on General and Complete Disarmament* tabled at Geneva in the spring of 1962.[81] The current proposal affords a systematic framework for discussing an actual reversal of the arms race.

Concerned groups within and outside of academic institutions can set up campus community-based coalition groups to document the activities of their college, and draw up plans for research and education for alternative social goals. This can serve as a document for organizing further coalitions, and generating debate about the academy. It can also become a touchstone for lobbying efforts at the national level. The formation of such plans should be through an iterative process facilitated through local, regional, and national fora among those interested in the fundamental issues: Knowledge for whom? Knowledge for what? Through what procedure? Who pays and how much? Networking can be accomplished through a variety of media: newsletter, video tape, a computer 'bulletin board', and existing organs willing to give these issues a hearing. The point is to begin to knit together the collective energies of groups and individuals in a sustained and strengthened effort which addresses the redistribution of institutional decision-making power.[82]

NOTES AND REFERENCES

1. Noam Chomsky, *For Reasons of State,* New York: Pantheon, 1973, p. 303.
2. Full text in Seymour Melman, *Pentagon Capitalism*, New York: McGraw-Hill, 1970, pp. 231–234.
3. 'Office of Naval Research Marks 40th Anniversary', *Science*, 21 November 1986, p. 932.
4. US DoD. *The Department of Defense Report on the University Role in Defense Research and Development for the Committees on Appropriations, United States Congress*, Washington D.C.: The Pentagon, April 1987, p. 5. Note these and subsequent data in this paper do not include money dispensed by the DoD through university-operated federally funded research and development centres (FFRDCs).
5. Jimmie R. Suttle, 'Basic Research From Lewis & Clark to Laser Physics', *Defense 82*, Washington D.C.: The Pentagon, p. 23.
6. Ibid.
7. Op. cit., 5, p. 24.
8. Op. cit., 5, p. 24.
9. Op. cit., 4, p. 14.
10. Computed from data in op. cit., 4, pp. 10, 14.
11. Computed from data in op. cit., 4, pp. 7, 10.
12. Op. cit., 4, p. 17.
13. Computed from data provided by the Strategic Defense Initiative Office of Innovative Science and Technology, the Pentagon, Washington D.C.; and the Federation of American Scientists, *Public Interest Report*, September 1986, Vol. 39, No. 7. Deflators from US Department of Commerce, *Survey of Current Business*, May 1987, Vol. 67, No. 5.
14. Edward Markey, 'Markey Releases Analysis of Reagan Energy Budget: The Militarization of Energy Department Budget Marches On', press release from the Office of US Congressman Edward Markey, 12 January 1987.
15. See, for instance, Federation of American Scientists, *Public Interest Report,* September 1986, Vol. 39, No. 7; communication by author with Jonathan Reichert, Department of Physics, State University of New York-Buffalo, July 1987.
16. Mark Zieman, 'Growing Militarization of the Space Program Worries U.S. Scientists', *Wall Street Journal*, 15 January 1986, p. 1.
17. Ibid.
18. Eric Bloch, Testimony before the US Senate Armed Service Committee, Subcommittee on Defense Industry and Technology, 9 March 1987.
19. Federation of American Scientists, *Public Interest Report,* September 1986, Vol. 39, No. 7, p. 14.
20. Computed from data in op. cit., 4, p. 7.
21. Op. cit, 5, p. 25.
22. Howard Ehrlich, 'The University-Military Research Connection', *Thought & Action*, Fall 1984, Vol. 1, No. 1, p. 118.
23. Op. cit., 5, p. 25.
24. Op. cit., 4, p. 7.
25. US DoD, Office of the Under-Secretary of Defense for Research and Engineering, Mimeo of completed GSA Form T-820-E for Fiscal Year 1986 indicating information about departmental committees, no date.
26. US DoD, Office of the Under Secretary of Defense for Research and Engineering, *Report of the Defense Science Board Task Force on University Responsiveness to National Security Requirements,* Washington D.C.: The Pentagon, January 1982.
27. Communication by author with Dr. John C. Crowley, July 1987.

108   *Robert Krinsky*

28. US DoD, Office of the Under Secretary of Defense for Research and Engineering, *Report of the DoD-University Forum: Calendar Year 1984,* Washington D.C.: The Pentagon, p. 2.
29. Op. cit., 23; and US DoD, *The Department of Defense University Research Initiative Research Program Summaries,* June 1987, Washington D.C.: The Pentagon, p. 2.
30. US DoD, *The Department of Defense Statement on the Science and Technology Program by the Deputy Under Secretary of Defense for Research and Advanced Technology to 100th Congress, 1st Session,* March 1987, p. 8.
31. US DoD, *The Department of Defense FY 1986 University Research Initiative Program Overview,* December 1985, pp. 1.
32. Op. cit., 26, p. 3.
33. Op. cit., 31, p. 48.
34. Op. cit., 31, pp. 49-50.
35. Quoted in op. cit., 19, p. 16.
36. See, especially, Seymour Melman, *Profits Without Production,* New York: Knopf, 1984.
37. Communication by the author with Dr. James Melcher, June 1987.
38. Op. cit., 4, p. 9.
40. Op. cit., 19, p. 13.
41. Carl Barus, 'Military Influence on the Electrical Engineering Curriculum Since World War II', *IEEE Technology and Society Magazine,* June 1987, p. 7.
42. Communication by author with Dr. Jonathan King, June 1987.
43. Ibid.
44. Op. cit., 4, p. 27.
45. Op. cit., p. 26.
46. US DoD, *The Department of Defense Report on the Merit Review Process for Competitive Selection of University Research Projects and an Analysis of the Potential for Expanding the Geographic Distribution of Research,* April 1987, p. 3.
47. Association of American Universities, *Beyond Growth: The Next Stage in Language and Area Studies,* Washington D.C.: AAU, 1984.
48. Ibid., p. 3.
49. Op. cit., 47, pp. 279-280.
50. Richard Lambert, *Points of Leverage: An Agenda for a National Foundation for International Studies,* New York: Social Science Research Council, 1986, p. vi.
51. Ibid., p. 50.
52. Information concerning the early funding of international affairs curricula after World War II is obtained from Gene M. Lyons and Louis Morton, *Schools for Strategy: Education and Research in National Security Affairs,* New York: Praeger, 1965, especially the Introduction and Chapter 7.
53. Ibid., p. 148.
54. Quoted in James William Gibson, *The Perfect War,* Boston: Atlantic Monthly, p. 22.
55. Op. cit., 52, p. 9.
56. Op. cit., 52, p. 152.
57. Op. cit., 52, p. 152.
58. Op. cit., 52, pp. 9, 160.
59. Communication by author with Dr. Seymour Melman who attended the conference, November 1986.
60. Thomas C. Schelling, 'What Went Wrong With Arms Control?' *Foreign Affairs,* Winter 1985/86, p. 226.
61. Donald G. Brennan, *Arms Control, Disarmament, and National Security,* New York: Braziller, 1961.
62. The first strategic arms limitation talks between the Soviet Union and the United States were an opportunity to prevent the introduction of multiple independently targetable re-entry vehicles (MIRVS). At the time the Soviet Union had not deployed any and the US had deployed 832. Rather than reduce these to zero, SALT 1 codified a combined increase to 1808 MIRVed missiles. (See, Robert Johansen, 'The Failure of Arms Control,' *Sojourners,* March 1981, p. 73.) Though the SALT II Treaty was never ratified, the Joint Chiefs of Staff found that the increases in weaponry permit-

ted therein, made the unratified treaty a useful planning document. (See, Joseph Nye Jr., 'Farewell to Arms Control?' *Foreign Affairs*, Fall 1986, p. 2.) The INF Accord occurs in a political and military context in which the US Government refuses to negotiate on SDI and has increased research funding for biological warfare six-fold since President Reagan entered office. The manner in which the US Government has pursued these military initiatives is of questionable consistency with the legality of the ABM Treaty and the Biological Weapons Convention, respectively. See Seth Shulman, 'Poisons from the Pentagon,' November 1987, pp. 16-18.

63. 'Avoiding Nuclear War Grants', *Carnegie Quarterly*, New York: Carnegie Corporation of New York, Vol. 30, No. 2, Spring 1985.
64. Ibid., 63.
65. Harvard University, *1986-1987 Catalogue of the John F. Kennedy School of Government*, p. 42.
66. The Harvard Nuclear Study Group: Albert Carnesale, Paul Doty, Stanley Hoffman, Samuel P. Huntington, Joseph S. Nye, Jr., Scott D. Sagan, *Living With Nuclear Weapons*, New York: Bantam, 1983, pp. 189–190.
67. Columbia University, Seminars on Media and Society, 'The Presidency and the Constitution: The Nuclear Balance of Terror, Part I,' (Video Tape), Show No. 105, New York: Columbia University, 1987.
68. Ibid., 67.
69. Communication by author with David Wright, Graduate Student, Department of Physics, University of Pennsylvania, June 1987. Wright is one of the initiators of the pledge.
70. On military state capitalism, see Seymour Melman, *Pentagon Capitalism,* New York: McGraw-Hill, 1970.
71. US GAO, 'University Finances: Research Revenues and Expenditures', July 1986, GAO/RCED-86-162BR, pp. 16, 19, 26–27.
72. Communication by author with Dr. David Noble, July 1987.
73. Seth Shulman, 'Poisons from the Pentagon', *The Progressive*, November 1987, p. 18.
74. The National Coalition for Universities in the Public Interest can be reached at P.O. Box 18372, Washington D.C., 20036.
75. Op. cit., 73.
76. Op. cit., 73.
77. Op. cit., 73.
78. Communication by author with Dr. Charles Schwartz, June 1987.
79. Danny Collum, 'Defying the Laws of Physics', an interview with Charles Schwartz, *Sojourners,* 22 May 1987, p. 24.
80. Ibid., p. 23.
81. Marcus G. Raskin, *Draft Treaty for a Comprehensive Program for Common Security and General Disarmament*, Washington D.C.: Institute for Policy Studies, 1986.
82. *Blueprint for the Peace Race*, US Arms Control and Disarmament Agency, Publication 4, General Series 3, Washington D.C.: Government Printing Office, May 1962.

Facing the Second Generation of the Nuclear Weapons Complex: Renewal of the Nuclear Production Base or Economic Conversion?

GREG BISCHAK

1. Nuclear disarmament and economic conversion

Disarmament proposals advanced by General Secretary Gorbachev and President Reagan calling for zero deployments for intermediate and short-range ballistic missiles in Europe, and 50% reductions in strategic nuclear weapons systems, seem to demand drastic reductions in nuclear force levels in the United States and the Soviet Union. Since such proposals were first advanced at the Reykjavik Summit and thereafter in Geneva, there has been very little public discussion as to the real effects of these proposals on the production and deployment of new generations of strategic and tactical delivery systems and nuclear warheads. On the surface one would expect the adoption of these proposals to require a gearing down of nuclear weapons production and new deployments. However, a closer inspection of the probable impact reveals that the adoption of both proposals would likely permit wide-ranging modernization of strategic nuclear forces.

Indeed, neither set of proposals addresses: (1) detailed staged reductions in any type of nuclear weapon which include the next generation of a strategic weapon system; (2) the setting up of an international inspectorate for zonal inspection, or (3) the need for detailed economic conversion of nuclear production facilities to guarantee the reversal of the nuclear arms race—that is, real disarmament as opposed to just another round of arms control.[1] An initial premise of this paper is that inspection and verification for nuclear disarmament requires, among other things, detailed planning for the economic conversion of those nuclear weapons production facilities which can be converted to purely civilian uses, and the shutdown and clean up of those facilities which cannot be converted. Industrial conversion of nuclear weapons production facilities should make it easier to verify the cessation of production of weapons-grade fissile materials.[2] Further, conversion and

111

economic diversification provide the means to mitigate the economic dislocation resulting from the termination of weapons production.

This paper focuses exclusively on the conversion planning problems for the nuclear weapons production complex which is owned and managed by the US Department of Energy (DOE). The complex embraces weapons research laboratories, nuclear weapons material production facilities, the weapons fabrication facilities, the nuclear weapons test sites, and the treatment, storage and disposal of radioactive wastes. The main objective of this paper is to understand the special problems of converting the nuclear weapons production complex, based on a critical review of the literature, and an assessment of the available economic studies for assessing the employment and income impacts of nuclear weapons conversion.

As a background to this discussion, I begin with an overview of the industrial and economic structure of the nuclear weapons complex, the missions of the main facilities currently comprising the complex, and the employment levels and degree of unionization within the complex. The next part of the paper discusses the historical determinants of nuclear materials and warheads production volumes and rates, focusing on the changes in the strategic policy, the budgetary trends and their effects on employment trends in the industry. In this part I document my opening assertion that the post-Reykjavik proposals would have little effect on nuclear weapon production rates. In the third part, I review the literature on conversion planning for the nuclear production complex in the United States and draw up a general assessment of available methodologies.

2. An overview of the nuclear weapons production complex

A brief overview of the US nuclear weapons production complex today shows that it is a far flung network of large industrial research laboratories and production facilities located in sixteen states, employing over 115,000 workers, scientists and engineers, with a budget for Fiscal Year 1987 of $8.7 billion dollars.[3] This complex is comprised of three main weapons laboratories, nine nuclear materials production facilities, seven nuclear warhead fabrication plants and two nuclear test sites.[4] Weapons research on design of nuclear and non-nuclear components and test instruments is done at the national laboratories. The production of weapons-grade nuclear materials (primarily uranium 235, plutonium 239 and tritium) is done at specialized uranium enrichment plants and military production reactors, while the feed materials to supply the fuel stock for these processes comes from facilities dedicated to such production. Fabrication of the fissionable materials (uranium 235 and 238 and plutonium 239) and fusion materials (lithium, deuterium and tritium) into components for bomb and warhead assemblies takes place at two specialized facilities, while the non-nuclear components are fabricated elsewhere and shipped to the Pantex plant outside Amarillo, Texas, for final assembly.

TABLE 1. *DOE research laboratories: primary nuclear weapons labs* (*)
(30 September 1986)

Facility & Location	Principal Contractor	Total Employment	Principal Unions
Argonne National Lab, Chicago, Illinois	University of Chicago	2,780	International Association of Machinists & Aerospace Workers, AFL-CIO
Brookhaven National Lab, Upton, New York	Associated Universities Inc.	3,154	International Brotherhood of Electrical Workers, Oil, Chemical & Atomic Workers
Idaho National Engineering Lab, Idaho Falls, Idaho.	EG&G Inc.	3,474	Oil, Chemical & Atomic Workers
	Westinghouse Idaho Nuclear	1,375	OCAW
	University of Chicago	686	OCAW
	West Valley Nuclear Services	444	International Association of Machinists
	Westinghouse Electric Co.	1,375	Metal Trades Council
Lawrence Radiation Lab, Berkeley, California	University of California	10,668	Alameda County Building & Construction Trades Council
Lawrence Livermore* Research Lab, Livermore, California	Sandia Corp.	1,061	International Association of Machinists & Aerospace Workers
	Rockwell International	203	
Los Alamos National Lab,* Los Alamos, New Mexico	University of California	7,727	None
Oak Ridge National Laboratories, Oak Ridge, Tennessee	Martin Marietta Corp.	5,001	Atomic Trades & Production Council
Sandia National Lab,* Albuquerque, New Mexico	Sandia Corp.	7,216	Metal Trades Council

Source: Metal Trades Council, 30 September 1986.

2.1. DOE national laboratories and nuclear weapons research

A profile of the DOE national research laboratories is presented in Table 1, which depicts for each research laboratory, the principal contractors and unions that represent the skilled craftsmen, technicians, operations and maintenance workers, designers and draughtsmen, toolroom and machine shop workers and computer operators.[5] Most nuclear weapons research on design, weapons applications, safeguards, and isotope separation is conducted at Lawrence Livermore, and Los Alamos Laboratory, while design work on the non-nuclear components is primarily done at Sandia National Laboratory. Approximately half of the total employment at the main nuclear weapons laboratories is directly weapons related; however, much of the balance of the service and support workers indirectly depend on weapons contracts for their jobs.[6]

In addition to these main laboratories, there are smaller nuclear weapons labs at Savannah River in Aiken, South Carolina, and the New Brunswick lab in Argonne, Illinois, and also the other DOE national labs that provide scientific and technical research support in key areas of weapons research. However, with the exception of the Savannah River and New Brunswick labs, the work load at these other labs is not primarily weapons oriented, with direct nuclear defence activities comprising only 1–5% of their 1987 fiscal budgets.[7]

2.2 Nuclear weapons materials production facilities

At the heart of the nuclear weapons production complex lie the facilities that supply the weapons-grade fissionable and fusion materials necessary to build nuclear fission and fusion warheads. The locations of these facilities, along with the principal operating contractors and unions that represent the workers, are presented in Table 2. Each of these facilities provides an industrial link in what is called the nuclear fuel cycle. The nuclear fuel cycle is graphically laid out in Figure 1 which depicts the input and output flows among the various industrial production processes that go into producing components for nuclear weapons.

Uranium mining and milling forms the beginning of the nuclear weapons fuel cycle, and is the only segment of the fuel cycle that is privately-owned and operated. All of the other phases of the cycle are government-owned and contractor-operated.

Federal procurements of uranium ore between 1949 to 1970 amounted to about 325,000 short tons, and provided the raw material to supply the federally-owned and contractor-operated enrichment plants. Uranium enrichment takes uranium fluoride-6 (which is a gas produced from milled and concentrated uranium oxide) and raises the percentage of the fissile isotope U-235 from its naturally occurring level of 0.7% to a 90% concentration for weapons applications. Light water reactor designs such as commercial nuclear power plants only require a 3% enrichment, while Naval submarine reactors require about 80% enrichment levels.

TABLE 2. *DOE nuclear materials production facilities (30 September 1986)*

Facility & Location	Principal Contractor	Total Employment	Principal Union
Ashtabula Plant, Ashtabula, Ohio	Reactive Metals Inc.	130	United Steel Workers
Feed Materials Production Center, Fernald, Ohio	Westinghouse Materials Co.	1,564	Fernald Atomic Trades & Labor Council
Hanford Reservation, Richland, Washington	Westinghouse	9,588	Hanford Metal Trades Council
	Battelle NW	2,597	"
	Boeing Computers	456	"
	Hanford Environmental Health Foundation	115	None
Idaho National Engineering Lab, Idaho Falls, Idaho	(See Table 1)	7,228	(See Table 1)
Oak Ridge Gaseous Diffusion Plant, Oak Ridge, Tennessee	Martin Marietta	2,451	Oil, Chemical & Atomic Workers
Paducah Gas Diffusion Plant, Paducah, Kentucky	Martin Marietta	1,212	Oil, Chemical & Atomic Workers
Portsmouth Gas Diffusion Plant, Piketon, Ohio	Goodyear Atomic Corporation	1,988	Oil, Chemical & Atomic Workers Local 3-689
Savannah River Plant, Aiken, South Carolina	E.I. DuPont de Nemours & Co.	7,635	No Union
Y-12 Plant, Oak Ridge, Tennessee	Martin Marietta	7,235	Atomic Trades & Labor Council

Source: *Approximate Current Employment On Operations & Maintenance at Department of Energy Installations, September 30, 1986,* by the Metal Trades Council of the AFL-CIO, from their annual conference proceedings, Washington D.C.

Currently there are three uranium enrichment plants based on the so-called gas diffusion process, which are located at Piketon, Ohio, Paducah, Kentucky and Oak Ridge, Tennessee. Only the Piketon plant currently produces high-assay enriched uranium for Naval reactor fuel, and no plant since 1964 has produced enriched uranium for weapons

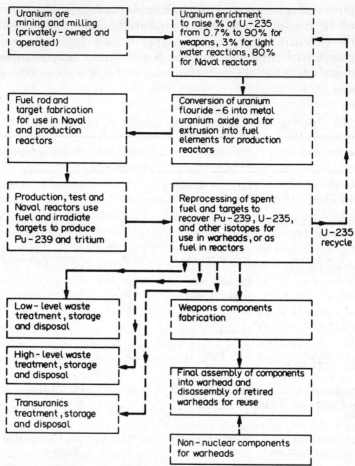

FIGURE 1. Military nuclear materials production and fuel cycle

applications. Stockpiles of highly enriched weapons-grade uranium make it currently unnecessary for enrichment plants to produce more. Indeed, the Natural Resources Defense Council has estimated that the US stockpile of highly enriched uranium at between 595 to 605 metric tons of U-235 enriched to 93.5% levels.[8] Thus, these enrichment plants are linked to the warhead production cycle by virtue of the stockpiles and the uranium supplies of slightly enriched uranium for fuel fabrication.

Fabrication of uranium metal into fuel elements and targets takes place at the Fernald Feed Materials Center, the Ashtabula plant and Savannah River. Through extrusion processes, the enriched uranium oxide is assembled into fuel rods and targets for insertion into plutonium production reactors at the Savannah River and Hanford facilities (all of which are either temporarily or permanently closed due to safety problems). The other target isotopes in fuel rods are made of lithium-6 for tritium production in the defence production reactors at Savannah River.

The specialized weapons production reactors use highly-enriched uranium and lithium-6 targets, which are bombarded by neutrons from the fission reactions of the surrounding fuel core of slightly enriched uranium, and transformed into isotopes of plutonium and tritium. Currently, the N-reactor at the Hanford Reservation has been shut down since January 1987. Originally, DOE officials hoped to renovate and improve the safety systems on the graphite-moderated N-reactor so as to extend its production capabilities through 1998. However, current DOE planning calls for the N-reactor to be permanently shut down. Meanwhile, the three heavy water production reactors at Savannah River capable of producing plutonium and tritium have been shut down since the summer of 1988 due to safety problems.[9] Prior to this shut down, the operational capabilities of the L, K, and P reactors were constrained by the reduction of their power levels to 26% of their rated capacity because of problems with their emergency cooling systems, and because of cracks in the reactor tank walls. The C-reactor is shut down because of cracks in the reactor tank walls, and the R-reactor has not operated since 1964.

Despite the current lack of production reactor availability, the national inventory of weapon-grade plutonium, estimated by the Natural Resources Defense Council to be about 93.1 metric tons, plus or minus 7 metric tons, makes it possible for warhead production to continue through the blending of super-grade plutonium with fuel grade plutonium so as to expand the available supply of weapon-grade material. Annual production of plutonium from all production reactors was about 2,000 kilograms annually from 1984 to 1986 for weapon-grade and super-grade. The national inventory of tritium production is estimated by the Natural Resources Defense Council to be 70 kilograms plus or minus 25 kilograms.[10] Of course, the recovery of the plutonium and tritium from production reactors depends on a chemical reprocessing of the spent fuel rods and targets to separate out the isotopes.

Chemical reprocessing of the spent fuel and targets from production and Naval reactors separates and removes the plutonium, tritium and uranium-235 for use in weapons fabrication or further fuel fabrication. Reprocessing takes place at the Hanford Reservation Purex plant (short for plutonium and uranium extraction), the Savannah River plant, and the Idaho Falls lab. A new special isotope separation process is being researched at Los Alamos National Lab using a laser separation process and it is planned to be built at the Idaho National Engineering Lab. Once these processes separate the plutonium, tritium, and uranium from the other usable isotopes, these materials are sent to the weapons component fabrication centres to make the nuclear structurals for the warheads. Meanwhile, the remainder of so-called high-level, low-level and transuranic radioactive wastes are treated, and then stored for interim and final disposal.

Fabrication of the nuclear components for warhead assemblies takes place at the Rocky Flats facility in Colorado, the Y-12 plant at Oak Ridge, and the Savannah River plant. In addition, non-nuclear components are fabricated at the Mound facility in Miamisburg, Ohio, the Pinellas Plant in Florida, and the Kansas City, Missouri, plant managed by Bendix. The facilities, contractors, employment, and unions are presented in Table 3. The figures for total employment levels include clerical workers, guards and other non-production workers, many of which are organized by other unions. While approximately half of the workforce at each facility is directly involved in nuclear weapons production, all of these workers depend on such military contracts to keep them employed at these facilities. As such, one should pay attention to total employment levels at each plant, since any alteration in capacity utilization will affect the other components of the workforce.

TABLE 3. *DOE nuclear warhead production facilities characteristics*

Facility/Location	Prime Contractor	Employment	Primary Unions
Kansas City Plant, Kansas City, Missouri	Bendix Corp.	7,287	International Association of Machinists & Aerospace Workers
Mound Facility, Miamisburg, Ohio	Monsanto Research Co.	2,274	Oil, Chemical & Atomic Workers
Pantex Plant, Amarillo, Texas	Mason & Hanger Silas & Mason	2,833	Metal Trade Council
Pinellas Plant, Clearwater, Florida	General Electric	1,972	No Union
Rocky Flats Plant, Golden, Colorado	Westinghouse Co. (formerly run by Rockwell International)	5,511	Oil, Chemical & Atomic Workers
Y-12 Plant, Oak Ridge, Tennessee	Martin Marietta	7,235	"

Source: *Approximate Current Employment On Operations & Maintenance at Department of Energy Installations, September 30, 1986,* by the Metal Trades Council of the AFL-CIO, from their annual conference proceedings, Washington D.C.

All nuclear and non-nuclear warhead components are shipped to the Pantex plant in Amarillo, Texas for final assembly into the warhead.

Warheads that are scheduled to be retired are sent to Pantex for dis-assembly so that the nuclear components can be reused in new generation warheads.

Throughout this process, considerable amounts of radioactive waste products are generated by the various production processes. Under the Defense Waste Management Plan of 1982, interim storage of high-level radioactive wastes generated from reprocessing and isotope separation is handled by Savannah River, Hanford and Idaho Falls. Defence trans-uranic wastes are stored at six sites, including Hanford, Savannah River, Idaho Falls, Oak Ridge, Los Alamos, and the Nevada Test site. Storage capacity of high-level radiation wastes (HLW) generated from reprocessing and isotope separation has been increased at Hanford, Savannah River and Idaho Falls, with the addition of new storage tanks to replace older tanks that are subject to corrosion and leaks. In addition, several new waste technologies are being developed to treat and store high-level wastes through waste immobilization and solidification. At Savannah River a high-level waste solidification plant is being completed that will be able to process 1,200 cubic metres of radio-active HLW sludge and produce 500 canisters of boro-silicate glass per year.[11] Also, a full-scale incineration programme for transuranic wastes is scheduled to begin at Savannah River by 1989. The incineration programme actually began in 1973, but was upgraded in 1984 with a $12 million investment to achieve supercritical combustion of transuranic wastes.[12]

Waste treatment and storage form the penultimate phase of the nuclear fuel cycle, preparing the wastes for final storage. A final depository for high-level wastes has yet to be determined, but the proposed site is located in the Yucca mountains of the Nevada Nuclear Test Site. An underground repository for transuranic wastes called the Waste Isolation Pilot Project (WIPP) has been constructed near Carlsbad, New Mexico at a cost of $700 million. Yet, this repository which is to store wastes contaminated by plutonium (or by other radioactive isotopes with an atomic number greater than uranium) was not opened as scheduled in 1988 because of geological instability due to the leakage of brine into the underground salt caverns. Because of these problems, the last link in the nuclear weapons fuel cycle has not been completed, and therefore the first generation of the fuel cycle has yet to achieve closure.

This overview of the nuclear weapons fuel cycle gives a sense of the technical complexity of the industry's structure and the size of employment within each segment. Let us now turn to examine the historical determinants of the production levels within the nuclear weapons production complex.

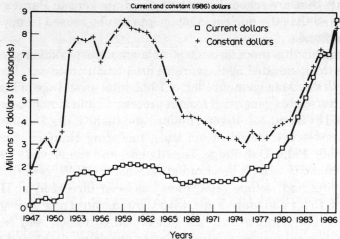

Years

FIGURE 2. Atomic energy defence expenditures

Source: *Nuclear Weapons Databook, US Nuclear Warhead Production* Vol. 2, by Thomas Cochran et. al., Ballinger Publishers, 1987, p. 4. The 1987 figure was updated with outlays from the *Department of Energy, FY 1988 Budget Requests, Estimates for Labs and Plants* by the Office of the Comptroller, Washington D.C., February 1987.

3. Historical determinants of production levels

Changes in strategic policy in the postwar period have accounted for the major shifts in production levels in the nuclear production complex. Four distinct cycles in nuclear weapons production levels can be tied directly to specific strategic policy decisions which required higher levels of funding of nuclear weapons R&D and production. Annual US atomic energy defence expenditures are depicted in Figure 2.

The first peacetime nuclear buildup began in 1947 as an effort to build up a stockpile of deliverable fission bomb designs, and lasted until 1950. Thereafter, President Truman made the decision to develop the thermonuclear bomb, which brought about a dramatic increase in expenditures on nuclear weapons research and development. The dip in expenditures in 1954 marked a brief period of austerity imposed under the first year of the Eisenhower Administration, which gave way to much higher levels of funding to support the development and deployment of a stockpile of new thermonuclear warhead designs. And by the mid-1950s, research had begun on light-weight warhead designs suitable for guided missiles.

Expenditures declined after 1962, reflecting the completion of the research and development phase of missile warhead buildup. Furthermore, in 1964 President Johnson announced a cutback in the capacity of utilization of all military production reactors as a means to underscore the US intention to negotiate further nuclear arms control agreements. Moreover, by 1964, the US had built up substantial reserves of highly enriched uranium and weapons-grade plutonium.[13] An upturn in expenditures during the mid-1970s coincides with the production of new warhead designs for Multiple Independently Targeted Reentry Vehicles (MIRVs) on ICBMs and SLBMs.

A fourth distinct phase of development occurs after 1979, when President Carter signed the Nuclear Weapons Stockpile Memorandum of 5 January 1979, setting higher warhead production levels. These production levels were raised again in 1982 after President Reagan took office and he put forth a five-year plan to modernize strategic and tactical nuclear forces. President Reagan's programme included new bombers, Air-Launched Cruise Missiles, a new Trident submarine missile and its D-5 warhead, the Pershing II missile and the MX missile. In addition, the designs of these new warheads have a higher yield-to-weight ratio, which requires more highly enriched uranium for the warheads. This warhead development, while in keeping with the general trend towards smaller, lighter warheads, has reversed the trend since the late 1960s towards less megatonnage per warhead. Thus, technological innovations in warhead design have made the next generation of warheads more accurate and powerful. Nonetheless, under the proposed START-type treaty, strategic nuclear weapons total megatonnage would probably be reduced by 50%.

It is in this context that one can understand the nature of the proposed five-year 50% reductions in strategic weapons systems under the Gorbachev and Reagan plans. Since the proposed agreement only sets numerical limits on warheads deployed, it does not restrict the modernization of the nuclear forces of either country. While the agreement would set a limit of about 6,000 warheads apiece, it does not preclude the production of weapons systems that are already out of the research and development stage. More importantly, the advertised 50% reductions in warheads excludes various nuclear bombs under 'special counting' rules, principally because of difficulties in establishing clear-cut verification procedures. Thus, the actual number of nuclear warheads on the US side would be reduced by 30% from 13,000 to 9,000, and the Soviets' nuclear warheads would be cut by 35% from 11,000 to 7,000. The total number of strategic nuclear delivery vehicles would be reduced from 2,000 to 1,600 for the US, and from 2,475 to 1,600 for the Soviets.[14] Yet none of the new nuclear delivery systems or warhead designs would be affected by the so-called 50% reduction proposal.

To be sure, the strategic nuclear weapons proposals would effect real reductions in strategic warhead deployment levels, but this would be achieved by retiring older systems for replacement by new systems. The net effect would be that the nuclear weapons production complex would still be producing at record high levels the new nuclear and non-nuclear components for the next generation of weapons. Perhaps more telling is the fact that the Soviet and US arms control negotiators cannot agree on the terms for the second five years of the proposal, which according to Mr. Gorbachev's rendering of the terms, would require an eventual elimination of all strategic nuclear delivery systems. However, the Reagan Administration understands the proposal not to cover strategic bombers during the second five-year period. While a lack of agreement about the meaning of the second five-year period disarmament proposal raises doubts about the likelihood of any treaty, the fact that the first five-year period does not preclude modernization of the strategic nuclear forces, illustrates the lack of seriousness of these proposals as a means to real disarmament.

Intermediate nuclear weapons reductions through the signing of the Intermediate Nuclear Forces Treaty only affects the Pershing II deployments and the Ground Launched Cruise Missile (GLCM). Since the Pershing II warheads are completed, a staged reduction and phasing out of the Pershing II should have little effect on the production levels of the nuclear production complex. By contrast, the Ground Launched Cruise Missile has only been 60% deployed, and therefore the Treaty restricting these deployments should mean 150 to 200 fewer warheads produced for GLCMs. Nonetheless, the agreement does not preclude compensatory modernization through the deployment of the Advanced Cruise Missile, including the air-launched and sea-launched versions of the Cruise Missile.

While these agreements might have a slight effect on the production levels within the complex, the overall effect is likely to be low, because the stockpile requirements that were set under the Reagan Administration have necessitated much higher production volumes than would be suggested by warhead requirements for new delivery systems.

Stockpiling of strategic nuclear materials has had a dramatic effect on total employment in the nuclear weapons production complex. A glance at the employment trends over the period from 1963 to 1986 shows how the changes in strategic nuclear policy have affected employment within the complex. As Figure 3 shows, the reductions in nuclear production that were brought about after the 1964 decision by President Lyndon Johnson to cut production of strategic nuclear materials by 20%, caused a drastic loss of employment among workers within the nuclear weapons production complex. Employment declined from about 38,000 workers directly involved in nuclear weapons development and production, to a low of about 28,500 workers. Thereafter, employment rose to a plateau of about 31,000 workers from 1969 through 1975, as the nuclear complex geared up to produce the MIRV warheads for the strategic missile launchers. But it was not until 1979, when President Carter signed an executive memorandum calling for higher levels of

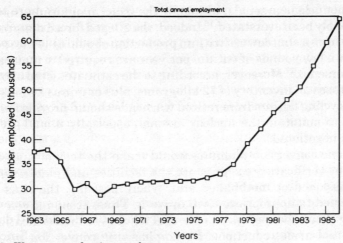

FIGURE 3. Weapons production employment
Source: *Occupational Employment in Atomic Activities*, by the AEC, ERDA, and DOE, 1968, 1975, 1985, 1987. This is a biannual survey conducted for the DOE. Intervening years are inputed by means of linear interpolation.

production of strategic nuclear materials, that employment grew rapidly. By 1986, total employment of workers directly involved in nuclear weapons production had reached about 65,000. I should note that these employment statistics are the only data compiled through an actual survey of government and contractor plants to discover the numbers of employees participating in nuclear weapons production. Also, these data do not include numerous scientists working in the National Laboratories in support of the principal weapons production researchers and workers, other maintenance and support workers, and workers in the uranium enrichment facilities. If one includes these other workers, total employment in 1986 stood at about 116,000 according to the DOE's Office of Industrial Relations.

Higher production levels of plutonium and tritium were begun so as to counter fears that there might be a shortage of these materials in the longer term. Nonetheless, as Frank von Hippel and others have shown, there is little reason for the US government to fear a shortage of fissile materials, especially if our leaders are committed to assuring real reductions in nuclear force levels.[15] For years many leading scientists have called for the end to production of strategic nuclear materials as a means to promote international cooperation for nuclear arms reduction. Furthermore, an elimination of plutonium and tritium production would make verification much easier, since only the commercial nuclear power sector would have to be policed by the International Atomic Energy Agency. It should be noted that since tritium decays by 5.5% per year, a cessation of its production would enforce a gradual reduction in thermonuclear arsenals, although the exact magnitude this effect has probably been overstated.[16] Indeed, the alleged forced disarmament scenario from a shutdown of tritium production should take into account that only a few pounds of tritium per year are required to maintain the nuclear arsenal.[17] Moreover, according to the estimates cited above, the US possesses an inventory of 72 kilograms, plus or minus 24 kilograms. Thus, recycling tritium from retired warheads should provide sufficient supplies to maintain the nuclear arsenal, especially if a START-type treaty is negotiated.

Economic conversion planning would make the task of nuclear disarmament verification easier, since the facilities and plants would be decommissioned or mothballed and, where possible, the sites would be converted to appropriate civilian work. Thus, economic conversion planning should be seen as an essential adjunct to the verification process for real arms reductions. By emphasizing conversion instead of modernization of nuclear forces, there is less resistance to taking the next step in arms reductions.

Clearly, any change in policy towards disarmament that requires the linking of nuclear weapons material production to treaty verification, will have wide-ranging effects on employment within the industry. While the total number of workers is not large, the regional effect of such a lay off would have a far more pronounced effect for people who work and live near these facilities. Thus, economic conversion for nuclear weapons facilities makes sense from an international perspective as a means to promote trust and cooperation, and in order to mitigate the regional economic dislocations. Let us turn to examine the literature and approaches to estimating the possible impacts of such a conversion project.

4. Economic conversion studies of the nuclear weapons production complex

Few studies have been conducted on economic conversion of nuclear weapons production facilities, and none has yet been systematically implemented. Nor have any of these studies addressed the issue of the impact of a complete cessation of production of weapons-grade nuclear materials. Most recently, in March of 1988, the state of Washington completed an economic diversification study for the Tri-Cities area located near the Hanford Reservation to analyze how the region might become less dependent upon nuclear weapons-related work.[18] This study was initiated as a result of legislation enacted by the state which recognized that the cessation of the Hanford N-reactor would have dramatic repercussions on the local economy.[19] While the study does not concentrate on the direct conversion potential of the Hanford operations, it does make an extensive evaluation of the feasible strategies available to diversify the regional economy. The study identifies numerous growth industries which are compatible with the Tri-Cities regional industrial base, as well as several import substitution markets. In addition, several key areas of public transportation, environmental and recreational infrastructural investment are identified which could promote economic growth and job creation in civilian industries.

Another conversion study was sponsored by the state of Colorado in 1981 to evaluate the impact of a shutdown of the Rocky Flats facility on the regional economy, and to evaluate alternative uses for the facility if production were relocated away from the existing area. The study was done by Battelle National Laboratories in Columbus, Ohio, and set forth a wide range of possible manufacturing and distribution operations that might best use the location and resources to build new businesses.[20]

Another case study was done in 1970 for the Hanford Reservation to evaluate the potential for diversifying the facility away from its dependence on military nuclear work and also to evaluate the potential effects of a complete nuclear disarmament treaty on employment in the region.[21]

Citizen and labour organizations in several states have attempted over the last few years to initiate their own economic conversion and diversification studies for several nuclear weapons facilities. Most recently, Citizen Alert in Nevada has begun preliminary research on economic diversification for the four county area continguous to the Nuclear Test Site in southern Nevada. In Idaho, the Snake River Alliance is also in the initial stages of launching a conversion and diversification study for the Idaho National Engineering Lab. In Ohio, trade unionists and community groups began a study of the conversion potential of the uranium enrichment plants at Piketon, Ohio and Paducah, Kentucky. The project, known as the Atomic Reclamation and Conversion Project (ARC), was begun in 1983 with the recognition that the decline of the commercial nuclear power industry posed a decisive threat to the future of these plants. Faced with the prospect of a stagnating commercial nuclear power industry, the trade unionists from the Oil, Chemical and Atomic Energy Workers Union set about to devise ways to respond to layoffs. Unfortunately, the ARC project never got beyond the proposal stage, largely because of financial limitations.[22]

In addition to these case studies, the Environmental Impact Statements and several economic impact analyses prepared by the Department of Energy to evaluate the effects of new construction projects at facilities within the production complex, provide important data to assess the regional impacts of each facility. Together, these studies provide some basis for estimating the regional impacts of changes in the utilization of these facilities. But before examining the results of these studies, let us consider the special nature of the problem.

4.1. Dimensions of the conversion problem

Nuclear weapons production facilities pose special problems for conversion planning, largely because of the specialized nature of the equipment and the radiological and environmental hazards that stem directly from the production processes and regulatory practices at the facilities. Under these conditions, direct conversion of such facilities may not be possible for many of the facilities. Indeed, the central conversion problem at many sites will be the environmental cleanup of the production plant and equipment, the removal of low-level, high-level, transuranic and toxic wastes, the environmental monitoring of on-site inactive waste repositories, and remedial action on many inactive waste facilities which have caused off-site ground, air and water contamination. In addition, off-site contamination will have to be cleaned up, while the remaining active nuclear production facilities would have to be upgraded to comply with existing environmental regulations to eliminate emissions from the plants. Inactive nuclear weapons facilities must be decommissioned and dismantled and safely disposed of in an environmentally sound manner.

In this context, economic conversion planners should focus on the potential employment and income impacts of these cleanup operations as one means to mitigate the dislocations stemming from a complete or partial shutdown of a facility. In addition, conversion planners could evaluate the direct conversion potential of the scientific, technical, engineering and production personnel, as well as the non-nuclear plant and equipment. Finally, diversification planning for the regional economy may be the most effective means of reducing the economic dependency of nuclear weapons production contracts. Diversification in this sense refers to state and local planning efforts to attract and develop new businesses in new markets and product fields suitable to the comparative economic advantages of the region.

Conversion analysis typically begins by estimating the baseline employment, income and output effects of a facility, which should be derived from the current status of operational plants and new construction projects already underway. Such a baseline analysis is an essential step for analyzing the economic impacts of a partial or complete shutdown of weapons production reactors and nuclear fuel cycle facilities. The alternative conversion scenario for reemploying and reusing people and resources at these facilities should consider four dimensions of conversion planning.

The first dimension of the conversion problem concerns the economic impact of decommissioning and dismantling (D&D) some or all of the nuclear weapons materials production reactors and fuel cycle facilities. Many surveys of reactor decommissioning have shown that dismantlement is more cost effective that either mothballing or entombment; therefore I will focus on D&D estimates.[23] Experience with commercial D&D at the Shippingport plant in Pennsylvania shows that it costs about $1.36 million per megawatt (electric) of installed capacity and usually takes about four years to complete. A lower-end estimate of D&D costs place the charge at $450,000 for decommissioning and dismantling the Dresden 1 nuclear power plant outside Chicago, Illinois.

As an example of the magnitude of these D&D costs let us examine the situation at the Savannah River Plant (SRP). Assuming that the five production reactors at SRP are rated at 860 megawatt(e), just like the Hanford Washington N-reactor, then the high-end total D&D costs comes to about $5.8 billion over a four-year period, while the low-end calculation places the charge at $2.3 billion. Surveys of D&D cost estimates also show that labour costs constitute between 25% and 50% of total costs, and that it takes about 300 work years to perform the dismantlement. In addition there is the time-consuming work of decontamination which must be estimated.[24] Clearly, reactor decommissioning and dismantlement will provide some immediate employment relief to the affected region.

Recent DOE economic assessments of the total costs for decommissioning and dismantling reactor and fuel cycle facilities before 1995 are estimated to amount $5 to $7 billion (in 1990 dollars) and another $3 billion for inactive enrichment facilities. In addition, D&D for facilities after 1995 are estimated conservatively to cost at least $10 billion.[25]

A second dimension of the conversion problem involves evaluating the costs and employment impacts of putting many of the nuclear weapons production facilities in compliance with the Clean Water Act standards and the Resource Conservation and Recovery Act requirements.[26] A recent GAO report has shown that several facilities are not in compliance with these civilian standards.[27] For example, groundwater contamination at the Savannah River Plant (SRP) by tritium is 2,500 times drinking water standards, and nitrate and mercury levels are elevated above acceptable levels. Since the SRP facilities are located above the Tuscaloosa aquifer, which extends into Georgia, Florida and Alabama, groundwater contamination requires immediate and careful clean-up. The DOE estimates that it will cost $50 million to provide additional waste water treatment for the reprocessing plant, and $30 million to close the seepage basins. Soil contamination at the SRP facilities of on-site areas by plutonium was found to be ten times the 'background' level, and soil under HLW storage tanks was contaminated. The DOE reports that overall cleanup costs are likely to be higher, costing about

$1,490 million (in 1990 dollars) before 1995, and perhaps another $349 million after 1995. In addition, upgrading operating facilities to comply with current environmental regulations could cost $2,872 million through the year 2045.[28]

On a national basis, the DOE estimates that it could cost $66 billion to $110 billion to clean up the sixteen major facilities in the nuclear weapons complex and bring them into compliance with environmental laws. These cleanup measures are estimated to extend through the year 2045, and therefore should have a long-run effect on employment for the regional economies near the nuclear weapons facilities.[29]

A third dimension of the conversion planning process should address the possibility of converting some of the complex to civilian work by transferring unused or 'excessed' resources to applicable projects. A conversion resource assessment should include the type and value of plant and equipment, and an inventory of the workforce skills and educational background. The inventories of plant and equipment at these sites should focus on the support facilities, which are less likely to be exposed to radiological contamination. Of particular interest are support facilities such as machine shops, communication facilities and computing and heavy equipment. In addition, some laboratories and fabrication shops may have direct conversion potential, especially if they were not integral parts of the fuel cycle production processes. Possible uses for the process-oriented facilities might include: ethanol fuel production; alternative energy R&D; municipal solid waste treatment and disposal; and hazardous waste treatment and disposal. Of course a careful inventory of the plant, equipment, and labour resources would have to precede any conversion study; followed by an engineering feasibility study and a marketing survey to assess the regional and national market.

A fourth dimension of conversion planning should evaluate economic development strategies that are independent of converting the facility because it may not be feasible or desirable to convert all or part of the complex to civilian work (though the workforce can always be converted). This type of diversification strategy depends on attracting and developing new businesses which are producing new products or opening up new regional markets. It should be emphasized that such a diversification strategy does not presuppose corporate diversification from military into civilian markets. Indeed, such an economic diversification strategy may work better through local and state initiatives to attract businesses to develop new products and markets which are compatible with the local economic resources and market potential.

4.2. Conversion and diversification case studies

Washington state launched an ambitious study in 1987 to promote the economic diversification of the Tri-Cities region comprised by the cities of Richland, Kennewick and Pasco and located adjacent to the DOE nuclear weapons complex at Hanford. State-wide peace and environmental groups were primarily responsible for initiating the legislation necessary to finance the study and inaugurate an on-going diversification process with some state assistance. The apparent catalyst for state support of the diversification study and programme was the prospective shutdown and closure of the Hanford N-reactor, which was expected to result in the loss of 6,300 jobs and $213 million for the Tri-Cities region. Losses of this magnitude would comprise about 11% of the employment and 14% of the income of the Benton-Franklin county regional economies. To date these losses have been delayed, as the DOE has yet to take definitive actions. However, timely planning by the state and local communities could mitigate the economic dislocations from a complete shutdown of the N-reactor. Furthermore, the economic significance and dependence of the regional economy is even greater, since the total direct employment at Hanford amounts to 14,500 jobs and is estimated to generate 21,500 additional jobs throughout the region and the rest of the state.[30]

Against this backdrop, the economic diversification study aimed to identify the opportunities for attracting new businesses to develop new regional, national and international markets for local production, as well as new products. An industrial screening model was used to match the regional economic assets of the Tri-Cities area with the operational and locational requirements of various growth industries. The results identified several key industries with market potential in agricultural food processing, biological products, pharmaceutical preparations, heating equipment, boat building and optical and surgical instruments and equipment. In addition, the study identified specific conversion potential for selected technologies utilizing the scientific and technological base of Hanford. The possible conversion fields included bioengineering, space systems design and communications, miniaturization of medical, space and energy technologies, ceramic and metallurgical R&D, alternative energy R&D and waste disposal technologies.

Import substitution for the regional and state economy was also explored as a strategy to encourage economic diversification. Import substitution occurs when a region begins to produce and market locally a good which had previously been imported to the region. Reducing regional imports generally tends to improve a region's income and stimulates growth. The study identified several industries with import substitution potential which included canned and preserved fruits and vegetables, fats and oils, wines, paper products, printing and publishing, plastic products, glass products, fabricated metal structures, and electronic equipment and components. Together, these products represent a market potential of over $21 million per year. In order to stimulate an import substitution process, the study recommended setting up a regional marketing agency, as well as providing more financial incentives and access to business loans.

As mandated by the enabling legislation for this study, a number of recommendations were made for concrete steps to diversify the regional economy. The study recommended that state and local resources be committed to establishing an agricultural development agency, a regional export programme and a business recruitment and venture capital programme. Specific public investments were recommended for the establishment of a molecular science centre, a new university centre for the Tri-Cities, and the development of waterfront and waterway improvements, as well as the widening of key highway arteries needed for expanded trade within the state.

The Washington state study provides an excellent model for state initiatives to diversify a regional economy and lessen its military dependence. It differs from traditional conversion strategies in that it emphasizes the development of civilian industries and regional economies which do not depend on direct conversion of the military production plant, equipment and personnel. The use of state legislation to promote economic diversification also promises to yield a real financial commitment on the part of the state to the lessening of the region's dependence on Hanford. The study contains many innovative ideas for financing and planning such regional economic diversification. Yet, the shortcoming of the study is that it does not explicitly deal with the extensive retraining problems faced by workers due to a partial or complete shutdown of the Hanford. Indeed, the study is rather overly optimistic about the re-employment potential of the Hanford workers, scientists and engineers. Finally, while it was beyond the scope of the study, it does not evaluate the repercussions on the regional labour market of an extensive environmental cleanup programme at the Hanford Reservation. The DOE has recently estimated that such a cleanup programme could cost as much as $45 billion through the year 2045.[31] Clearly, such a programme would have a pronounced effect on regional labour markets for many years to come.

One of the most comprehensive conversion studies of a nuclear weapons production facility was done by Battelle Columbus Laboratories for the Department of Energy and Rockwell International for the Rocky Flats Plant in Colorado. The object of the study was to assess the impact of relocating the production facility out of region, and to assess the possible reuses of the facility. The strength of this study was that it used an input-output model to estimate the regional direct, indirect and induced effects on income, employment and output due to a shut-down of the facility, and to assess the impact of its possible reuse. Direct employment effects are those gains or losses due to hirings or layoffs at the plant in question. Indirect employment effects are due to layoffs from subcontractors or suppliers who no longer have these contracts and must adjust production. Induced effects are the consequences of the lower income and spending that result from the shutdown of a facility in a region, which in turn may have a significant effect on the employment, income and earnings of the surrounding community. The relationship between the primary, or direct effects, and the secondary, or indirect and induced effects is characterized by economists as multiplier relationship. For example, an employment multiplier of 1.5 implies that for every two primary jobs, there is an additional one job created.

The Battelle study of the Rocky Flats installation analyzed two case studies for the impact of a partial relocation of plutonium operations, and a complete relocation of the whole facility. Estimates were devel-oped for the income, output and employment impacts of these two cases. The output multiplier was estimated to be 1.21, which means for every dollar of output produced at the facility, there is an additional 21¢ of output indirectly attributable to the effects of the facilities operation. The employment multiplier was estimated to be 1.42, thus on average, for every job loss or gain at the facility, the region experiences a corres-ponding 0.42 loss or gain in employment. The income multiplier was estimated to be 1.71, thus for every dollar change of income produced at the facility, there is a corresponding change of 0.71.

The importance of these figures is that they provide a method for calculating the effects of the annual changes in employment, income and output on the surrounding community or region. These input-out-put relationships change very slowly over time, thus these estimates may be used to calculate, for example, the employment impact on the surrounding community of a shutdown of the Rocky Flats plant. Accord-ing to this estimate the total loss of employment due to a complete shutdown would be 8,507 jobs regionally. Within the Denver-Boulder standard metropolitan statistical area, this loss of jobs would not be a significant impact when compared to total employment, but when measured in relation to manufacturing employment, it could amount to about 4–6% of all new industrial jobs in the region. Thus there are some grounds to be concerned over the industrial employment impacts.

Perhaps the more interesting aspect of the study is that it develops a methodology for identifying industries to target for potential reuse of the site and its facilities. First it analyzes the regional growth industries to identify potential industrial and service sectors that provide good opportunities. Next, the study evaluates the regional supply and demand relationships by industry, so as to assess whether there is specific advantage to locating in the region. The study then screens the industries in terms of several operational and locational criteria that make a difference to potential entrants to the field, such as the academic background of the workforce, occupational structure, transportation and infrastructural requirements of the industry relative to local and regional infrastructure.

Parallel to this assessment, the Rocky Flats contractor drew up a list of the plant, equipment and facilities that would be available for reuse after the site has been decontaminated and the property made available for lease or sale. It is noteworthy to mention here that the contractor and government officials estimated that cleanup could take seven to ten years, and the process of transferring the government property could take another three to five years. Clearly, there are many obstacles to converting such a site to industrial reuse, especially if the time horizon for conversion planning must be ten to fifteen years.

Based on a breakdown of the physical plant and facilities by category of use for administration, manufacturing, laboratory service, maintenance, warehousing, storage and materials handling, a conversion score was computed for the total square feet of plant and facilities that would be available for reuse after decontamination and removal of property and equipment that the government and contractor will retain. From this partial list of resources, the study looked to match these resources to the list of best-bet growth areas in the regional economy. The general model of industrial redevelopment was to make the site into an industrial park. There was no attempt to look at an integrated facility on the site. In general, the study identified several manufacturing product fields in electronics, electrical machinery, non-electronic machinery, pharmaceuticals, transportation equipment, and scientific and mechanical instrumentation.

The shortcoming of this study was that it did not evaluate the conversion planning problems for the workers and managers who had worked for years at the plant under the strict security regime of a major defence installation, and had become accustomed to the non-competitive norms of government defence contracting. There is also the problem of retooling scientists and engineers for work in civilian fields. None of these problems were addressed by the study, and in order to address them properly, there must be national legislation in place to provide income support and financing for such retraining and conversion planning.

The Atomic Reclamation and Conversion Project in Ohio and Kentucky was an attempt at advance planning by a citizen group composed of workers and members of the community, who were concerned about the prospect of their plants closing in ten to fifteen years. Clearly, with the sagging nuclear power industry, and the old high-cost gas diffusion technology in these plants, the ARC project was a timely application of conversion planning.

Funding limitations led to the demise of the ARC project, yet the preliminary proposal for research had many interesting ideas about possible startup projects that were tied to local infrastructural needs. The study advanced such ideas as an ethanol fuel production facility, an industrial biomass gasification plant, municipal solid waste management and sorting, recycling research and waste incineration research, and possibly the storage of low-level radioactive wastes or hazardous wastes. Generally, this project took a more active interest in analyzing how the conversion would affect and serve the local community. In that regard the preliminary analysis stated possibilities that might be technically feasible, but would also have to be acceptable to the community.

The last conversion case study considered here is by Aris Christodoulou, which focused on the Hanford Nuclear Reservation and efforts to diversify its operations so as to make the locality less sensitive to the fluctuation in federal operations at the facilities.[32] Unfortunately, many of the conversion applications suggested by this study depended on moving into civilian nuclear power research. When the study was conceived in 1969–70, civilian nuclear power may have seemed like a growth industry, but today, many of the proposals put forward by this study are no longer feasible. In many ways, the idea behind this type of conversion goes back to the early days of nuclear energy, when many saw the peaceful atom as a means to convert the military uses of nuclear energy to serve civilian needs. But today the links between the military and civilian atom are clearer, and it is evident that the intertwining of the industrial infrastructure of one lends strength to the other. Therefore, industrial conversion to civilian nuclear power should be viewed somewhat sceptically.

Various regional economic impacts are analyzed in the Environmental Impact Statements for a number of facilities that are undergoing major construction projects related to the expansion of the nuclear production complex. The shortcoming of these studies in evaluating the regional employment, income and output impacts is that they do not use economic modelling to analyze the effects of changes in the capacity utilization or expansion of these facilities. Generally, the employment and income multipliers seem to be inflated, and tend to be on the order of 2.32 for income multipliers. When compared to input-output generated multipliers, which are on the order of 1.6 to 1.8, there must be some questions about the reliability of the Environmental Impact Statements estimates.[33] Perhaps the best method for estimating the regional impacts of such conversion studies is to use a regional input-output model.

4.3. Economic impact analysis

Regional economic modelling of the income and employment changes based on input-output (I-O) analysis would be the preferred method to estimate the multipliers for such a study of the shutdown, conversion and economic diversification of nuclear weapons facilities. Direct, indirect and induced income, employment, and output impacts can be calculated from a given change in demand through an I-O framework like the Commerce Department's RIMS II model.[34] There are many other I-O models which can perform the same calculations as the RIMS II model. For example, George Treyz of Regional Economic Models, Inc. has developed an input-output model that is co-joined to a regional econometric model, which supplies fairly reliable regional economic estimates.[35] It should be noted that such modelling is expensive, and therefore requires some organizational funding. However, if the United States government was committed to using conversion planning as a necessary and complementary activity for a verifiable disarmament treaty, then cost would be a small matter.

On a national scale, the number of workers employed in nuclear weapons production facilities might seem relatively small, even when one calculates the indirect employment effects. Taking the current total employment at the nuclear weapons facilities in 1987 at about 116,000 workers, including enrichment plant and operation and maintenance workers and other supporting research scientists, and assuming a low- and high-end employment multiplier of 1.4 and 1.8, the total direct and indirect employment effect attributable to nuclear weapons production is between 162,400 to 208,800. Nationally, taking an income multiplier which ranges between 1.75 and 2.0, results in a total income multiplier for Fiscal Year 1987 of between $15.2 billion to $17.4 billion. Of course, the regional impact of this employment and spending is bound to be far more pronounced locally than it is nationally. Nonetheless, major adjustments in the scale and scope of such spending and employment would require careful planning both nationally and regionally. Certainly, the government should take some responsibility for conversion planning in an industry which it owns and manages. But more importantly, if nuclear disarmament is to be taken seriously, we must begin to take economic conversion planning as part of the disarmament process. This is especially true in the nuclear field, where the process of checking the inventory of nuclear materials is made easier without military production reactors.

5. Conclusion

The United States faces a critical strategic decision as to whether it should replace the aging and unsafe nuclear weapons production facilities with a second generation of plutonium and tritium production reactors and reprocessing plants, or convert them, where possible, to civilian use. Currently, Department of Defense planners and the Department of Energy have begun to build waste separation, incineration and disposal facilities for military radioactive wastes, thus completing the first generation of the nuclear-industrial-complex. In addition, the DOE plans a second generation of the nuclear weapons complex with two new production reactors and a special isotope separation facility. One of the proposed reactors would produce plutonium at a site provisionally located in Idaho at the INEL, while the other proposed reactor at SRP in South Carolina would produce tritium. Preliminary DOE estimates for building these two reactors come to about $6.8 billion. However, these estimates seem conservative since the new plutonium production reactor design involves an entirely new modual concept linking several small gas-cooled reactors together. Moreover, these new reactors would use an entirely new type of fuel element and fuel assembly.[36] This reactor design is widely regarded by nuclear industry analysts as a prototype for a new so-called inherently safe design for the next generation of commercial reactors.

These plans unfold in the context of the strategic nuclear build-up since 1979 which has led to a revival of the aging nuclear production facilities, a growth in total employment in the nuclear weapons complex, and an increased awareness of environmental hazards of the existing facilities. The accelerated usage of these obsolete and environmentally unsound facilities has led to a breakdown in critical linkages of the nuclear weapons fuel cycle. Most prominent are the shutdown of the production reactors, warhead fabrication plants, and the unresolved waste disposal problem. Despite the current crisis affecting the whole complex, these decisions to restart and rebuild the nuclear weapons production base are having wide-ranging effects on the income, employment and environmental safety of the people living and working in and around these facilities. More importantly, these actions by the US nuclear planners presage the development of a whole new generation of nuclear weapons systems, which will likely block the path to disarmament.

It is overdue that the peace movement press the issue of conversion as a central component of any staged disarmament process. Such conversion will help to establish trust and international cooperation, as well as making the verification process easier. However, conversion on this scale needs the institutional framework of national conversion legislation and local initiative and planning to provide the ways and means to effect a successful conversion and diversification process.

NOTES AND REFERENCES

1. For a discussion of zonal inspection, see L. B. Sohn, 'Disarmament and Arms Control by Territories' in the *Bulletin of Atomic Scientists*, Vol. 17, April, 1961, p. 130. Also see David Inglis, 'Region by Region System of Inspection and Disarmament' in *Journal of Conflict Resolution*, Vol. 9, 1965, p. 187.
2. See Frank von Hippel, David Albright and Christopher Paine, 'The Danger of Military Reactors' in the *Bulletin of Atomic Scientists*, October 1986, pp. 44–48.
3. Budget data are from the Office of Controller of the Department of Energy for budget requests for Fiscal Year 1987.
4. Data are drawn from a number of sources, but the best general source is the *Nuclear Weapons Industry* by Kenneth Bertsch et. al., published by Investor Responsibility Research Center, Washington D.C., 1983, especially Chapter 3.
5. Data are from the annual conference report of the Metals Trades Council of the AFL-CIO, Washington D.C.
6. Estimates of the defence load of the research labs is based on an estimate from DOE budget requests for Fiscal Year 1987 for each lab's atomic defence activity request.
7. For a more detailed description of each of these research labs, see the *Nuclear Weapons Databook*, Vol. II, *U.S. Nuclear Warhead Production*, by Thomas Cochran et. al., Cambridge Mass.: Ballinger Books, 1987, Chapter 3.
8. Ibid., Appendix D, p. 197, Table D-7.
9. General Accounting Office, Testimony by Keith O. Fultz, Associate Director of Resources, Community and Economic Development, 'Management and Safety Issues Concerning DOE's Production Reactors at Savannah River, South Carolina', 12 March 1982. Before the Committee on Government Affairs of the US Senate.
10. Natural Resources Defense Council provided the estimates in the *Nuclear Weapons Databook*, Vol. II, op. cit., pp. 67–76 and p. 91.
11. *Spent Fuel and Radiation Wastes Inventories, Projections and Characteristics*, by the DOE/EIA, September 1983, pp. 234–38.
12. *Radwaste* by Fred Shapiro, New York: Random House, 1981, pp. 58 and 112.
13. See 'Conversion of Nuclear Facilities from Military to Civilian Uses: A Case Study of Hanford Nuclear Reservation' by Aris Christodoulou, in *Conversion of Industry from a Military to Civilian Economy*, edited by Seymour Melman, Lexington, Mass.: Lexington Books, 1970.
14. *START and Strategic Modernization* by Robert Norris, William Arkin and Thomas Cochran, Natural Resources Defense Council, Washington D.C., December 1987, pp. 13–16.
15. von Hippel, op. cit.
16. See 'The Tritium Factor' by Paul Leventhal and Milton Hoenig in *The New York Times*, 4 August 1988, op. ed. page.
17. See 'Major Fight Seen on Bomb Reactors Proposed by U.S.' by Michael Gordon in *The New York Times*, 5 December 1988, p. 12.
18. See *Tri-Cities Economic Diversification Study* by the Department of Trade and Economic Development of Washington State, March 1988, Washington State, Olympia, Washington.
19. Ibid., Appendix A.
20. See *The Social and Economic Impacts of Changing Missions at the Rocky Flats Plant* by Battelle Laboratories, Columbus, Ohio, for the Department of Energy, 1981.
21. Christodoulou, op. cit.
22. Unpublished draft of *Proposal for Atomic Reclamation and Conversion Project* by Employment Research Associates for the Atomic Reclamation and Conversion Project, Piketon, Ohio, 1985.
23. *Worldwatch Paper No. 65*, 'Decommissioning: Nuclear Power's Missing Link' by Cynthia Pollack, pp. 29–30.

24. Ibid.
25. See *Nuclear Health and Safety: Dealing with Problems in the Nuclear Defense Complex Expected to Cost Over $100 Billion* by the US General Accounting Office, July, 1988, p. 22.
26. General Accounting Office, *Nuclear Energy: Environmental Issues at DOE's Nuclear Defense Facilities*, September 1986, pp. 2–10.
27. Ibid.
28. See *Environment, Safety and Health Report for the Department of Energy Complex* by the US Department of Energy, 1 July 1988, Washington D.C., pp. Q1–Q7.
29. Ibid., pp. 34–35.
30. Tri-Cities Study, op.cit., p. ii and pp. 11–12.
31. *Nuclear Waste: Problems Associated With DOE's Inactive Waste Sites*, US General Accounting Office, August 1988, p. 31.
32. Christodoulou, op. cit.
33. See *Final Environmental Impact Statement: Defense Waste Processing Facility, Savannah River Plant, Aiken, S.C.*, February 1982, by the US DOE, Washington D.C. pp.4–4 through 4–14. Also see the Final EIS for *The Y-12 Plant Site, Oak Ridge, Tennessee,* December 1982, US DOE, pp.III-11-14 and Section IV. Also see the Draft EIS on the *Pantex Plant Site, Amarillo Texas,* December 1982, pp.2–17, 3–37, 4–21. And see Volume 2 of the draft EIS for *Disposal of Hanford Defense High Level, Transuranics and Tank Wastes,* March 1986, by US DOE, pp. 1-23. Also see *The Social and Economic Impact of the Department of Energy on the State of New Mexico, FY 1986* by the US Department of Energy, Albuquerque Operation Office, June 1987, pp. 17–21.
34. See *Regional Input-Output Modeling System (RIMS II): Estimation, Evaluation, and Application of a Disaggregated Regional Impact Model*, US Department of Commerce, Regional Economic Analysis Division, Bureau of Economic Analysis, Washington D.C., 1983.
35. See 'Using a Multi-Regional Forecasting and Simulation Model to Estimate the Effects of the Military Buildup from 1981–85 on State Economies' by George Treyz et al. of Regional Economic Models, University of Massachusetts, Amherst, 1986.
36. See 'Experts Call Reactor Design Immune to Disaster' by William Broad, in *The New York Times,* 15 November 1988, p. 25.

Converting the Military Economy Through the Local State: Local Conversion Prospects in Massachusetts

JONATHAN M. FELDMAN

1. Local conversion initiatives

Throughout the 1970s and 1980s, peace organizations in the United States began to organize a number of factory-based, state or municipal initiatives in support of economic conversion. In local conversion initiatives, the state has been the key arena for building coalitions around conversion legislation—pressuring state economic development agencies to try to carry out retraining, fund feasibility studies, assist in the transfer of civilian technology and provide economic assistance for local conversion projects. There have also been attempts at lobbying state political leaders to take over defence facilities.

Two important strategic questions have confronted conversion proponents in actions which attempt to pressure the local state as a lever in support of conversion. First, what opportunities and obstacles are presented by organizing on this political terrain, i.e., in non-federal political initiatives? In answering this question we will examine the role of the military economy, political lobbying groups, and business interests in shaping the state of Massachusetts. The second strategic question is: should local conversion advocates push for the use of incentives such as traditional economic development tools, or constraints such as laws which require alternative use committees and punish defence firms that fail to undertake planning for civilian production?

The state of Massachusetts provides a useful case study for examining the role of the local state in advancing and limiting local conversion initiatives. Massachusetts is one of the largest recipients of contract awards from the Pentagon, ranking fourth in dollars received in Fiscal Year (FY) 1985, after California, New York, and Texas. However, Massachusetts is also one of the most 'liberal' states in the US, having a large university population, and is second to California in the number of peace organizations.[1]

In the 1970s and 1980s, Massachusetts has been confronted with the twin problems of accelerated deindustrialization of traditional basic industry and increased militarization of key economic sectors. Relative to the first set of problems, there was a major struggle by labour and community organizations to gain passage of comprehensive plant closing legislation.

In response to increased militarization activists have attempted to regulate nuclear defence contractors in Cambridge, Massachusetts; organized a commission to study defence dependency at the Massachusetts Institute of Technology; and passed state and city 'Jobs With Peace' referenda that raise questions about the detrimental impact of national defence spending on communities. There have also been statewide activities in support of a 'nuclear freeze'. However, the most important local conversion initiative was the attempt by peace activists, community groups and progressive rank-and-file trade unionists to push General Dynamics, the state government and the local union leadership into supporting conversion of the Quincy Shipyard, a producer of Navy vessels in Quincy, Massachusetts.

The Quincy case illustrates both the limits and possibilities of promoting conversion planning, given the legal and institutional infrastructure provided by liberal state industrial policy measures. But, in judging how such *existing* measures were used in Quincy and what stands in the way of more comprehensive state conversion legislation, it is important to examine the economic and political forces which have prevented more radical, comprehensive conversion and reindustrialization planning by the local state.

2. Obstacles to state action I: the Massachusetts military economy

There has been a good deal of debate as to what role defence spending has played in creating rapid growth in the Massachusetts economy in the 1970s and 1980s. How much is attributable to economic development initiatives, the expansion of the service economy and growth in civilian high technology sectors as opposed to national defence spending? There is evidence that the dramatic turnaround in the Massachusetts economy from 1975 to 1985 was not based on economic development programmes and that the state's links to defence sectors played an important role. Public plus private (non-farm) employment in Massachusetts increased by 16% between 1975 and 1983, in contrast to only 4% between 1967 and 1975. In explaining this pattern of sustained and accelerated growth after 1979, Ronald F. Ferguson and Helen F. Ladd at Harvard's John F. Kennedy School of Government concluded:

... The state's disproportionate share of federal defense-related spending, the special attractiveness of Massachusetts for high technology industries and exportable business services, and the increased spending associated with rising income probably account for the bulk of the above-average performance of key Massachusetts sectors during this period.[2]

The link between Massachusetts' growth in the 1970s and the military economy can be seen in statistics which show the expansion in the Massachusetts' military economy outpacing the national defence economy's growth. After falling from a peak of $1.6 billion in FY 1968, annual defence spending in Massachusetts increased from $1.2 billion in FY 1970 to about $3 billion in FY 1979 (in current dollars). But 'the growth in military contracting in Massachusetts was not simply a reflection of national increases. Total US defence spending in FY 1979, in constant dollars, was actually 34% lower than spending in FY 1968'.[3]

The greater growth of the Massachusetts military economy is based on the state's disproportionate share of the fastest growing military economic sectors. The fastest growing sectors in the Massachusetts economy from 1975 to 1983 were services and high technology. Among the latter group, Table 1 shows that over this eight-year-period, high-tech jobs contributed 70.2 thousand net new jobs to the Massachusetts economy.[4] Evidence that defence-linked sectors grew faster than the economy as a whole is seen in a comparison of data collected from the census and Annual Survey of Manufacturers, and information collected from the MA-175 Series whose population is primarily industries shipping to the federal government. From 1972 to 1983 the total value of state industrial shipments increased by 440% in the MA-175 survey. For the general census the comparable figure was 165%. In sum, the government-linked industries grew 2.7 times as fast as state industries as a whole.[5]

TABLE 1. *Massachusetts high technology sectors: 1975-1983*

	Growth Rate (%)	Job Growth (000's of Jobs)
Non-electrical machinery (including computers)	38	27.8
Electrical and electronics	34	28.8
Instruments	31	13.6
TOTAL		70.2

Source: R. Ferguson and H. Ladd, *Economic Performance and Economic Development Policy in Massachusetts*, Cambridge, Massachusetts: John F. Kennedy School of Government, May 1986.

TABLE 2. *Defence market share (1979, 1982, and 1987)*

SIC code	Title	Defence share of output			Defence output growth
		1979	1982	1987	
383	Optical instruments	21.6	28.0	30.7	38.0
3811	Engineering instruments	23.5	27.7	33.6	59.9
3679-9	Electronic components	12.0	17.0	19.8	49.3
3825	Instruments to measure electricity	5.6	8.4	9.8	49.7
3573	Computers	3.6	7.1	12.7	141.0
3674	Semiconductors	9.5	12.5	12.5	51.4

Source: *US Industrial Outlook, 1983*; Ann R. Markusen, 'Defense Spending: A Successful Industrial Policy?' Working Paper No. 424, Institute of Urban and Regional Development, University of California, Berkeley, June 1984.

TABLE 3. *Shares of average annual change in US electronics production*

Time period	Share taken by: Military spending	Capital spending	Exports
1976-1980	19%	52%	29%
1980-1981	34%	48%	18%
1981-1984	51%	26%	23%

Source: *Whatever Happened to Job Security*, West Somerville, Massachusetts: The High Tech Research Group, 1986.

TABLE 4. *Prime contracts for top ten and total Massachusetts recipients FY80–84 ($ millions)*

	FY80	FY81	FY82	FY83	FY84	5-year total
Raytheon	$1250	1428	1636	1948	2499	8761
General Electric	1003	1357	1259	1446	1851	6916
GTE	151	211	287	279	482	1410
MIT	154	164	218	250	264	1050
Avco Corp	106	137	191	242	211	887
MITRE Corp	110	136	167	204	238	855
Draper Labs	77	86	124	111	288	686
RCA Corp	55	93	148	113	82	491
Chamberlain	69	80	88	81	86	404
Honeywell	30	45	171	36	40	322
Top 10, Total	3005	3737	4289	4710	6041	21782
All Other	724	859	1012	1618	988	5201
Total	3729	4596	5301	6328	7029	26983

Source: Data Resources Incorporated data, Lexington, Massachusetts, as published in Robert Leavitt, *By the Sword We Seek Peace*, ms., Boston, Massachusetts, 1986.

The link between the growth in the general economy and the military economy during the 1970s can be seen in the dependency of the high technology sector on military expenditures: 'defense-oriented private sector employment represents substantial proportions of nonelectrical machinery, electronics, and instruments, precisely the three manufacturing sectors that have grown most rapidly in Massachusetts'.[6] The defence output share and projected output growth of these military industries *nationally* is illustrated in Table 2. Table 3 illustrates how military spending is taking an increasing share of national electronics production.

The growth in high-technology defence spending, together with the Reagan military build-up as a whole, is reflected in increased employment in primary and secondary defence industries. According to the Massachusetts Division of Employment Security (DES) total defence-oriented employment increased by 15,300 or 16% from 1980 to 1984.[7] Various analysts suggest differing estimates for the military's impact on Massachusetts employment. Using estimates from DES, the Federal Reserve Bank of Boston calculated that defence spending 'appears to be responsible for at most 5-10% of the 330,000 jobs created in the state' in the years 1980-1985.[8]

There is clear evidence that the military economy is not the dominant force shaping the Massachusetts economy and that the conversion of military to civilian resources could provide more jobs with greater aggregate wages.[9] However, because defence spending is one of the growth centres of the Massachusetts economy and military spending is concentrated in a few prime contractors, serious political obstacles are created which limit state intervention in support of economic conversion. Table 4 shows how defence spending has been concentrated among Massachusett's top ten defence contractors. From FY 1980 through FY 1984, almost $27 billion was injected into the state through such prime military contracts.[10]

The incentive among military contractors to continue their ties with the military is illustrated in Figures 1 and 2. Figure 1 illustrates the proportion of total industrial shipments represented by shipments to the three military serving agencies: the Department of Defense, the National Aeronautics and Space Administration and the Department of Energy (and its predecessor agencies). Figure 2 illustrates how five of the principal defence contractors in Massachusetts are growing more dependent on military contracts as seen as a proportion of total sales.

In 1984, about 80% of Raytheon's total prime contracts were awarded to Massachusetts affiliates. The corresponding figures for General Electric and AVCO were 41% and 24% respectively. But even for companies like RCA and Honeywell where less than 10% of total prime contracts received by these firms were awarded to Massachusetts affiliates, mili-

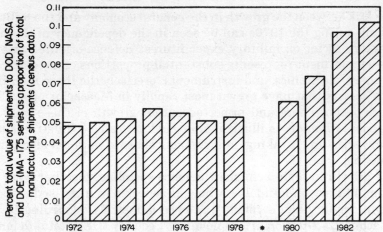

FIGURE 1. Military shipments in Massachusetts: ratio of total manufacturing shipments

Source: *Shipments to Federal Government Agencies*, various years, Current Industrial Reports MA-175, US Department of Commerce, Washington D.C.; *Annual Survey of Manufactures* and *Census of Manufactures*, various years, US Department of Commerce, Washington D.C.

*No state census done in 1979.

tary dependency still represents a political barrier. Precisely because leading firms like Honeywell and RCA are becoming more defence-dependent nationally, they will fight any precedents which seek to promote conversion *even in states where they may not have a major stake in defence work*.[11]

TABLE 5. *Comparison of Massachusetts annual wages per employee in defence-linked industries and average annual pay in Massachusetts (1983)*

SIC code	Title	Annual wages per employee (Dollars)
3671	Electron tubes, receiving type	20,582
3673	Electron tubes, transmitting	25,816
3674	Semiconductors and related devices	25,025
3721	Aircraft	29,365
3724	Aircraft engines and engine parts	30,597
3728	Aircraft equipment, nec	23,244
3731	Shipbuilding and repairing	24,103*
3761	Guided missiles and space vehicles	27,344
Average Annual Pay		17,347

*National Annual Wages only.

Source: *Employment and Wages: Annual Averages 1983*, Washington D.C.: US Department of Labor, May 1985; *The State & Metropolitan Data Book*, Washington D.C.: US Department of Commerce, April 1986.

The interest of state economic planners and labour in defence spend-

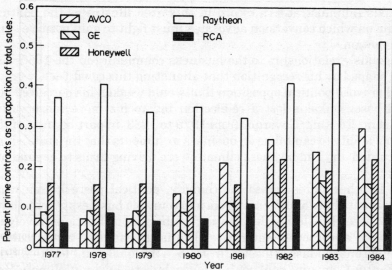

FIGURE 2. Military dependency of top contractors with operations in Massachusetts

Source: *100 Companies Receiving the Largest Dollar Volume of Military Prime Contract Awards*, Fiscal Years 1977-1984, US Department of Defense, Washington D.C.; Data on total corporate sales collected from company annual reports, *Standard Corporate Description*, Standard & Poors, New York, 1987 and *Stock Reports*, New York Stock Exchange, Standard & Poors.

ing is also reflected in data which show that the average state worker in key defence-linked economic sectors makes more than the average worker in Massachusetts (see Table 5).

3. Obstacles to state action II: military and corporate barriers to economic reconstruction

The economic incentives for continued ties to the military translate into political barriers which limit political intervention by the local state on behalf of conversion. One report on the Massachusetts military economy summarized the position of the state's Governor as follows:

> . . . On the one hand, admitting to any significant aid from military spending would both lessen the accomplishments of the Governor's own economic incentives and undercut the credibility of his critique of the 'Reagan Revolution' in federal budgetary policy. It might also lead to increased peace movement attention to state complicity in the Reagan military buildup. On the other hand, any negative attention to military contracting in the state would antagonize many of the high tech business leaders for whom the Governor has worked so hard in improving the state's 'business climate'.[12]

The ability and willingness of the local state to regulate local capital is a central issue in how conversion legislation is drafted and the extent to which the state will intervene on behalf of conversion. A look at the

Dukakis Administration's record in this area illustrates the political terrain on which conversion advocates must fight to gain positive state intervention.

Dukakis's relationship to the business community in the 1980s has been shaped by his recognition that alienating this constituency group could provoke political opposition that would weaken his perceived political base. Dukakis lost a re-election bid to his more conservative opponent, Ed King, Governor from 1979 to 1983, in part because of the latter's ability to capitalize on business arguments that the state's high tax burden and bad business climate were driving firms to expand out of state.[13]

As in other states across the country, political posturing on what factors contribute and detract from a favourable business climate have shaped local legislative debates and gubernatorial actions involving regulation of corporate enterprise. The issue has been a particularly sensitive one in Massachusetts. In 1975, a national plant location firm, the Fantus Company, ranked the Massachusetts business climate 46th among 48 states: 'This ranking remained a standard statistic in the debate over the state's business climate for the next four years.'[14]

State mobilization in support of business interests has been aided by what could be defined as capital flight's 'discipline effect' on local progressive policy initiatives. In almost every year from 1955 to 1975, New England 'had a higher incidence of business failures than either the South Atlantic region (containing Maryland, Virginia, Georgia, and Florida) or the West Central region (dominated by the state of Texas)'.

Plant closures, as well as technological and regional displacement in critical industries such as women's apparel, shoes and paper mills helped create unemployment rates in New England in the three decades following World War II that were higher in most years than in the rest of the country (although this pattern would be reversed by 1978).[15]

The new wave of economic growth that began in New England during the 1970s was in part conditional on the creation of a new labour force in the 1960s which was more flexible and open to corporate decisions governing work hours, work rules and wages. For example: 'In 1979 union success rates in certification elections were lower in New England than in any other region in the country—including the Deep South.'[16] One requirement then for the region's favourable business climate and accompanying growth was the weakening of labour.

Political mobilization around the detrimental impact of progressive labour legislation and the need to maintain a favourable business climate has been instrumental in blocking the adoption of comprehensive federal and state plant closing legislation. This story is important to conversion efforts which also depend on the regulation of capital both to prevent capital flight blackmail in response to conversion efforts and to ensure the integrity of the civilian industrial base (e.g., by keeping open auto plants communities *may* become less dependent on attracting military production).

Economists differ on the impact which plant closing legislation would have in encouraging capital flight or discouraging new businesses from coming to a state. In their studies on plant closings, economists Barry Bluestone and Bennett Harrison have argued that 'the elasticity of response to regulation is quite low'. The states also decrease their ability to affect business location decisions by competing with one another to offer exemptions and subsidies to firms choosing to locate within their borders.[17] Although plant closing legislation may not affect business location decisions, business interests have mobilized their resources to block this legislation; some local labour bureaucracies have given it only lukewarm support. After the failure of national plant closing legislation to pass Congress in 1974, and in anticipation of increased business opposition at the national level, plant closing advocates turned to the states.[18] By 1983, plant closing legislation had been introduced in 24 states and many cities. However, that year saw only two states (Wisconsin and Maine) and one city (Philadelphia) which had passed laws regulating plant closings.[19]

The defence-business complex has played an important role in limiting the scope of plant closing legislation in Massachusetts. After Dukakis's re-election for a second term in 1983, the Governor appointed 38 representatives from business, labour, government and academia to a commission designed to address the revitalization of regions dependent on mature industries and 'to head off a divisive showdown looming over plant closing prenotification bills in the legislature.' The delegation of responsibility to this Commission on the Future of Mature Industries helped deflect responsibility from the Governor. Among the members were representatives from the Massachusetts High Technology Council (MHTC); they were appointed 'to keep MHTC from being a vocal critic'.[20]

MHTC played a key role in the electoral victory of proposition 2&½, a state initiative that limited the growth of property tax levies (and tended to shift tax burdens away from business property).[21] During the debate over plant closing legislation and the Commission's position on this issue, the President of the Council claimed that 40 of its 75 members planning expansions were delaying their plans until decisions were reached on plant closing legislation.[22] The Council also pushed a set of alternative guidelines to labour's positions on plant closing legislation. These proposals made no mention of prenotification or state intervention to save a facility.[23]

The Council is closely integrated with military interests. In 1987, the Council had 145 members and 42 associate member corporations (which included two of the state's leading banks, Arthur D. Little, AT&T Bell Laboratories, Hewlitt-Packard, IBM, Lotus Development Corporation and Motorola Incorporated). Not counting the Charles Stark Draper Labs Incorporated, 17 of the Council's members and one associate member collectively received over $62 million in contracts for research and development work won by Massachusetts affiliates that was sponsored by the Defense Department in FY 1983. Draper's 1984 prime contracts represented an additional sum of more than $288 million in prime contracts from the Defense Department.[24]

Pressure from such business interests inside and outside the Commission helped prevent mandatory prenotification in plant closings from being adopted as Commission policy. In the press, they threatened that the verdict on this question would 'provide either positive or negative signals . . . that [would] affect job growth for years to come'.[25] Rather than advocate punishments for firms refusing to give notification, the Commission came to favour open-ended notification language and a package of unemployment benefits. The acceptance of the Massachusetts plant closing law in the business community 'reflects largely the fact that it is voluntary'. Employer refusal to pay benefits makes the general taxpayer liable for supplementary benefits, even when a firm can afford to pay.[26]

In February of 1986, the defence-linked conglomerate United Technologies announced the closing of the 76-year-old American Bosch Company manufacturing plant, a subsidiary whose closure led to the lay-off of 900 manufacturing workers. The closure rekindled the debate over plant closings in Massachusetts:

> . . . At issue in this case was not whether United Technologies had complied with the letter of the law (which contained no mandatory restrictions on plant closing procedures, but only recommended voluntary actions), but whether the existence of the law had any effect at all on companies' layoff, closing and relocation decisions and procedures.[27]

In sum, the combined efforts of the local corporate-military industrial complex helped limit the utility of plant closing legislation.

The power of military interests in Massachusetts has recently received a more coherent expression in the establishment of the 'Military Affairs Council' in March of 1985. The Council includes some of the state's largest military contractors (including Raytheon, GTE, Northrop and MIT's Lincoln Labs). One of the initiators of the Council says that its goal is to 'maintain and preserve the presence and long term power' of the state's defence industry by lobbying public officials and through campaigns to improve the public's perception of the military. By the close of 1985, the Council had lined up more than 100 corporate members.[28]

4. Conversion and the Quincy shipyards

Against this background of political and economic forces we can better examine the limits of state and local response to conversion initiatives at the Quincy Shipyard. These efforts, begun in the early 1980s, were led by the South Shore Conversion Committee (SSCC), an alliance of in-plant union members, peace advocates and community supporters. The Committee sought to encourage the conversion of the shipyards towards a more diversified set of civilian uses, leaving open the possibility of repair work on Navy vessels.

What were the possible areas of state intervention in support of economic conversion? The Mature Industries Law, which grew out of the work of the Mature Industries Commission, *did provide* local state planners with some legal and financial room for intervening in support of conversion planning at the Quincy Shipyard facility. The 1984 law provided for the establishment of an economic stabilization trust:

> . . . to provide flexible high risk financing necessary to implement a change in owner-
> ship, a corporate restructuring, or a turnaround plan for an economically viable, but
> troubled business which faces the likelihood of a large employment loss, plant closure,
> or failure without such change in ownership, corporate restructuring, or turnaround
> plan.[29]

Corporations or businesses seeking such financial support are required to show, among other things, that without trust funding the business is likely to experience a large loss in employment, plant closure or failure. However, the initial legislation capitalized the economic stabilization fund at only $2 million. In comparison, total state government expenditures in 1983 were $9.3 billion, defining the limits of this legislation.[30]

The Industrial Services Program was the state agency which contracted Booz-Allen Hamilton (BAH), a financial services corporation, to carry out an alternative use study for the Quincy facility. However, the utility of state intervention here was limited in two important respects. First, SSCC argued that the BAH study did not consider important conversion possibilities. Secondly, other critics have argued that the delay in getting a study commissioned and circulated to the public weakened efforts to build the case for conversion planning among the trade union and other constituency groups.[31]

The Booz-Allen & Hamilton study focused on shipyard wage levels as the main determinant in shaping the kind of work which could be carried out at the Quincy facility, whether it be shipbuilding or alternative products. However, the SSCC argued that the state should have focused on having the new facility sustain industrial employment as well as the good wages which were available to Quincy workers. The sale price of the facility was a key political issue which shaped the alternatives open to Quincy. For example, a lower sale price would have made more likely alternatives such as construction of modular housing.

Lower wages might have been needed to ensure the economic operation of a converted facility. However, SSCC advocates argued that the state's BAH study allowed wages to become the key issue in debates over the future of the facility. The study did not examine various scenarios for the facility under different sale prices or profit levels. As a result, the state's conception of alternative use planning rested more on labour sacrifices than on corporate sacrifices, i.e., the state could have made the sale price and profit levels a *political issue* by such alternative scenarios and thus created pressure on General Dynamics. This approach would also have increased the likelihood that the future use of the shipyard would have been on terms favourable to labour.[32]

The state also failed to intervene in a timely fashion to support the organized efforts of the SSCC to guarantee maximum retention of union wage-scale jobs. Massachusetts state legislation requires the Industrial Services Program to oversee: 'an early warning system to identify industries, businesses likely to experience large losses in employment or plant closures.'[33]

In July 1985, General Dynamics announced that it would close the yard the following spring; the state commissioned the study by the consultants BAH in October 1985. However, the state could have intervened even earlier by acting on the mandate provided by state legislation for an early warning system. Most industry analysts had identified shipbuilding as a troubled industry even before the passage of this enabling legislation. Early state intervention would have facilitated the economic planning and political mobilization needed for economic conversion planning.[34]

Another area of possible state intervention was the use of eminent domain proceedings against General Dynamics. A state takeover of the yards would have preserved the integrity of the facility and prevented the company from breaking up the yard, demolishing buildings and the like. State control would have allowed control of the selling price of the property, thereby the costs faced by potential buyers of the facility.[35] Thus, state control could have facilitated employee ownership of the site, encouraging increased employee performance. This would also have made wage levels less of an issue in the firm's competitiveness.

In August of 1985, the state's Secretary of Labor indicated that the state might seize the shipyards through eminent domain to prevent General Dynamics from selling the yard to a developer. However, the state later claimed that such a step would not be necessary. In part, the reversal was motivated by the ability of General Dynamics to draw out the process in the courts for about two years. However, the state *did use* eminent domain 'as a way to keep the company cooperative, rather than as something actually to use'.[36]

Another area of state intervention that could have been used to facilitate conversion planning was the application of existing statutes regulating the shipyard as a marine-based facility, as well as relevant zoning laws. The yard is considered 'environmentally hostile' which means that the accumulated waste from the construction, painting and finishing has ruined the land and surrounding waterways for all but industrial uses. Under state wetlands and waterways regulations, the shipyard is considered a 'Designated Port Area' in which 'waterways regulations give preference to marine-related industrial uses'. New owners of such facilities have 'to go through an elaborate licensing process if they desire to use or to alter' the facilities.[37] The towns of Quincy and Braintree have zoning powers which can be used to limit use of the site primarily to certain industrial uses: at the time of the announced closure, development for mixed-use commercial and residential purposes was not permitted and would have required re-zoning.[38]

The state did face some pressure to intervene to provide jobs for the shipyard workers or otherwise appear to come to their aid. In addition to the mandate of the Mature Industries Law, the state needed to maintain its political legitimacy with the communities and workers dependent on the shipyards. The state was also motivated to 'save' Quincy in order to keep in place an important source of state income. When in operation, the yard employed 6,300 workers for an annual payroll of $114 million. The facility paid about $18 million in federal and $8.1 million in state income taxes per year. In 1984, General Dynamics estimated that its contribution to the state economy exceeded $353 million.[39]

The combination of such economic and political pressures to intervene in some fashion, together with the economic and political interests which opposed conversion, led the state to support a salvage operation which encouraged worker retraining but did not actively support local conversion initiatives. In testimony before the state-sponsored task force on the re-use of the Quincy Shipyard, Steve Meachem, Co-Chair of SSCC, explained that the Industrial Services Department 'leads a big effort to retrain shipyard workers, involving millions of dollars. Yet this effort is totally divorced from re-use planning for the shipyard. Why wasn't money set aside to retrain workers for on-site jobs?'[40]

The state's intervention was limited not only by its calculated responses to corporate and military lobbies but also by the opposition to conversion by the company's conservative local union leadership. An organizing question which emerged in the SSCC was whether or not you could mobilize Local 5 to save the shipyard facility and the bargaining unit. If the progressive rank-and-file slate had won control over the union, it would have advocated conversion planning at Quincy. In addition, if the proconversion union slate had won, the SSCC and in-plant organizers could have secured the assistance of sympathetic officials in the various state offices dealing with labour affairs.[41]

5. The political response to conversion obstacles: building economic development coalitions

What political strategy should conversion activists follow, given the large influence on the local state by military and business interests? The Quincy case illustrates that there are a number of existing tools available to the state which can be used to further conversion planning. However, the problem confronting conversion activists is to develop political coalitions with sufficient power and consciousness to push the state to use these tools in a responsive manner; coalitions are also needed to pass comprehensive conversion legislation (see below).

The political obstacles to conversion on the local level are substantial; they are represented by a coalition of military-linked firms, corporations hostile to state regulation, conservative labour leaders and state bureaucrats fearful of alienating the constituencies linked to high-wage defence jobs. Some peace activists, community development groups and progressive legislators have argued that these conversion obstacles require a change in political strategy. They argue against mobilization around the ideas of alternative use committees, eminent domain, disarmament and the creation of a legal machinery which attempts to effect conversion through formal constraints on defence firms.

The basic argument employed is that conversion can be facilitated by first mobilizing constituencies around more limited objectives and goals. Three examples serve to illustrate how these arguments have evolved. In the South Shore Conversion Committee a debate emerged over how much General Dynamics and the state should be pushed towards all-out conversion of the Quincy facility, i.e., the development of new product lines keeping the existing bargaining unit intact. Others supported more moderate approaches which might have accommodated the state or company by allowing for mixed uses on the site which did not guarantee the integrity of the bargaining unit, e.g., the building of an industrial park facility.[42]

In Philadelphia, after failing to win the support of city political leaders and congressional representatives for conversion planning at the local Naval shipyards, local peace activists changed their approach. Rather than call for outright conversion of the Navy yard, activists are working in coalitions which link economic development and peace initiatives. This group has adopted a strategy of organizing around *economic development* as a means to facilitate conversion planning.

Local peace and community activist proponents of this idea argue that before issues of alternative investment and conversion planning can be tackled outright, a broad political base should be created that involves neighbourhood groups and communities suffering from economic underdevelopment, unions and defence workers concerned with plant closures, bankers, as well as corporate and political leaders sympathetic to peace concerns.[43]

In initial legislation before the Massachusetts State House, state representative David P. Magnani has proposed the creation of a commission that would study the feasibility of economic conversion strategies. Rather than explicitly call for conversion planning outright, the bill allows a commission of local state representatives and private and public officials to first collect information and build support for conversion planning. This approach to conversion is based on the assumption that the conversion constituency is 'not yet coherent' and allows the conversion movement to 'generate consensus'. An implicit assumption is that legal constraints that immediately enforce conversion would require significant political mobilization that has not yet materialized. As Magnani explains, 'to develop the political support necessary to pass mandatory types of conversion legislation, there first needs to be a period of voluntary options and positive incentives. If it has been shown that an incentive program fails to encourage conversion, there will be less resistance to pass mandatory legislation.'[44]

Each example presented here purports to confront the reality of conversion obstacles by first creating a political base not explicitly tied to mobilization around disarmament and alternative use planning. The political base is created by job creation or preservation which does not immediately threaten corporate and military interests. Alternatively, a commission of inquiry provides documentation and public hearings that could conceivably be used to rally peace supporters and attract press attention.

In some formulations, these political approaches are employed to reach out to constituencies not accessible to disarmament organizers, e.g., banks, corporations and local political leaders. Another interpretation offered is that there should be a division of labour between peace and conversion activists on the one hand, and broader more pragmatic organizing of the kind enumerated above. The coalition is built first around economic development concerns, then, once it has amassed significant political clout it can move on to conversion planning issues.[45] Each of these approaches may break new ground for local conversion efforts by expanding their political base. However, there are limitations to using traditional economic development incentives and coalitions as a vehicle to facilitate economic conversion planning. First, national economic development is itself retarded by military spending, and the resources the state has available for local development are limited by their diversion into Pentagon coffers. In other words, there are limits to how much development can be achieved without conversion.[46]

Second, there are clear divergences between strategies useful to peace advocates and those which build the political base in the model advocated by economic development organizers. One divergence is based on the choice of allies. It is not clear that once economic development coalitions begin to focus on conversion planning, they will be able to win the support of their allies among corporations, bankers and local politicians.

A second divergence is based on the kinds of political education that can be projected by traditional community organizing and economic development approaches. The burden of the military economy requires corporate restructuring and alternative planning. Limiting the terms of debate to gain consensus and to create a political base risks putting off today what you must do tomorrow, i.e., there are no short-cuts around the necessity to educate people about the immediate need for conversion planning. The Quincy case illustrates this need.

Within the South Shore Conversion Committee, conversion proponents argued that a victory which did not maintain the existing bargaining unit and did not have these workers in place producing alternative products was not worth much.[47] Among the concessions such a victory would create was the failure of a local conversion effort to create a model for alternative use that could be sold to other union locals. Workers in military projects would be less convinced that conversion meant job security. In general, strategies that create jobs at closed defence facilities but do not preserve a bargaining unit and challenge the character of investment decisions and corporate planning in support of military activities do not provide workers or communities with a vision that alternatives to the military economy are possible.

Third, in contrast to the belief of some economic planners that traditional economic development incentives could facilitate conversion among prime contractors, the accumulated economic evidence suggests the contrary. Military firms reap substantial economic rewards from defence work; their dedication to military production makes them incompetent for civilian production and burdens them with significant economic and political barriers to exit, keeping them economically and ideologically committed to defence work.[48]

In Massachusetts, the limits to economic incentives in facilitating economic conversion can be seen in state industry's growing dependency on military contracts. As Figures 1 and 2 illustrate, in the present militarized economy, industrial firms have extended their ties to the Pentagon. Because such firms have shifted towards *increased* reliance on the military, state incentives such as tax breaks, rent subsidization and loans will prove insufficient in promoting conversion.

Economic incentives *may* prove successful in encouraging civilian diversification among subcontractors. Unlike the prime contractors, the smaller contractors are 'required to supply their own plants, equipment and money'. The smaller defence contractors realize a lower return on investment in comparison with both the prime contractors and smaller civilian contractors, 'frequently at a level where bankruptcy is common'.[49] The fluctuations in defence contracting, lower profits and less favoured position faced by subcontractors create incentives for diversification into civilian production. The targets here should be smaller firms on the periphery of the military economy, now owned by prime contractors.

The economic literature on the military economy and state data for Massachusetts indicate that prime contracting military firms will resist conversion unless they are forced by legal and political means to undertake conversion planning. Steps towards a legal mechanism to apply such constraints locally have been taken in the city of Berkeley, California. In November of 1986, voters there overwhelmingly passed the Nuclear Free Berkeley Act. The Act requires the cessation of nuclear weapons work within city limits, the divestment of city funds from businesses that engage in nuclear weapons work and involves the city in the promotion of 'educational activities . . . to advance public awareness and understanding' about the dangers of nuclear weapons.[50]

Significant incentives for conversion and penalties for defence contractors exist if peace coalitions are able to mobilize their resources in targeting the local state. For example, in 1983, 12% of state and local government expenditures representing $68 billion were on capital outlays, i.e., spending on construction, equipment, land and existing structures.[51] Such funding (together with state pensions) could be divested from military contractors. Alternatively, states could reward converting firms with targeted infrastructure investments.

6. The future course of local conversion organizing

The opposition of the local state defines the barriers confronting efforts to implement local conversion planning. However, such efforts are critical to national mobilization around alternative use planning. One lesson from the movement to pass plant closing legislation is that corporations and other forces opposing conversion planning are equally able to project their resources at the national and local levels.

The opposition of the conservative local union leadership was instrumental in blocking the development of a broader coalition effort for conversion of the Quincy Shipyards. By educating the rank-and-file about the importance of conversion, local conversion groups and labour activists can help break down the resistance to disarmament in the ranks of labour.

Local conversion efforts are also important because the Pentagon itself is organizing constituencies locally to increase the links of small businesses and communities to the military economy. The Defense Department has established 'procurement outreach' centres and programmes to generate employment in states and localities by assisting firms in attracting defence and other government work.[52] If local peace groups fail to challenge such efforts, they will allow the constituency for defence-linked development to grow broader.

Conversion groups built around statewide legislation and local projects can make the case for national conversion legislation. They can document the local impact which defence spending has had on their communities in terms of jobs, housing and other needed resources lost in diverted tax expenditures. Local conversion constituencies can be mobilized around national legislative hearings which take testimony on national conversion bills.

As seen in the Quincy conversion effort, the issue of building a large political base is a central problem in confronting the local state's resistance to conversion planning. The South Shore Conversion Committee was limited by a lack of awareness of the importance of conversion among other social groups and among many in the state's large peace movement. However, the Committee *was* successful in broadening this awareness through its organizing efforts.[53]

There are ways to amass political power in support of conversion without sacrificing the constraints and political educational work needed to build the conversion movement. These involve the creation of coalitions which share a common radical programme. These coalitions can operate networks with other social groups which are accustomed to pressuring the local state to apply legal constraints on corporate actors to accomplish their objectives. Such constituencies include movements by women, people of colour and rank-and-file labour, as well as activists concerned with environmental degradation, disarmament and intervention in the Third World.

Other coalitions can be formed which link conversion to legislation aimed at the civilian economy such as plant closing initiatives. In addition, conversion can provide a vehicle for employment and resources to those professions negatively impacted by the diversion of federal resources away from their base of employment and into the military economy. Public employee unions facing cutbacks, unions linked to professions which could gain employment if money were spent on a revitalized infrastructure rather than war, professional societies of urban planners, architects and civil engineers could be mobilized if the case for how conversion could benefit them were made. Until such new coalitions are forged, local organizing efforts will be unable to project the political power needed to push the local state to adopt the constraints and responsive planning needed to facilitate a national conversion programme.

NOTES AND REFERENCES

1. Correspondence from Lynn E. Browne, Federal Reserve Bank of Boston, 14 May 1987; Robert Leavitt, *'By the Sword We Seek Peace'; Military Spending and State Government in Massachusetts*, ms., Boston, Massachusetts, 1986
2. Ronald F. Ferguson and Helen F. Ladd, *Economic Performance and Economic Development Policy in Massachusetts*, Discussion Paper D86-2, Cambridge, Massachusetts: John F. Kennedy School of Government, May 1986, p. 25.
3. Leavitt, op. cit., p. 25.
4. Ferguson and Ladd, op. cit., pp. 25ff.
5. *Shipments to Federal Government Agencies*, various years, Current Industrial Reports MA-175 US Department of Commerce, Washington D.C.; *Annual Survey of Manufactures and Census of Manufactures*, various years, US Department of Commerce, Washington D.C. The calculations performed here do not account for inflation and are based on comparisons of 1972 and 1983 as base years only. In the MA-175 survey, total military shipments from the three defence-serving agencies increased from $920.1 million in 1972 to $5,085.8 million in 1983, or 453%, similar to the 440% figure for total shipments.
6. Massachusetts Division of Employment Security Data as cited in Ferguson and Ladd, op. cit., p. 38.
7. Field Research Department, 'Employment Trends in Defense-Oriented Industries, Massachusetts, 1980-1984', Boston, Massachusetts: Massachusetts Division of Employment Security, February 1987.
8. Browne, op. cit.
9. A report by Massachusetts Jobs With Peace found that about 128,000 state residents were employed directly or indirectly by the military, representing only 4.4% of the workforce. The study also found that a $1 billion reduction in state military contracts together with a redirection of this money to civilian programmes like housing, education, and health would have increased total state employment by 39,000 and total wages by $429 million. See *Massachusetts and Its Military Industry*, Boston, Massachusetts: Massachusetts Jobs With Peace, May 1987.
10. Data on percent of total defence contracts awarded to Massachusetts affiliates based on data compiled by Data Resources Inc. cited in Leavitt, op. cit., p. 29 and Defense Department data. An important clarification should be noted here. In Fiscal Year 1979, the last year for which data are available, of all subcontracts distributed, 17% of Massachusetts subcontracts were distributed intrastate. However, subcontracts represented less than 10% of prime contracts for that year. See Table 10 in E. J. Malecki, 'Military Spending and the US defense industry: regional patterns of military contracts and subcontracts', *Environment and Planning C: Government and Policy*, Vol. 2, 1984, pp. 31-44.
11. A story on the defeat of a recent peace referendum in Los Angeles noted that opponents raised money 'from military contractors across the country' which 'apparently feared the California proposition would set a precedent'. See Dan La Botz, 'Military Contractors Defeat "Jobs With Peace" Proposal', *Labor Notes*, December 1986.
12. Leavitt, op. cit., p. 47. In an interview with a state house staff member, this researcher was told that a bill directly pushing for economic conversion was regarded as politically taboo. In an interview with a leading state economic development official, this researcher was told that conversion planning was unrealistic given oppo-

158   *Jonathan M. Feldman*

sition by trade unions and corporations and that the high wages paid by defence firms was an important consideration shaping state policy.

13. Ibid., Ferguson and Ladd, op. cit., p. 87.
14. Ferguson and Ladd, ibid., p. 51.
15. Bennett Harrison, 'Regional Restructuring and 'Good Business Climates': The Economic Transformation of New England Since World War II' in L. Sawers and W. Tabb, eds, *Sunbelt-Snowbelt: Urban Development and Regional Restructuring*, New York: Oxford University Press, 1984, pp. 62, 62-63.
16. Ibid., p. 68.
17. Nancy R. Folbre et al., 'Legislation in Maine' in P. Staudohar and H. Brown, eds., *Deindustrialization and Plant Closure*. Lexington, Massachusetts: Lexington Books, 1987, p. 296; Barry Bluestone and Bennett Harrison, *The Deindustrialization of America*, New York: Basic Books, 1982.
18. Lawrence E. Rothstein, *Plant Closings: Power, Politics and Workers*, Dover, Massachusetts: Auburn House Publishing Co., 1986, p. 29.
19. Judith Leff, 'The Plant Closing Debate in Massachusetts', Harvard Business School Case no. 9-386-173, Rev. 5/86, Cambridge, Massachusetts: Harvard University, 1986, p. 2.
20. Ferguson and Ladd, op. cit., pp. 113-114.
21. Ibid., Paul Starobin, 'Business Lobbying in the Bay State: The Massachusetts High Technology Council: Sequel', Kennedy School of Government Case no. C14-83-500S, Cambridge, Massachusetts: Harvard University, 1983.
22. Ferguson and Ladd, op. cit., p. 127.
23. Leff, op. cit., p. 9.
24. '500 Contractors Receiving the Largest Dollar Volume of Prime Contract Awards for Research, Development, Test and Evaluation', FY 1983, Department of Defense; Massachusetts High Technology Council, Inc. Membership List, 1 May 1987; *The Cambridge Case for Diversification Planning*, Cambridge, Massachusetts, December 1986.
25. Ferguson and Ladd, op. cit., p. 116.
26. Ibid., p. 121.
27. Judith Leff, 'United Technologies and the Closing of American Bosch', Harvard Business School Case no. 9-386-174, Rev. 5/86. Cambridge, Massachusetts: Harvard University, 1986.
28. Leavitt, op. cit., p. 48.
29. Mature Industries Law, Chapter 23D, Section 11; Paquita Zuidema, *State Mature Industry Policy: Massachusetts' Response to the Closing of the Quincy Shipyard*, Master's Thesis, Technology and Policy Program, M.I.T., February 1987.
30. Mature Industries Law, op. cit.; Table No. 462, *Statistical Abstract of the US*, Washington D.C.: Department of Commerce, 1986, p. 279.
31. Zuidema, op. cit.
32. Interview with Steve Meachem, South Shore Conversion Committee, Hingham, Massachusetts, Spring 1987; Steve Meachem, 'Presentation to the Task Force on the Reuse of the Quincy Shipyard', Quincy Shipyard Save the Jobs Coalition, 9 April 1986.
33. Zuidema, op. cit.
34. Ibid.
35. Interview with Meachem and Meachem, 'Presentation . . .', op. cit.
36. Zuidema, op. cit., pp. 43ff. Eminent domain is based on state laws in which the state, for reasons of public interest, can purchase a site or facility and manage, lease or sell it so that benefits are maintained for the public welfare. Even conservative state legislators in Quincy openly called for the use of eminent domain. A precedent for the use of eminent domain occurred on 24 December 1985 when Governor Dukakis took over 35 acres in Framingham, Massachusetts. However, this took place against local community objections. See Elizabeth Sherman, 'Saving Quincy Shipyard', *Plowshare Press*, Vol. 12, No.1, Winter 1987; Zuidema, op. cit.
37. Ibid., pp. 27ff.
38. Ibid., p. 29.

39. Ibid., p. 6.
40. Meachem, 'Presentation . . .', op. cit.
41. Interview with Meachem, op. cit.
42. Ibid. Meachem notes that given the termination of Navy contracts, the gap between arguments for alternative use planning and more moderate proposals was narrowed considerably, e.g., it was harder to argue against proposals which involved alternative product lines.
43. Interview with George Lakey, Pennsylvania, Jobs With Peace and Jon Brandow, League Island Development Corporation, Philadelphia, Pennsylvania, 15 April 1987. The coalition has been used to rally support for alternative use of a Naval hospital threatened with closure and a programme of 'full use' of the city's Naval Yards. Under the full use plan, organizers have advocated bringing additional civilian work into the Navy yard without attacking military work directly. See also Jon Brandow, 'The Philadelphia Story', *Plowshare Press*, Vol. 12, No. 2, Spring 1987. The city of Cambridge, Massachusetts, has an official peace commission which is attempting to encourage 'diversification planning' as a way of promoting increased civilian production and reduced defence dependency among the City's high technology firms. It is believed that such firms could diversify if provided help with management, marketing and economic development assistance. See *The Cambridge Case for Diversification Planning*, op. cit., and Note 49 (below). Again, the problem here is whether the capital incentives are present for diversification even if (as the report documents) many defence contractors feel military work involves cumbersome government reporting and is unstable.
44. H. 1485, State of Massachusetts; Based on a conversation with State Representative David P. Magnani, 16 June 1987.
45. Interview with John Brandow, op. cit.
46. See Seymour Melman, *The Permanent War Economy*, New York: Simon & Schuster, 1974; and *Profits without Production*, New York: Alfred A. Knopf, 1983.
47. Interview with Meachem, op. cit.
48. See Melman, op. cit.; Jacques Gansler, *The Defense Industry*, Cambridge, Massachusetts: MIT Press, 1980; Fred Kaplan, 'Defense Profits are Double Commercial Profits, Study says', *Boston Globe*, 13 May 1987; Gordon Adams, *The Iron Triangle*, New York: Council On Economic Priorities, 1981; *DOD Revolving Door*, Washington D.C.: Government Accounting Office, March 1986.
49. Gansler, op. cit. Richard Hatch, a professor at New Jersey Institute of Technology, has proposed the adoption of the networking principles used by local Italian manufacturers as a means of facilitating conversion among defence subcontractors. This approach is most useful for firms which carry out both civilian and defence work and have flexible production systems. An analysis suggestive of this approach appears in R. Hatch, 'Reviving Local Manufacturing, Italian Style', *City Limits*, April 1986.
50. Nancy Skinner, City Councillor, Memo on 'Implementation of Measure K, The Nuclear Free Berkeley Act', 12 January 1987; Ordinance No. 5784-N.S., 'The Nuclear Free Berkeley Act', City of Berkeley. The possible avenues of peace law are explored further in Ann Fagen Ginger, 'Finding Peace Law and Teaching It', *Nova Law Journal*, Vol. 10, No. 2, Winter 1986. Especially for nuclear-linked contractors, the legal basis for constraints on defence firms can be found in state police powers and enforcement of health and safety.
51. Table No. 452, *Statistical Abstract*, op. cit., p. 270. Such targeted procurement may involve changes in state law regarding competitive bidding.
52. Judith C. Hackett, 'Procurement Outreach Programs: Strengthening Existing Businesses Through Government Contracts', *CSG Backgrounder*, Lexington, Kentucky: Council of State Governments, November 1985.
53. See Sherman, op. cit.

Law for Economic Conversion: Necessity and Characteristics

SEYMOUR MELMAN

1. Planning economic conversion

On 28 January 1987, Congressman Ted Weiss (Democrat, New York) submitted to the US House of Representatives a proposal for a law on economic conversion, co-sponsored (until December 1988) by 60 of his fellow members of Congress. What are the assumptions of this proposed law and why is it required?

There are two solid reasons for economic conversion planning: first, to facilitate reconstruction of the damage owing to a permanent war economy; second, to relieve disarmament negotiators of the fear that a reversal of the arms race carries unacceptable economic penalties.

On the face of it these considerations seem to be powerful, compelling. Hence, why are laws needed to require the necessary actions for these useful purposes?

Economic conversion law is required because major barriers must be overcome to set in motion the necessary planning process for reliable conversion operations. Managers in military industry, bases and laboratories fear a loss of power and privilege that would be caused by a reversal of the arms race and drastic reductions in military spending. Military-serving managers have markets that are guaranteed by the federal government. They direct the production of goods and services that are sold before they are produced. The profitability of their operations is guaranteed by contract and tradition in the military economy. The top managers serving the military draw upon the finance capital capabilities of the entire society to facilitate their operations. Their proposals for weapons design and functions have far-reaching effects on both domestic and foreign policy of the government. These positions of power and privilege would indeed be diminished or eliminated if the arms race were reversed and military budgets reduced.

There is a further genuine fear among many of the people in military-serving industry, laboratories and bases: the expertise which they wield in the service of the military could become largely obsolete in the event of a major reduction in military requirements. It is normal for many men and women to regard a requirement for occupational retraining as

161

fraught with personal and professional discomfort. Insofar as military-serving occupations have received higher pay and more rapid promotion than civilian-serving counterparts, the men and women in the service of the military often fear a reduction in income as well.

Finally, the whole society has been taught by economists, from right to left, that military goods and services are a source of wealth—like anything else with a price tag. Propelled by this myth, there is a fear that reduction in military spending could entail a loss of both employment and wealth.

Accordingly, there are no grounds for expecting that the managers of military economy would, on their own, set in motion the competent planning process that is required for moving from military to civilian work. For these reasons law is needed to make the necessary action mandatory, to compel the actions that are in the economic and political interests of the larger society.

2. Major components of law for economic conversion

The following are ten major components of law for facilitating economic conversion planning and operations.

2.1. Mandatory alternative use committees

Every military-serving factory, laboratory and base above a given size—say, 100 employees—should be required to establish, as a condition of its military service, an alternative use committee with responsibility for preparing blueprint-ready plans for civilian work in the event that the military service of the people and facilities is no longer required. This committee is best composed—equally—of representatives of management and the working people, all occupations. This sharing of responsibility and authority is designed to assure not only a maximum flow of ideas, but also responsibility to both the administrators and to the working people of a factory, laboratory or base. The alternative use committee must be guaranteed access to whatever data and facilities it requires for fulfilling this function. The availability of alternative use plans, reviewed periodically—say, every two years—assures the people of the military-serving facility that competent attention has been given to their economic prospects beyond the service of the military.

2.2. Advanced conversion planning

Planning for economic conversion cannot be left to be set in motion at the time when, say, a military contract has been cancelled or production quantities seriously reduced. The basic reason is the time period required for planning alternative use of buildings, equipment and people. There is no simple formula for making a competent selection of new products for a military-serving facility. Careful attention must be given not only to market requirements but also to the suitability of people and equipment for prospective new work. Beyond product selection there are the further tasks of refashioning machinery and production layouts; investigating new materials and arranging for sources of supply; and pre-testing materials, equipment and whole processes prior to new production operations. A period of two years is a reasonable time allotment for these functions.

2.3. Advanced notification of contract termination

Government top managers must be required to give reasonable notification, say a year in advance, to factories, laboratories and bases when major projects are to be terminated. Such advanced notification is essential for facilitating orderly changeover and avoiding chaotic conditions and crash programmes.

2.4. Mandatory occupational retraining

Professional retraining is a particularly important matter for the managerial and engineering-technical occupations. Managers have become highly specialized, as required by the particular rules and modes of operation suitable for the service of the military. Thus, a marketing manager who has been long experienced in the service of the military is skilled in the political-diplomatic requirements of that vocation, differing considerably from the skill necessary for selling to civilian department stores. Engineers who have become skilled in design and related operations that are carried out with indifference to cost must be fundamentally reoriented to the design problems that must be solved where cost minimizing and civilian reliability requirements dominate the scene. For these reasons, occupational retraining for administrators and engineers who have been long in the service of the military must be made mandatory as a part of economic conversion law. Available evidence indicates that only a minority of production workers may be so specialized in their occupational skills as to require retraining for suitability to civilian work.

2.5. Community economic adjustment planning

Where military-serving industry, laboratories and bases are present in significant clusters, then the characteristics of entire communities are subject to major reshaping as part of economic conversion. For example, conversion to civilian work of many industrial facilities will entail a significant reduction in the number of engineering-technical people required, or a major movement in and out of the community of these occupations. In either event, major costs are entailed for the communities involved. Accordingly, planning funds should be made available for blue-printing the necessary adjustment operations.

2.6. Decentralized control of alternative use planning

There is no standardized formula or blueprint that can be universally applied for economic conversion planning. The work must be done with attention to the requirements of specific products and the capabilities and limitations of particular workforces, plant and equipment, surrounding infrastructure and resources. Accordingly, the operation of alternative use committees and related activity for conversion planning is most effectively carried out at the point of operation of the facilities concerned. This does not, in any way, detract from the feasibility or importance of calling upon specialized skills from any other place to facilitate the work in hand. But this does emphasize that a remotely positioned centralized organization is emphatically unsuited for economic conversion planning.

2.7. Income maintenance during civilian conversion

Even with blueprint-ready plans and schedules in hand there will still be a significant time period needed to change over from military to civilian work. Under best conditions months are required to set in motion even the best prepared plans. Moreover, it is prudent to understand that time is needed for discovery of error and correction. Accordingly, preparation for economic conversion should provide for income maintenance to the people involved. This can be done by rules that are socially validated by previous practice. For example, in the US auto industry the combination of unemployment insurance and income support systems agreed by management and the unions have provided for as much as 90% of previous pay during a period of scheduled unemployment. Such provisions do not preclude the use of unemployment time as professional training and upgrading time.

2.8. Relocation allowances

Military-serving industrial units are often overloaded with administrative and engineering-technical people. Therefore, major industrial and geographic relocation is to be expected as part of conversion to civilian economy. The moving expenses for entire households can be substantial and one or another form of subsidization of these costs should be an integral part of economic conversion law.

2.9. A national network for employment opportunity

Precisely because of the predictable requirement for major relocation of engineers, administrators and many production workers, a sensible part of economic conversion planning should be provision for a national network for employment opportunity. This will be especially important to production workers of those facilities that are not readily convertible to civilian use. This must be expected for the more exotic military-related operations, e.g., remotely-located facilities for testing warheads and rocket engines, and the production and stockpiling of unusually volatile and dangerous munitions. It is therefore reasonable to expect that concentrations of need for new employment sites will be a characteristic condition of military civilian conversion. A national employment network should help to solve this problem.

2.10. Capital investment planning by government

The operation of a large military economy for more than forty years has entailed major underinvestment in the facilities and services called infrastructure (the roads, water systems, waste disposal operations, education plant and work forces, libraries, public health operations, parks, communication and transportation systems, etc.). Reversing the neglect of these facilities and their staffs typically requires large capital investments. Detailed planning for these purposes by the local and national government bodies that are responsible for infrastructure facilities and operations will make a major contribution to competent conversion planning. The large markets that are opened up by infrastructure maintenance and renewal are part of the alternative product system towards which many military-industry firms, laboratories, and bases can be reoriented. Hence, capital investment plans by governments at all levels will comprise a major contribution towards defining new markets and jobs for converting factories, laboratories, and bases.

3. Reshuffling people and responsibilities

There is a further characteristic of economic conversion law that can have a major effect. That pertains to the location of the national economic conversion commission, or similar body within a national government. To many of the people connected with one or another aspect of military economy, the prospect of conversion planning suggests that it be located within the very agency that is responsible for administering the existing military economy. In the United States this would mean assigning major administrative responsibility for conversion operations to the Department of Defense. Indeed, this seems to be a prudent way to address these problems in the eyes of many lawmakers and others who have had long careers developing liaison with the Pentagon in the service of local military industry, research, and base operations. The elemental logic of these people comes down to this: why not locate responsibility for conversion to civilian work precisely in the place that organizes all the military-serving work?

Alas, this apparent convenience also entails strengthening the decision power of the war-making institutions, and the prospect of continuing the criteria of decision-making and methods of operation that have become characteristic of permanent military economies. These methods are wholly unsuited to the civilian economy. Indifference to cost and product reliability assures incompetence and failure in the civilian sphere. Also, continuity of style of working is bolstered by continuity of organization. Hence reshuffling people and responsibilities is a necessary part of assuring a change, a conversion, from military to civilian methods of working. Indeed, if responsibility and authority for administering economic conversion planning and operations were vested in the directorate of military economy, that would be tantamount to creating a Ministry of National Economy, with an enlargement of military economy rather than a conversion.

4. No subsidies to management

A vital feature of economic conversion law is the absence of subsidies to the managements of converting enterprises. Subsidies in the form of guarantees of capital, or markets, or profitability would tend to reinforce cost-maximizing and associated inefficiency and incompetence that are precisely the reverse of the requirements for competent conversion to civilian economy.

The implementation of these characteristics of economic conversion law may be facilitated or made more difficult by one or another surrounding condition of economy, politics, or ideology. However, the essential law requirements for competent economic conversion are specific to the common characteristics of modern military economy, wherever located.

The specifications discussed here for desirable components of economic conversion law are fulfilled in H.R. 813, a proposed law submitted in the House of Representatives of the United States Congress on 28 January 1987 by Congressman Ted Weiss (Democrat, New York) and co-sponsored, at this writing, by 60 of his fellow members of Congress.

III. Armaments and the Economy

Arms Conversion and the Defence Industry in the United Kingdom: A Review of Recent Developments

TOM WOODHOUSE, STEVE SCHOFIELD AND PETER SOUTHWOOD

1. Re-evaluation of the conversion debate

For many years speculation about the desirability of converting military resources to civilian use has been lacking two vital dimensions or resources. Firstly, there has been no reliable database of information about the detailed impact of defence contractors on the UK economy. Secondly, there was no credible policy at central and local government levels sufficiently well worked out to ensure that the concerns of people whose livelihood comes from working in defence industries are taken seriously.

Both the proponents of a strong defence economy, and peace movement opponents of high military expenditure, have tended to speak on behalf of defence workers—in the first case promising security from new weapons contracts, and in the second holding out the panacea of arms conversion.

In the UK, arms conversion and defence industry research has been seriously inhibited by the paucity of information available from central government and from defence contractors. With the partial exception of the Lucas campaign in the mid and late 1970s, the idea of arms conversion has not been part of the main agenda of policy makers in government, or even (again with partial exceptions) the labour movement. In the absence of concrete progress the idea of arms conversion has itself come under attack: by Gordon Adams who has argued that the whole approach is basically misguided;[1] and by Jan Oberg because it does not go far enough in the direction of building a radically new demilitarized international economy linked to development objectives.[2]

This article re-evaluates the conversion debate in the light of recent experience in the UK. Specifically it reviews progress in filling the critical gaps in knowledge mentioned above. Policies for arms conversion in the UK are viewed as part of a broader preoccupation with disarmament and defence policy, linking alternative (non-nuclear) defence policies to a more long-term idea of economic regeneration and security. Section 1 reviews the progress of work into understanding the problems of measuring and controlling defence industries both at a theoretical and practical (public policy) level. Section 2 looks at research into key defence industry sites in the UK and the product and policy proposals emanating from this research. The section will concentrate especially on the Trident submarine construction yard at Barrow.

Sections 3 and 4 provide an account of the development of database and information network on the extent of the UK industry. The publication of Nicole Ball and Milton Leitenberg's *The Structure of the Defense Industry: An International Survey* in 1983 represented an important advance in its discussion of the salient characteristics of the arms industries in a wide variety of countries. The only major arms producer omitted from the survey was the United Kingdom. This omission was at least in part a result of the difficulty of obtaining comprehensive information on the UK industry, and of the consequent underdeveloped state of research into the structure of the arms industry in the United Kingdom.

In the UK the Economist Intelligence Unit carried out a survey of 142 companies operating in defence production in 1962. Then in the mid and late 1970s the results of work undertaken on behalf of the Labour Party Defence Study Group was published *(Sense About Defence* (1977) and *Democratic Socialism and the Costs of Defence* (1979)). This work did not add substantially to knowledge about the overall structure of the UK arms industry, but it was significant in that it focused attention on the policy implications of transferring resources from military to civilian production. It also developed a series of local studies which looked in detail at the prospects and techniques for providing alternative, non-military, employment for naval shipbuilding workers, and for aerospace engineers working on the Tornado Multi Role Combat Aircraft. It is unfortunate, though perhaps understandable, that this work was not followed through in the form of a national policy developed by government to encourage and support diversification and conversion initiatives.

Hopes for a breakthrough on conversion (or more properly, diversification) tended, unrealistically, to fall on the shoulders of the Lucas Aerospace Shop Stewards Combine Committee, whose campaign for the manufacture of socially useful products became internationally recognized. It is demanding rather too much to expect that the Lucas campaign might itself somehow have solved at a stroke all of the problems concerning social control of the defence industries; but it did provide invaluable insights into the possibilities of producing an imaginative range of viable products given proper support. For this to happen greater knowledge must be developed of the working of the defence industries and of the relationship between defence industries and security policy. This knowledge once developed must be utilized in a policy-effective manner.

The domestic political climate has been hostile to the implementation of worker participation in defence production decisions. Although the government has completely failed to deal with unemployment resulting from excess capacity in the defence industries, nevertheless, there has been significant progress made by researchers into the problems posed by defence industries, and into conversion and diversification policies.

The publication of the proceedings of the Alternative Defence Commission (*Defence Without the Bomb*, 1983) and a general heightening of awareness of defence policy issues in public debate, resulted in increased dissatisfaction with a nuclear-dependent defence strategy. A valuable supplementary paper published on behalf of the Commission (*The Economic Consequences of Non-Nuclear Defence*) identified the main defence related nuclear production facilities in the UK and estimated that less than 60,000 jobs were sustained by the nuclear weapons programme, a very small proportion of the total defence employment figure. The largest single item in the expansion of nuclear defence will be the Trident nuclear submarines now under construction at the Barrow-in-Furness shipyard of Vickers. Trident costs will consume such a high proportion of the planned defence budget that severe economies will have to be made in other areas, and Chalmers has calculated that by 1990 total spending on new equipment will fall by up to 36%.[3] In these circumstances there will be a dual crisis in defence spending employment and defence related production.

The decision to proceed with the Trident submarine contract, effectively confirmed by the Conservative victory in the June 1987 general election, will mean that there will be an increased probability of the cancellation of other major defence contracts in the late 1980s and early 1990s. Should future political circumstances change in favour of the opposition Labour Party then there is the likelihood of a move to a policy of non-nuclear defence, and consequently of a major reorientation of labour and capital resources in the nuclear sector of the defence industry. In this event the work carried out at Barrow-in-Furness on conversion and diversification will be of critical importance. This research is described in section 2.

For the immediate future it seems clear that Trident construction will continue, and indeed will be followed by other expensive follow-on systems, especially in aerospace. In this situation it becomes even more imperative for peace and disarmament researchers to develop data and information resources. They must be of a sufficient quality to anticipate diversification and conversion opportunities likely to emerge as a consequence of the cancellation of a range of defence contracts, whether for financial reasons or because of changes in defence policy following changes in international or national perceptions. Progress of research in this area is described in sections 3 and 4.

In any event research will be of little consequence if it does not have some utility for policy-making. Once again there are indications that significant progress has been made. In 1983 the Trades Union Congress committed itself to support for defence conversion planning. In 1984 a National Trade Union Defence Conversion Committee was formed from seven trade unions with members in the defence sector. Most significantly, in 1986 the National Executive Committee of the Labour Party not only declared its support for defence conversion, but elaborated on a national policy through which it would implement the commitment should it come to form a government. In essence, the policy involves the establishment of a National Agency for Industrial Conversion and Recovery within the Department of Trade and Industry. This agency would provide assistance to those areas heavily dependent on defence contracts through a conversion fund and would have the general responsibility of helping employers and trade unionists to develop policies for diversification, conversion and industrial recovery. The document in which these proposals are put, *Defence Conversion and Costs*, represents the most detailed policy statement yet adopted by a major political party on the conversion issue.

Of course the adoption of the policy depends on the ability of the Labour Party to form a government. Yet even in the absence of this prospect for the immediate future, there are pressures occurring that will create the climate in which conversion and diversification issues will have to be confronted. Indeed it may be argued that it would be irresponsible for policy makers and managers in the defence sector not to examine product alternatives on commercial grounds alone. Common to all defence companies is the escalating cost of the new generation of weapons which makes it increasingly likely that research, development and production costs will have to be shared between countries—a process which is already occurring. This is likely to result in the need to cut back on plant and workforce, creating high levels of unemployment among defence workers. Already between 1984 and 1987 nearly 25,000 jobs were lost among Britain's major defence contractors, and this process will accelerate as defence spending in real terms is cut.

Yet of even more concern than the decline in employment are the signals of industrial decay indicated primarily in the failure of government support for research and development programmes in industry. Government funded research and development devoted to defence is now more than half of total government investment in research. Britain ranks very low in Europe in terms of the proportion of national wealth devoted to non-defence purposes. There are already signs of disquiet about this and the concern will heighten. Indeed the whole problem of Britain's military burden will manifest itself as a pressing one for government, industry, and trade unions as the burden becomes more and more detrimental to general economic well-being. The development of diversification and conversion policies, and of expertise in these areas, will be a critical part of the agenda for economic development in the closing decades of the century.

2. Conversion projects in the UK

Barrow Alternative Employment Committee—(North West England). The Barrow project represents the most important industry-based initiative in the UK because of the participation by trade unionists and the relative importance of the Trident submarine programme locally as well as in the context of national defence policy. Vickers (VSEL since privatization in 1986) is Britain's leading naval defence contractor and the monopoly producer of nuclear-powered submarines. The Trident programme requires all four submarines to be constructed at Barrow. The contract for the first was received in April 1986.

Local trade union concern centred on the growing dependency of the company and the local economy on a programme that was vulnerable to cancellation. In 1984, this resulted in the Trades Council forming the Barrow Alternative Employment Committee, made up of a broad cross-section of workers in the yard, to look at possible alternatives to Trident. Research for the committee centred on the impact of Trident expenditure on the defence budget, alternative defence policies and programmes and possible diversification into new marine-based, commercial production. It was clear that Trident was having a severe effect on conventional defence procurement within a declining overall budget. Yet Trident in national terms represented the worst return in employment because of the high proportion of the Trident budget spent (mainly on the missiles) in the USA. Even in Barrow, the government projected an average of 4,000 jobs sustained by Trident during the lifetime of the programme, in comparison to a workforce of 12,300.

Alternative defence policies, centring on non-offensive conventional defence (including submarine construction), would have provided a similar level of employment for the company. However, the defence spending crisis would have continued. The need to end excessive defence dependency of the company is great if employment and production capacity are to be maintained.

The Committee's report made a strong case for a major expansion of non-military research, development and production in the marine sector, re-orienting government support from military to civilian R&D.[4] Using international comparisons of large shipbuilding and engineering programmes, it concluded that substantial areas of potential new activity existed in sea-based renewable energy programmes, marine technology developments such as submersibles and specialist ship-building production. Although there are some technical and industrial problems in such a programme, since Vickers is the largest integrated shipbuilding and engineering facility left in Europe, it could begin the process of change in a gradual but sustained fashion. The real barriers are institutional, emanating from central government and local management both of whom emphasize the importance of the Trident programme in particular, or the specialist role of the company in defence work in general.

Alternative Employment Study Group— (Dumbarton—Scotland). In contrast to Barrow, this project reflects a community-based concern about the impact of a major defence site, the Clyde Submarine base, on the local economy, as well as the lack of other local economic opportunities. A variety of trade union and peace groups from the Dumbarton area formed the Alternative Employment Study Group in 1984 to assess the role of the base. Research has focused on the general decline in employment in the Dumbarton area, in the light of drastic cuts in shipbuilding and engineering. Employment prospects at the base are poor, even with the expansion of facilities to accommodate the Trident submarines once they become operational in the 1990s.

Because of the specialist facilities and the distance of the base from major population centres, the emphasis has been on local and regional economic policy which would provide new economic opportunities. The focus has not really been on alternative use of the base facilities as such. More recently, research has been expanded to a full investigation of the Scottish defence industry. This has included issues of employment, location, regional spending as a proportion of the national budget, etc. Such work should form the database necessary to identify various sites vulnerable to cutbacks in defence procurement and guide appropriate responses to the threat of closures and redundancies.[5]

Llangennech—(South Wales). Llangennech is a Royal Naval Stores Depot facing closure under Ministry of Defence plans, with the loss of several hundred jobs. Since the announcement of the decision to close the depot, a Joint Action Committee (JAC) was established by the unions to campaign against closure. But the JAC also decided to consider plans for alternative use. The government has stated its intentions to close all facilities from 1987 through to 1990, and the conversion element has now taken priority for the unions.

Emphasis has been placed on conversion to a network of small businesses based on the current and potential skills and resources of the workforce. This is considered to be the best means of lessening dependence on external capital and providing firmer roots and closer identity with the local economy. In 1986, the JAC (after consultation with the

Welsh Development Agency and the Wales Co-operative Centre) formed Alterplan 87, registered as a company to design, fund-raise, and commission studies into alternative employment initiatives. The Ministry of Defence agreed to second two members of JAC to work full time as permanent staff and Alterplan 87 now has its own office on site. This is very significant in terms of the historical aversion of the Ministry of Defence (MoD) to trade union work on conversion. It clearly reflects the strength of national trade union support for the Llangennech initiative which the MoD found difficult to ignore.

Already, internal study groups are discussing the following specific areas: joinery, specialized packing, vehicle repair, agriculture/horticulture and industrial painting. The next stage of activities is to identify the most promising ideas for new uses and their technical and infrastructural requirements. An application for support from the European Economic Community has also been made. This would be to fund research on the skills base of the workforce, management services, financial services and marketing for new projects.[6]

The Greater London Conversion Council. The Greater London Conversion Council (GLCC) is an organization of trade unionists and researchers in the London area concerned with the defence sector in London and the impact of defence spending on the London economy. Created initially with the help of the Greater London Council (itself now abolished by the Conservative Government), it has produced a series of reports. The first of these was an overview of the defence industries in London and the potential job losses resulting from national government policy.[7] More recently, work has focused on the leading sectors of aerospace[8] and electronics.[9]

Other projects active in the UK include a trade union based initiative in the South West;[10] and groups involved in product research and in research for local authorities, recognizing the role new production can make in the area of local economic planning.

Arms Conversion Group. All of these groups are represented on the Arms Conversion Group (ACG), an umbrella organization based at the School of Peace Studies, which serves as a focus for these and other initiatives around the country. It also includes groups and individuals whose main work is not directly on conversion but who share an interest in the promotion of such activities. The ACG has served as a forum on these various conversion issues, and has also produced reports itself dealing with a variety of research topics. The first in the series was a survey of the attitudes of defence workers at Barrow.

The Barrow survey covered four unions at Vickers Shipbuilding and Engineering Ltd (VSEL). Although there is an extensive literature on defence conversion and a background of trade union and political campaigns to promote a conversion programme, a scientifically based survey of the opinions of those most directly affected had not been attempted in the UK. Defence workers at VESL, Britain's biggest naval defence contractor (at present constucting the first Trident submarine) were considered a good population to sample in testing attitudes to military and civilian work, as well as appropriate measures to safeguard jobs.

Security and union membership confidentiality were obvious difficulties in carrying out this research. But these were overcome by concentrating on industrial and employment issues like work preferences, knowledge of and support for civilian alternatives to military work, and Trident. As far as work preferences were concerned only 4% preferred defence work, 35% preferred civilian work, with the majority expressing no preference. For a company which has been and continues to be so heavily dependent on defence contracts, the low level of preference for defence work is very surprising, especially as there is frequently a presumption that the higher skill content, greater job security, etc., of defence work creates a positive commitment on the part of the defence workers.

Trident was considered essential to job security by 64% of respondents. However, in a follow on question a greater majority (83%) agreed that their job security did not depend on Trident but on VSEL having enough defence orders in general. The fact that a minority agreed with both statements indicates respondents were 'hedging their bets', i.e., if there were no alternatives Trident would be essential but for the vast majority, as long as an adequate alternative was offered, Trident had no special quality in terms of job security.

The options put forward should Trident be cancelled included defence, civilian and government civilian contracts. The overwhelming priority choice was other Royal Navy submarine contracts. This is consistent with the questions on Trident and demonstrates how present political and economic realities influenced respondents' choices. However, the support for an expansion of civilian work was also strong. 73% of respondents would support a pilot project involving the development of more civilian products and there was a clear majority who felt that more scope existed for civilian production at VSEL.

On conversion, the results provide contrasting findings. A majority would support plans for alternatives as a form of insurance policy should defence contracts be cut. But when asked what words would best describe the process of changing from defence to civilian production the largest group were 'don't knows', suggesting that the concept was a difficult one. Of those who chose a description, conversion was one of the least popular (at 10%), with technology transfer and diversification getting much greater support, (21% and 25% respectively), presumably because these terms are more neutral and do not require the kind of drastic changes implied by conversion.

Only a minority had heard of the Lucas Plan (24%) and, although many people knew of the Barrow Alternative Employment Committee's existence, we specifically asked if they knew of the *work* of the Committee. Only a minority (41%) said yes and of this group a majority (56%) felt that their work was either useful or very useful.

In summary then, while recognizing the importance attached to defence work, we can take a positive message on civilian production, as far as our respondents are concerned. Work preferences show clearly that there is no prior commitment to defence work, as is commonly assumed. The commitment is simply to work. The clear support for a pilot project on civilian products demonstrates that the workforce expect every avenue of investigation to be considered by management, and the success of such a project could create a groundswell of support for further development.[11]

It is clear that considerable efforts have been made locally and nationally to place conversion on the political agenda. Practical initiatives have emerged in several key defence locations, each providing their own emphasis on the direction conversion planning should take in order to accommodate particular circumstances and local issues. At a national level, detailed proposals were, for the first time, incorporated into the industrial policy of a major political party. Had the Labour Party been elected in June 1987, this would have provided a framework in which all the local projects could have played a positive role. The return of a Conservative Government, committed to the Trident programme, means that the overall decline in defence employment will continue, as will the need for conversion initiatives to be sustained and encouraged.

Without an overall policy framework this will clearly be difficult, but our existing projects can serve as models for responses to the different types of industrial and employment dislocations caused by the continued defence spending squeeze. If the results of the Barrow survey are indicative of the attitudes of defence workers in all sectors of the defence industry, this would represent encouraging evidence that a broadening of the product base in defence dependent companies would be a popular policy option in the medium and long term. There is scope here for further comparative research into workers' (and managers') attitudes at other defence sites. Therefore, as the problems facing the defence sector become more and more intractable, the role of conversion initiatives will be seen as increasingly relevant and important. The detailed work already done provides the most comprehensive base ever achieved in this country for an understanding of the issues involved in conversion and the mobilization of people directly affected at a local level.

3. The UK defence industry at national level: a survey of current employment trends

Any realistic assessment of the impact of reductions in the size of defence industries, due to cutbacks in defence spending, has to begin with the role played by these industries today. Yet comparatively little is known about the major companies which comprise the core of the UK defence industry. Such information as exists is widely distributed amongst many sources. The computerized database established in the School of Peace Studies at Bradford University is an attempt to go some way towards filling this gap in the literature, within the constraints of national security and commercial secrecy.

The database is the result of a 12 month study of the empirical data on the UK defence industry in which essential information on arms manufacturers (concerning their defence contracts, funding from the Ministry of Defence, sites and numbers employed) was collated. While this database is far from complete it is thought to be of sufficient quality and reliability to be a worthwhile contribution to future work on the economic effects of disarmament or reductions in defence spending. It should also be useful in the subsequent development of a policy on arms conversion to prevent redundancies. The emphasis of this database is on what defence firms do; on their existing work and specialities rather than the conversion possibilities.

The database covers 37 top contractors to the MoD in terms of:

—the location of their most significant MoD oriented sites;
—their degree of dependency on the MoD in terms of sales and employment;
—the nature of the specific MoD contracts they are known to be working on.

These 31 UK companies and 6 foreign-owned subsidiaries together cover some 21 divisions and 80 subsidiaries involving about 300 sites.

A location map is provided in Figure 1 showing the main MoD oriented sites of the 37 principal contractors across the UK. Further location maps, contained in the interim report on the database,[12] illustrate the sites with the largest number of employees amongst the top aerospace, shipbuilding and ordnance firms. The counties with the greatest concentration of defence sites are (in descending order): Greater London; Hampshire; West Midlands; Hertfordshire; Essex; Surrey; Lancashire; Somerset; Strathclyde; Bedfordshire. The cities and towns with the largest number of defence contractors are (by number of sites): Coventry; Bristol; Portsmouth; Edinburgh; Glasgow; Preston; Watford; Bracknell. Apart from these places contractors,

KEY

Town/city in or around which the following contractors are based

CONTRACTORS
(listed by size of MoD payments in 1982/3)

Over £100 million
A = British Aerospace PLC (Aircraft Group)
B = British Aerospace PLC (Dynamics Group)
C = British Shipbuilders
D = Ferranti PLC
E = The General Electric Company PLC
F = The Plessey Company PLC
G = Rolls Royce PLC
H = Royal Ordnance PLC
I = Westland PLC

£50–100 million
J = BL PLC
K = Hunting Associated Industries PLC
L = Racal Electronics PLC
M = Thorn EMI PLC
N = Vauxhall Motors Ltd.

£25–50 million
O = British Manufacture & Research Company Ltd.
P = Dowty Group PLC
Q = Guest, Keen & Nettlefords PLC
R = Lucas Industries PLC
S = Marshall of Cambridge (Engineering) Ltd.
T = Philips Electronics & Associated Industries Ltd.
U = Pilkington Brothers PLC
V = Short Brothers PLC
W = United Kingdom Atomic Energy Authority
Y = United Scientific Holdings PLC
X = Vickers PLC

£10–25 million
a = British Electric Traction Company PLC
b = BTR PLC
c = Cable & Wireless PLC
d = Cambridge Electronic Industries PLC
e = Hawker Siddeley Group PLC
f = Standard Telephones and Cables PLC
g = Cossor Electronics Ltd.
h = The Singer Company (UK) Ltd.
i = Smiths Industries PLC
j = The Weir Group PLC

Others
k = Pearson PLC (£5–10 million)
l = Perkins Engines Ltd. (£?)
m = Yarrow PLC (£5–10 million)

( ) = number of sites (*if greater than 1*)

GREATER LONDON
Chessington = L(3)
Chiswick = B
Enfield = H
Feltham = L.M.P. (2)
Hayes = M (4)
Hounslow = k
Ilford = F (2).i
Inner London = E.R. (3) c.f.
Kingston-on-Thames = A
New Malden = L(6)
Raynes Park = L
Ruislip = L
Stanmore = E (2)
Surbiton = d
Wembley = E.L.
Willesden = R

FIGURE 1. The main MoD oriented sites of the 37 principal contractors across the UK
Source: Arms Conversion Group.

though concentrated in the South East, South West, West Midlands, North West and Scotland, are generally spread fairly evenly across many towns within the regions.

Over 70% of the firms investigated have a dependency of 5% or more on MoD contracts, in terms of sales and employment. Moreover, this defence work tends to be concentrated within a few divisions or subsidiaries where most of the defence work is undertaken. The firms with the heaviest MoD dependency, of probably at least 33% of sales, are:

  (i) *In aerospace:* British Aerospace, Westland, Marshall of Cambridge, Hunting Associated Industries;
 (ii) *In electronics:* Ferranti, Cossor Electronics, Singer Company (UK);
(iii) *In shipbuilding:* British Shipbuilders (before privatization of the warship yards in 1985–86), Yarrow Shipbuilders (now owned by GEC);
 (iv) *In ordnance:* Royal Ordnance, British Manufacture and Research Company.

The sample of defence contracts was estimated to account for between 166,000 and 180,000 of the 225,000 jobs which the MoD calculated were *directly* supported by its own equipment programmes in 1984. This represents between 74 and 80% of total *direct* employment on MoD equipment programmes.

A detailed analysis of the major aircraft and shipbuilding programmes illustrates the extent to which defence companies have specialized even in the industry sectors (e.g., electronics) where there is some competition. While smaller defence budgets and a renewed government emphasis on competition may well produce more intense rivalry between those companies, it must be doubted whether these factors can substantially affect procurement patterns. There are, after all, a very limited number of domestic UK producers of high technology equipment and the government is committed to maintaining an indigenous defence industry base.

There appears to be little scope for the government to respond to budgetary pressure by cancelling major MoD contracts underway at the moment. Most programmes are too far advanced or are too crucial to perceived military requirements and maintenance of UK industrial capacity to make cancellation politically feasible. In December 1986 the government did, though, announce the cancellation of the Nimrod Airborne Early Warning aircraft programme and the SP-70 self-propelled gun in quick succession. However, this was due to serious technical, not budgetary, problems. In fact the need to find more money to pay for replacement equipment programmes will add to the MoD's budgetary difficulties rather than reduce them.

Postponements of decisions, or reductions in the size of further orders, are the most likely means for the government to attempt to achieve its spending targets. A list of expected forthcoming contracts over the next 15 years was provided in the interim report. In particular it included contracts for: a supersonic Harrier programme; anti-tank helicopters; various missile programmes; a future Main Battle Tank; command and control systems; various warships and submarines. Collaborative projects are extremely prominent except in the naval area.

4. Employment implications of MoD procurement plans

The Conservative government's options in coping with an increasingly tight defence budget over the next few years have been made worse by the onset of the peak years of expenditure on the Trident nuclear missile system. Politically, the options are likely to be restricted to putting back rather than cancelling existing programmes, and postponing decisions on new equipment. This in turn is bound to have an effect on jobs.

Indeed, over the three years since 1984 about 25,000 jobs have been lost from the principal MoD contractors and their defence-oriented subsidiaries. This is quite apart from reductions in employment levels due to natural wastage. Approximately 11,500–15,500 of these job losses can be directly attributed to diminished MoD procurement demands and altered purchasing policies. These figures must be seen in the context of a long-term decline in UK defence-related industrial employment, due to the increasingly capital-intensive nature of equipment procurement. Yet, they also reflect the harsher climate the UK defence industry had entered after seven years of rapid growth in military expenditure. Although the job losses may not seem very high, compared to those in other industries like steel and automobiles, it is worth noting that within three years they have exceeded the 7,500 direct jobs which the Trident programme is expected to maintain over its twenty-year procurement cycle.

The defence spending squeeze and the new Trident programme appear to have hit the warship building sector hardest. All the warship yards, except those in the VSEL consortium where the Trident submarines will be built, have experienced an erosion of employment. If this process continues, as seems likely, one or more warship yards may have to close. The ordnance sector is also facing grave difficulties at the moment. The Royal Ordnance factories were sold to British Aerospace in April 1987, except for the site at Leeds which manufactures tanks. They now face the prospect of further rationalization after thousands of redundancies in the ammunition and explosive factories caused by reduced procurement requirements and the application of competitive tendering practices by the MoD. The tank factory at Leeds, whose future had looked doubtful, was incorporated into Vickers PLC in 1986. Vickers owns the only other UK tank factory (at Elswick on Tyneside) and therefore now has a monopoly in the manufacture of tanks. Even military aerospace sites are likely to face a run-down in employment levels despite the anticipated European Fighter Aircraft (EFA) programme and a huge export deal involving the sale of Tornado and other aircraft to Saudi Arabia. This arises principally from the smaller size and UK share of the EFA programme and doubts about whether the government could afford to fund a supersonic Harrier programme in the 1990s as well. Lastly, the electronics sector is also likely to experience reduced defence-related employment. Where this occurs will depend on which firms are the winners, and which the losers, within key market segments, at home and abroad.[13]

5. Conclusion

The extent of the likely job losses emphasizes the importance of developing arms conversion strategies now to enable companies and communities with a significant or heavy reliance on the MoD to adjust to cuts in defence spending. The existence of a computerized database will greatly aid in monitoring the effects of the defence spending squeeze over the ensuing years. The Arms Conversion Group is hoping to extend the database to cover other major Western defence industries in the USA, West Germany, France and Italy. This seems a logical move, following the greater prominence that collaborative weapons programmes have been given, and will enable more attention to be focused on the need for international conversion planning.

NOTES AND REFERENCES

1. Gordon Adams, 'Economic Conversion Misses the Point', *Bulletin of the Atomic Scientists*, February 1986.
2. Jan Oberg, 'Is the Conversion Idea to be Converted', in H. Tuomi and R. Väyrynen, eds., *Militarization and Arms Production*, 1983.
3. Malcolm Chalmers, 'The 1987 Defence Budget: Time for Choice?' *Peace Research Reports*, No. 17, May 1987.
4. Steve Schofield for BAEC 'Employment and Security-Alternatives to Trident; An Interim Report', *Peace Research Report* 10, July 1986, School of Peace Studies, University of Bradford.
5. Russell Fleming, 'Polaris and Trident—the Myths and Realities of Employment', Alternative Employment Study Group, 1985.
6. Llangennech Trade Unions Joint Action Committee, *Alterplan 87—A new approach*, 1987.
7. Greater London Conversion Council, *Arms Conversion*, 1985.
8. Bernard Harbor, *British Aerospace—A Kingston Perspective*, 1986.
9. Sue Willett, 'Lost Jobs, Wasted Skills–The Impact of Defence Procurement on the Electronics Sector in London', GLCC, 1987.
10. Arthur Taylor, *A Better Future for Future Defence Jobs in the South West*, 1987.

11. Peter Southwood and Steve Schofield, 'Warship Yard Workers—A survey of attitudes to defence and civilian production at VSEL, Barrow' ACG Report No. 1, 1987.
12. Peter Southwood, 'The UK Defence Industry: Characteristics of the main UK defence equipment manufacturers which are also relevant to a credible arms conversion strategy', *Peace Studies Research Reports,* No. 8, September 1985.
13. This section is based on Peter Southwood, 'Arms Conversion and the United Kingdom Defence Industry: An evaluation of policies for the diversification and conversion of military industries', PhD thesis, University of Bradford, 1988.

High Technology Programmes:
For the Military or for the Economy?

MARIO PIANTA

1. Different directions in state-of-the-art technology

High technology is an increasingly important part of the economy in advanced countries and has become the object of a new type of policy designed to speed up technical change and the diffusion of innovation. Large research and development (R&D) programmes, directed and financed by governments, are reshaping the innovative activities of industries, laboratories and universities.

The United States, Europe and Japan have all developed major programmes in the same areas of new technologies—microelectronics, computers, telecommunications, materials, biotechnologies. However, there are deep differences in the direction of their efforts and in their institutional setting. In the US most programmes are military-related and have become a part of the current arms race. In Japan these projects have successfully aimed at the economic needs of civilian sectors. In Europe high technology is pursued in a somewhat indiscriminate way between civilian and military applications.

This paper reviews the development and characteristics of the major high technology programmes in these countries, focusing on three case studies, the US Strategic Defense Initiative, the European Eureka programme and the Japanese Human Frontiers Program, in order to show the different directions that progress in state-of-the-art technology can take as a result of political choices, economic policies and military pressures. The increasing emphasis on military technology is discussed, arguing for an alternative orientation of innovative efforts, and for a strategy of conversion of high technology programmes to the needs of the civilian economy.

2. The new technological landscape

The years since the Second World War have been marked by the technological leadership of the US. Combined with economic strength and military power, US control over the more advanced technology has been a pillar of the postwar hegemony of the United States over the West, and a major factor in fuelling the arms race between East and West.

Over the years, the US technological lead has been eroded by the growth of Europe and Japan. All technological and economic indicators—R&D expenditures, patents, number of scientists, high technology trade, investment, Gross Domestic Product (GDP)—show that the US leadership has been replaced by converging performances of the US, Europe and Japan, with an increasing specialization at the technological frontier, and a fragmented pattern of relative advantage in different sectors.[1]

TABLE 1. *Military and civilian research and development expenditures in advanced countries as a share of GDP, 1960s-1980s*

Military R&D (MIRD), civil government R&D (civil GOVRD) and gross domestic expenditure on R&D (GERD): percentages of gross domestic product, 3-year averages 1961–63 to 1982–84.

	1961-63	1964-66	1967-69	1970-72	1973-75	1976-78	1979-81	1982-84
USA								
MIRD	1.32	1.09	0.97	0.79	0.67	0.62	0.62	0.79
civil GOVRD	0.62	0.97	0.89	0.70	0.60	0.63	0.62	0.45
GERD	..	3.06	3.02	2.66	2.42	2.36	2.46	2.73
Japan								
MIRD	0.01	0.01	0.01	..	0.01	0.01	0.01	0.01
civil GOVRD	0.45	0.49	0.48	..	0.58	0.58	0.61	0.62
GERD	1.31	1.31	1.52	1.93	2.03	1.99	2.23	2.40
FR Germany								
MIRD	0.12	0.16	0.19	0.15	0.14	0.13	0.12	0.11
civil GOVRD	0.49	0.65	0.75	0.93	1.07	0.98	1.03	1.05
GERD	..	1.51	1.77	2.16	2.16	2.19	2.44	2.58
France								
MIRD	0.42	0.53	0.46	0.34	0.36	0.34	0.43	0.46
civil GOVRD	0.59	0.87	1.01	0.84	0.80	0.72	0.74	0.92
GERD	1.58	1.98	2.11	1.89	1.79	1.76	1.89	2.15
UK								
MIRD	0.78	0.73	0.56	0.52	0.58	0.61	0.68	0.63
civil GOVRD	0.52	0.60	0.67	0.75	0.79	0.67	0.69	0.69
GERD	..	2.36	2.33	2.12	2.18	2.19	2.42	2.27
Sweden								
MIRD	0.36	0.40	0.37	..	..	0.27	0.19	0.19
civil GOVRD	0.44	0.54	0.58	..	0.77	0.93	0.97	1.01
GERD	..	1.23	1.27	1.46	1.65	1.84	2.20	..

From: *SIPRI Yearbook 1986, World Armaments and Disarmament,* p. 303.

Table 1 summarizes the evolution of R&D expenditures as a percentage of GDP in six major Western countries, from the 1960s to the mid-1980s, comparing total R&D, military R&D and non-military government-funded R&D. While in the 1960s the US commitment to R&D was above 3% of GDP, far higher than the other countries, in the 1982-84 period Japan and the Federal Republic of Germany have reached the US level. Moreover, military R&D is 0.8% of GDP in the US, eight times higher than in Germany and eighty times higher than in Japan, and the share of expenditure for civilian R&D in these two countries is now higher than in the US.

TABLE 2. *Major high technology programmes in the United States Defense Department programmes (data in million US dollars)*

Programme	Strategic computing programme	Very High Speed Integrated Circuits (VHSIC)	Strategic Defense Initiative (SDI)
Institutions involved	Defense Department, DARPA	Defense Department, DARPA, other agencies	Defense Department, SDIO
Key decision power	DARPA	Defense Department	Defense Department SDIO
Where R&D is done	US firms, laboratories, universities	US firms, laboratories, universities	US firms, laboratories, universities (1% is done in Europe)
Period and funding	Five Years, 1984-1989, $600m	1980-1985, $300m 1980-1989, $700m	1984-1987, $9,000m 1984-1990, $33,000m 1984-1994, $90,000m
Areas of research	Microelectronics, artificial intelligence, expert systems, computers, software	Microelectronics, gallium arsenide chips	Space, lasers, electromagnetics, microelectronics, supercomputers, software
Type of research	Applied, development	Applied, development	Applied, development
Products developed or considered	Autonomous land vehicle pilot's associate, Battle management system: new military systems	Very fast, miniaturized microprocessors for new weapons and control systems: new military systems	Space and BMD weapons control systems: new military systems
Objectives and likely outcome	Development of new military technologies in artificial intelligence and computers	Development of new military technologies in microelectronics	New generation of strategic weapons, first strike capability, new arms race in space

In this context, a technological strategy in the more advanced countries cannot aim at reaching (or restoring) an overall leadership, nor, for the weaker countries, can it be an indiscriminate effort to imitate the technological model offered by the leading country. Rather, the new objective of technological strategies becomes targeting the best position for the national economy in the international division of labour at the technological frontier. This is the purpose of the increasing number of high technology programmes in all advanced countries.

3. The proliferation of high technology programmes

In the new international context of technological competition, high technology programmes have combined the resources and strategies of governments with the research efforts of national laboratories and the production capacity of national firms. They can be defined as large R&D projects targeted to specific technological advances or to the development of industrial or military systems. With budgets of hundreds of millions of dollars, they are a major force shaping the development and applications of new technologies in the areas of microelectronics, computers, telecommunications, materials, biotechnology.

Since the mid-1980s in all advanced capitalist countries the number of these programmes has swelled,[2] their importance in governments' technological strategies has increased and their impact over the direction of technological change has become deeper. By concentrating large R&D resources, and developing major innovations, they have a unique influence on economic and military systems. They are a key factor in the process of restructuring of advanced countries.

Tables 2 to 5 provide an overview of the major high technology programmes in the US, Europe and Japan, with a summary of their institutional setting, the time scale, the funds available, the sectors involved and the likely results. Although only the most important and coherent programmes (13 in all) have been considered, the amount of resources they are expected to mobilize is remarkable. By 1990 it can be estimated at $60–70 billion, roughly the same amount the United States spent in 1981 for all (private and public) R&D. This represents an unprecedented concentration of world innovative resources and decision power in the hands of few governments, agencies and large firms.

3.1. The US programmes

In the United States two types of programmes can be identified, those directed by the Defense Department (such as the Strategic Computing Program, the Very High Speed Integrated Circuits (VHSIC) and the Strategic Defense Initiative), shown in Table 2, and those developed by

US firms, shown in Table 3. The former have massive funds and a much broader scope, while private sector programmes appear to fill gaps in the R&D activities of firms through cooperative projects.

In many Defense Department programmes a key role is played by DARPA (Defense Advanced Research Projects Agency), an agency specialized in directing technological change towards military applications. Launched in 1983 as a response to the Japanese Fifth Generation Computer Program (see below), DARPA's Strategic Computing Program has pioneered the new strategic role of high technology programmes in the US. With a budget of $600 million over five years, it aims to develop artificial intelligence and computer research. From $50 million in fiscal year 1984, its budget was planned to rise rapidly to $95 million in 1985 and $150 million in 1986.[3] The total costs are expected to be greater than one billion dollars if the programme continues to be funded for a decade.[4]

The specific projects under way are an autonomous land vehicle, an aircraft pilot's associate and a battle management system for the Navy. They combine 'machine intelligence technology', expert systems, machine vision, speech understanding, and parallel processing in new technological developments that are tailor-made for the military needs of the projects. DARPA's assertion that 'these military applications collectively pull the basic research efforts and focus them in the most rewarding area'[5] shows the the driving force in this programme is the performance requirement of the military system, rather than the development of an advanced technology base with wider applications.[6]

A second major project directed by DARPA aims to create the hardware and software for fast, large and 'intelligent' computers, with the Very High Speed Integrated Circuits (VHSIC) programme. DARPA has spent $300 million over the past five years on military VHSIC and plans to spend one billion dollars for research on supercomputers.[7] The VHSIC programme is scheduled to run for ten years at the cost of $700 million and aims not only to make the traditional integrated circuits more miniaturized and faster, but also to develop entirely new systems such as gallium arsenide microchips and optical computing. Research is also devoted to expert systems, artificial intelligence and computer architecture.[8]

Little economic benefit is expected from this programme. A study of the Atlantic Institute for International Affairs reported that

the organization, structure, and objectives of VHSIC are now inappropriate for high technology firms competing commercially on a global scale . . . The limited applications of integrated circuits produced for the military, and their narrow share of the world semiconductor market, mean that spillover benefits from VHSIC participation will probably not improve competitiveness in global semiconductor markets.[9]

TABLE 3. *Major high technology programmes in the United States, private sector programmes (data in million US dollars)*

Programme	Microelectronics and Computer Technology Corporation (MCC)	Semiconductor Research Corporation (SRC)	Semiconductor Manufacturing Technology Corporation (Sematech) (planned)
Institutions involved	21 US private firms in a cooperative project	13 US private firms in a cooperative project	US semiconductor firms in a project sponsored by the Defense Department
Key decision power	Firms	Firms	Defense Department, firms
Where R&D is done	MCC laboratories (400 scientists)	US universities	New plants and laboratories
Period & funding	Started in 1983, annual budget $75m	Started in 1982, annual budget $35–40m	To be started in 1987, funded with $1,000m by the Defense Department over five years
Areas of research	Microelectronics, systems architecture, software, VLSI superconductivity	Semiconductors, VLSI	Semiconductor production technology
Type of research	Applied, precompetitive development	Basic, applied	Applied, development
Products developed or considered	New advanced microelectronics: new means of production	New semiconductors: new means of production	New semiconductor productions systems: new means of production
Objectives and likely outcome	Development of new technologies by US firms; more competitiveness	Advances in semiconductor technology; more competitiveness	US self-reliance in chip production; national security, more competitiveness

While the role of the US Defense Department in funding and directing technological change in areas such as aerospace, materials, and manufacturing automation is very extensive[10] it has usually been performed through its generous research and procurement contracts, rather than through a unifying programme with a well-defined technological strategy.[11] This has dramatically changed in 1984 with the Strategic Defense Initiative (SDI), the new model of US military-oriented high technology programmes. SDI is analyzed in some detail in section 4.

TABLE 4. *Major high technology programmes in Europe (data in million US dollars at 1987 exchange rates)*

Country	European Community	European Community	European Community	European Community	All West European countries
Programme	Science and Technology Framework Programme (planned) (includes all EC programmes)	ESPRIT, European Strategic Programme for Research in Information Technology	RACE, R&D in Advanced Communications Technologies for Europe	BRITE, Basic Research in Industrial Technologies for Europe	EUREKA European Research Coordination Agency
Institutions involved	EC and member states, laboratories, firms (including US affiliates)	EC, member states, European firms (including US affiliates)	EC, member states, European firms (including US affiliates)	EC, member states, European firms	States' governments and firms, High representatives, Eureka secretariat
Key decision power	EC and member states, firms	Firms	Firms, telecommunications agencies	Firms	Firms, governments
Where R&D is done	European laboratories, firms and universities	European firms, universities	European firms	European firms	European firms, laboratories, universities
Period and funding	Five years, 1987-1991, to be funded with $6,200m by the EC	Ten years, 1984-1994 total EC funds $1,840m in 1987-91 to be matched by firms; in 1984-86, 240 projects funded with $655m by EEC	Five years, 1987-1991, $632m by the EC; Phase II planned, 1991-1996	Three years, 1985-1987, $140m by the EC, to be matched by firms; in 1985-86, 102 projects funded; $460m for 1987-91	Started in 1985, in 1985-87 165 projects funded with $4,500-5,000m (50% firms, 50% governments)
Areas of research	Information technology, telecommunications, materials, manufacturing, nuclear energy, etc.	Microelectronics, computers, software, office and factory automation (CAD-CAM-CIM)	Telecommunications, optoelectronics, Integrated Broadband Communications (IBC) and ISDN	Materials, manufacturing technology and automation; focus on auto and chemical industries	Microelectronics, computers, software, telecommunications, lasers, robots, transportation, biotechnologies, environment
Type of research	Basic, applied	Applied, precompetitive development	Applied, development	Precompetitive development	Applied, development
Products developed or considered	Nuclear reactors, information systems, computers, materials: new means of production, new public infrastructure	Advanced information technologies, automation systems: new means of production	Introduction of IBC and ISDN: new public infrastructure, new means of production	Advanced materials and new production technologies in auto and chemicals: new means of production and consumption	Advanced electronics and information systems, new production technologies, etc.: new means of production, new public infrastructure
Objectives and likely outcome	More integration and competitiveness in Europe	More integration and competitiveness in information technologies	More integration and competitiveness in telecommunications	More integration and competitiveness in production technologies	More integration and competitiveness in Europe

MPP—G*

TABLE 5. *Major technology programmes in Japan (data in million US dollars at 1987 exchange rates)*

Programme	Fifth-generation Computer Program	Frontier Research Program	Human Frontiers Science Program (planned)
Institutions involved	MITI (Ministry for International Trade and Industry); ICOT (Institute for new generation computer technology)	STA, Science and Technology Agency; RIKEN Institute of Physical and Chemical Research	MITI, STA
Key Decision power	MITI	STA, RIKEN	MITI, STA
Where R&D is done	Japanese firms, laboratories, universities	New RIKEN laboratory (involving foreign scientists)	Laboratories, firms, universities, in Japan and abroad
Period and funding	Ten years, 1982-1992, $450m; in FY 1987, $40m	Ten years, 1986-1996, in FY 1986, $7.7m, in FY 1987, $10m	Twenty years, 1987-2007, in FY 1987 $1.4m preliminary study; to be funded with $250m per year; Japan offered $3,500m to be matched by others
Areas of research	Parallel computers, artificial intelligence logic programming, software	Biosciences, ageing, homoeostasis, materials, optics, bioelectronics	Biosciences, artificial human functions, sequencing the human genoma, robots
Type of research	Applied, development	Basic, applied	Basic, applied
Products developed or considered	New computers and information technology: new means of production and consumption	Biotechnologies for pharmaceuticals and agriculture, new materials, sensors, biochips: new means of production, consumption	Biotechnologies and new advanced instrumentation: new means of production
Objectives and likely outcome	Development of a new generation of computer technology	Advances in basic research in bioscience and materials	Development of a new generation of biotechnologies and biosciences

A second type of US high technology programme, shown in Table 3, has recently been developed by private firms through cooperative projects, especially in microelectronics. The most important one is the initiative of 21 US electronics firms—all the major ones, with the exception of IBM—that pooled together resources and in 1983 formed the Microelectronics and Computer Technology Corporation (MCC). Each company contributes to the $75 million annual budget, financing the research performed by 400 scientists in the new MCC laboratories in Austin, Texas. The four initial areas of research are systems architecture, software engineering, manufacturing of microprocessors and computer-aided design of Very Large Scale Integrated Circuits (VLSIC). Research in superconductivity has recently been added.[12]

As US legislation prevents a full cooperation among firms in product development, MCC focuses on precompetitive research; MCC will own the patents on the results and will licence them to the individual companies of the pool, which will carry out development and production. MCC has not been very successful so far, mainly for the reluctance of the partners to share their research. It was not until June 1987 that the first product of MCC cooperation appeared, a software system for chip design developed by NCR. Furthermore, four firms have announced their withdrawal from MCC in 1988.[13]

The semiconductor industry is another example of the growing cooperation among US firms. The first step has been the establishment of the Semiconductor Research Corporation, a nonprofit consortium of 13 companies funding university research on advanced integrated circuits at the level of $35 million a year.[14]

The next step, after a major intervention of the US government in support of the domestic chip producers faced by increasing Japanese competition,[15] is the project of the Semiconductor Industry Association, the US trade group, for creating a Semiconductor Manufacturing Technology Corporation (Sematech) along the lines of the MCC described above. All large US manufacturers of semiconductors would join in a major programme for developing the manufacturing system of the next generation of chips. The one billion dollars needed for the project may come from the new funds the US Defense Department is prepared to spend in support of US semiconductor firms. Initial funding of $100 million a year was approved by Congress early in 1987.[16]

3.2. European programmes

The EC countries have shown a growing interest in developing a European 'Science and Technology Community', pooling their R&D efforts, unifying standards and markets under the pressure of increasing competition from the US and Japan. The European Community has taken the initiative in this process; its objective is 'to strengthen the technological bases of European industry and to develop its international competitiveness'.[17]

European programmes usually fund 50% of an R&D project proposed by an international consortium of European firms that are requested to match the EC contribution. However, other programmes are directly managed by the EC and its agencies, with the participation of some of the EC countries, as in the case of the large European nuclear power programme.

The areas of EC-sponsored research include resources, energy, information technology and telecommunications, biotechnologies, new materials and 'quality of life' issues. Table 4 summarizes the major European high technology programmes, starting with the 1987-1991 'Framework Programme' of the European Communities Commission, designed to include all EC innovative activities. From a proposed budget of 10,000 million ECUs (European Currency Units), about $11,500 million, the final agreement, after long disputes among the EC governments, resulted in September 1987 in a halved budget of 5,396m ECUs, about $6,200m. [18]

The Framework Programme gives a major emphasis to industrial competitiveness (60% of the funds, twice as much as the 1984-87 programme), followed by energy (21%) and 'quality of life' (7.5%).[19] European competitiveness is pursued through projects in information technologies (with an estimated $1,840 million); telecommunications ($632 million); new services using computerized telecommunications ($800–$1,000 million); manufacturing technologies ($460 million); biotechnologies ($138 million). In the energy field nuclear power absorbs almost all funds, with the fusion project ($702 million) and the nuclear fission programme ($506 million). Only $140 million are planned for research in other energy sources.[20]

The major projects sponsored by the EC and summarized in Table 4 include the ESPRIT programme in information technology, RACE in telecommunications and BRITE in industrial technologies.

ESPRIT (European Strategic Programme of Research in Information Technology) covers a wide area of precompetitive research[21] and is funded by $1,840 million for 1987–91. A consortium of at least two firms of different European countries has to be established, with the possibility of partnership with research institutions and universities. Half of the funding for the projects has to come from the firms involved and the other half is provided by the EC. Started in 1984, ESPRIT has led in its first year to 104 cooperative projects that have involved 270 European firms, including affiliates of US multinational corporations.[22]

ESPRIT projects are not proposed by the Commission of the European Communities—the initiative remains with firms. The range of sub-programmes include advanced microelectronics, software technology, information processing, office systems, computer integrated manufacturing. Its focus after 1987 will be on microelectronic and peripheral technologies (silicon, compound semiconductors, CAD, peripherals, storage, printers and displays); information processing systems (design and architecture, knowledge engineering, signal processing); integration of information technologies into application systems (support systems, factor automation); dissemination of the results; participation of small firms.[23]

In telecommunications, the EC project is RACE (R&D in Advanced Communication Technologies for Europe) aiming at the introduction of Integrated Broadband Communication (IBC) by 1995, taking into account the evolving Integrated Service Digital Networks (ISDN). After a definition phase in 1985-86 to focus the programme, Phase I (1987-1991) will lay the groundwork and will be followed by a second phase ending in 1996. The first phase has been funded with $623 million.[24]

BRITE (Basic Research in Industrial Technologies for Europe) is a project for manufacturing technologies with an intersectoral and interdisciplinary approach. It is tailor-made to the needs of industry and focuses on reliability of materials and components, reduction of deterioration, laser joining techniques, membranes, CAD-CAM systems, and materials. By 1986, 550 projects proposals had been received, with an average of four participants. However, only 102 were funded due to budget constraints. The budget for 1987-1991 is $460 million.[25]

The other important European-wide programme, Eureka, has been developed outside the EC framework and will be analyzed in section 5.

3.3. The Japanese programmes

The classical model of high technology programmes is offered by the Japanese tradition of cooperation between the government, industry and universities on well-defined projects targeted to achieving industrial leadership in specific world markets. Many projects and policies by the Japanese Ministry for International Trade and Industry (MITI) share some elements of this approach. We will consider here the three major programmes developed at the high technology end of Japanese policies (see Table 5). The Fifth Generation Computer Program, launched in 1981, is directed by the Institute for New Generation Computer Technology (ICOT) and coordinated by the specialist Electro-Technical Laboratory (ETL); it involves an expenditure of $450 million over ten years.[26]

This is the project that, with its long-term commitment and imaginative proposals, put pressure on the US and Europe to develop similar initiatives, such as the Strategic Computer Program, MCC and ESPRIT. Unlike the previous radical changes in computer technology, the Japanese project aims not only to innovate the devices, introducing Very Large Scale Integrated Circuits (VLSIC), but also to change the design philosophy of computers, with an emphasis on logic programming, highly parallel computer architecture, the development of artificial intelligence software and human-machine interface natural to human beings.[27]

The project is now in its intermediate phase when experimental small-scale subsystems are being produced. While by 1991 a final prototype system is expected to be completed, some proposals stress the need for further exploration of the basic technologies required for the project.[28]

The other Japanese programmes that are discussed here are more recent and, again, radically innovative. The Frontier Research Program is a relatively small project for basic research in bioscience and materials, starting with a budget under $10 million. Four laboratories investigate the biological problems of biohomeostasis, focusing on the molecular biology of ageing, the ageing process, intestinal flora and plant biological regulation. The materials programme has three laboratories studying quantum materials, optics and bioelectronics. While research will be carried out in Japan, in the new laboratories for the Institute of Physical and Chemical Research (RIKEN), three of the seven laboratories will be headed by non-Japanese scientists, opening a new major international collaboration.[29]

The declared aim of the project is to advance basic research; RIKEN argues that 'Japan must now break away from the catch-up type of research and instead must plan a pioneering role in the discovery of new scientific knowledge, so as to contribute to the prosperity of the world'.[30] Nevertheless, there are evident applications of the research undertaken by the Frontier Science Program in biotechnologies for pharmaceuticals and agriculture, and in new materials for industrial production.

The Frontier Science Program is considered as a preliminary initiative in the direction of the much larger and more important Human Frontier Science Program currently planned in Japan and examined in section 6.

*   *   *

After this preliminary overview of the major high technology programmes by the US, Europe and Japan, a few elements are already evident. Very large innovative resources are concentrated in programmes associated with key national strategies, addressing a large spectrum of new technologies. While these programmes show many, often surprising, similarities,[31] their institutional setting and direction of research remain different, linked to the national technological strategies of the US, Europe and Japan. Similarities and differences will be highlighted now in the analysis of the three most important high technology programmes under way: the US Strategic Defense Initiative, the European Eureka and the Japanese Human Frontier Science Program.

4. The US Strategic Defense Initiative

SDI is the largest single research programme ever developed by a Western government. It is managed by the US Defense Department through the SDI Organization (SDIO). Its aim, the development of anti-missile defence, is still unclear in its scope and feasibility,[32] but SDI funds have rapidly increased from 1 billion dollars in 1984, to 1.6 billion in Fiscal Year 1985, 3 billion in 1986 and 3.5 billion in 1987 (with an administration's request of 5.4 billion). For Fiscal Year 1988 the administration's request of 5.7 billion has been reduced by the House of Representatives to 3.1 billion.[33]

TABLE 6. *Strategic defence funding (million US dollars)*

Programme	Strategic Defense Initiative Organization			
	FY 1985	FY 1986	FY 1987	FY 1988
Surveillance, acquisition, tracking & kill assessment	546	857	1,262	1,558
Directed energy weapons	378	844	1,615	1,582
Kinetic energy weapons	256	596	991	1,217
Systems concepts & battle management	100	227	462	564
Survivability, lethality & key support technology	108	222	454	524
Management HQ, SDI	9	13	17	18
Total	1,397	2,759	4,808	5,463

	Department of Energy		
	FY 1985	FY 1986	FY 1987
Strategic defence-related programmes	224	288	603

From: Waller et al., 1986, op. cit., p. 15.

4.1. SDI funds and contracts

Table 6 shows the growth of the administration's requests between 1985 and 1988, broken down into the five categories of the programme: surveillance, acquisition, tracking and kill assessment (absorbing almost 30% of the funds); directed energy weapons (about 30%); kinetic energy weapons (about 20%); systems concepts and battle management (less than 10%); survivability, lethality and key support technology (about 10%).

The projected funding for SDI amounts to $33 billion between 1984 and 1990 and to 90 billion in the 1984-1994 decade.[34] By 1990, SDI may well absorb one-quarter of all R&D funds of the US Defense Department.[35]

Seven billion dollars have so far been spent for Star Wars. The funds have been distributed in contracts with firms, laboratories and universities. Studies from the Council on Economic Priorities (CEP), in New York, have documented their distribution. Table 7 shows the 20 companies that received the largest SDI contracts in the period 1983-1986. Together, they received $5.4 billion, three-quarters of total expenditures. Lockheed, General Motors (through its Hughes division), the Lawrence Livermore National Laboratory, Boeing and TRW are the first five recipients; all of them are companies which are already of major importance in the list of Pentagon contractors; one-third of SDI contracts has so far gone to these five companies.

Among the first eight SDI corporate contractors there are six of the seven largest contractors of the DoD and five of the first six DoD contractors for RDT&E.[36] The concentration is also geographical; 83% of all SDI contracts between 1983 and 1986 have gone to five states: California ($3,264 million, 44% of all SDI expenditures); New Mexico ($1,230 million); Massachusetts ($718 million); Alabama ($535 million); and Washington ($403 million).[37]

In spite of the US invitation to its allies to join in SDI research—an offer that has been accepted so far by Britain, the Federal Republic of Germany, Israel, Japan and Italy—few SDI contracts have reached Europe. Britain has received $40 million, with nine contracts to private firms for $15.5 million; a $10 million contract to the British Ministry of Defence for the European architecture study (85% of which has been subcontracted to 18 private companies), and a $10 million contract for laser research at a government laboratory. West Germany has received $30 million; $21 million went to Dornier and $4 million to Messerschmitt-Bolkow-Blohm.[38]

In December 1986 seven contracts, worth $2 million each, were awarded to consortia of different firms for studying the architecture of a European strategic defence. The seven groups include 51 companies, 29 of which are European. The groups are headed by Messerschmitt-Bolkow-Blohm of Germany; Aerospatiale and Thomson of France; Snia BPD, a Fiat subsidiary, of Italy; and by four US companies: LTV Science Applications International; RCA; Lockheed; and Hughes, a division of General Motors.[39] The total value of the European contracts for Star Wars for the five years up to 1990 is expected to be not more than $300 million, 1% of total SDI expenditures.[40]

Military industries, however, are not the only beneficiaries of SDI contracts; US universities are increasingly involved in Star Wars research, with $200 million received from SDI by 1986. The Massachusetts Institute of Technology, with its off-campus Lincoln Laboratory, in 1985 received contracts for $60 million. In 1986, Utah State University received $8 million; the University of Texas, $6 million; Georgia Tech $5.2 million; Johns Hopkins $4.8 million; Stanford $3.3 million.[41]

TABLE 7. *The top 20 SDI contractors, FY83-FY86 (thousands US dollars)*

Company	$ value of contracts FY 1983-FY 1986	% of total contracts FY 1983-FY 1986
Lockheed*	720,961	9.8%
General Motors	612,698	8.4
DOE Lawrence Livermore National Lab*	375,433	5.1
Boeing	373,697	5.1
TRW	373,117	5.1
EG&G*	360,300	4.9
McDonnell Douglas	338,224	4.6
MIT Lincoln Lab	327,542	4.5
DOE Los Alamos National Lab*	285,588	3.9
General Electric	260,797	3.6
DOE Sandia National Lab*	226,530	3.1
Rockwell International	197,405	2.7
Teledyne Inc.	181,145	2.5
Gencorp Inc	175,455	2.4
SDI Institute	125,000	1.7
Textron	120,331	1.6
LTV Corp.	105,657	1.4
Flow General	90,226	1.2
Raytheon Co.	81,819	1.1
Martin Marietta	77,781	1.1
TOTAL	$5,409,706	73.8%

*Data are from FY 1983–June, 1986. Since the last four months of FY 1986 are not included in the estimates, final figures may differ from those listed here. Figures also include $549 million in FY 1987 priced contract options that have yet to be exercised. Of this, Lockheed is to receive $34 million, Lawrence Livermore $140 million, EG&G $154 million, Los Alamos $123 million and Sandia $99 million. These values will increase significantly after Congress determines SDI appropriations.

From: Council on Economic Priorities, 1987, op. cit.

To encourage SDI research in universities and in small laboratories, SDIO set up a separate agency, 'Innovative Science and Technology' (IST), funded with 5% of the total SDI budget. IST gave $28 million to universities in 1985 and $100 million in 1986. Sixty-two million dollars have been assigned to six research consortia, including 29 universities in 16 states, working in the areas of non-nuclear space power, optical computing, electronic circuits, high speed electronic systems, composite materials and chemical lasers.[42]

With such large funds, SDIO has been able to attract a very large number of academic researchers; by autumn 1985 SDIO had already received 2,600 applications from individuals and universities.[43] For many academics, in fact, SDI represents one of the few available sources for new funds. The price to pay, however, is an increasing militarization of research in US universities, and the arrival on campus of classified research and security clearances.[44]

4.2. SDI's technological outcome

The technological results of Star Wars are highly controversial. On the one hand, its supporters claim that the new SDI technologies – electronics, lasers, materials—will lead to major innovations in all fields, with a major impact on the whole of the economy. On the other hand, SDI raises in an exemplary way the widely debated question on the use of military expenditure as an industrial and technological policy for the US economy.[45]

Such a role of the Star Wars programme is documented by the growing share of R&D expenditure that is devoted to SDI in the US. SDI is expected to account for 30% of the new military research, 10% of all military R&D and possibly 5% of the total private and public R&D expenditure of the United States.[46] SDI will also continue to drive more scientists and engineers away from commercial work and is expected to control about one-fifth of US high technology venture capital.[47]

The narrow focus on military problems and applications is the major limitation of Star Wars. Ann Markusen argued that 'there is little chance that the Strategic Defense Initiative will provide many commercial spinoffs',[48] and a British committee reviewing R&D policy stated that 'we remain unconvinced by the argument that the SDI will produce valuable civil spin-off'.[49]

According to Nathan Rosenberg, SDI 'represents a highly inefficient way of organizing support for the civilian economy'. Secrecy and the specific military requirements of SDI raise major problems: 'the substantial divergence between the needs of the civilian economy and the military goal of strategic defense provides a formidable array of concerns which casts further doubt on the efficacy of SDI' for the civilian economy. Furthermore, 'the vast bulk of the funds appears to be devoted to downstream military applications, as well as to achieving a high degree of survivability of that hardware under extreme circumstances'.[50]

With all these doubts on its effectiveness as a domestic technological strategy, SDI may still show its greatest results in the international arena. In the new technological landscape, SDI represents a major attempt to influence the direction of progress at the technological frontier towards the areas (military systems, space, supercomputing) where the US still has a large advantage over Europe and Japan. In the current competition among the most advanced capitalist countries, asserting the American 'style' of military-oriented high technology appears as a major objective of SDI, a form of US policy that can be described as a 'Technological Star Wars' strategy against Europe and Japan.[51]

TABLE 8. *Eureka programme, description and cost of the projects (data in million US dollars at 1987 exchange rates)*

Sector	No. of projects	%	Cost (US$m)	%	Nature and likely outcome of the projects
Microelectronics and computers	14	19.4	443.2	13.8	Development and new applications of existing technologies. Emphasis on rationalization
Software and information technology	7	9.7	578.2	18	and control. A few military spinoffs possible. Leading mainly to new means of
Telecommuni-cations	4	5	477.3	14.9	production and a few final products.
Robots, lasers and manufacturing	14	19.4	650.1	20	Massive application of new technologies to production. Emphasis on automation
Materials	7	9.7	143.2	4.5	and rationalization. A few military-oriented projects. Leading to new means of production.
Transportation	5	6.9	272.7	8.5	Use of existing technologies to rationalize the transport system. Leading to new means of production and new infrastructures.
Health and biotechnology	8	11.1	158.7	5	New applications and new research in biotechnology. Leading to some final products and new means of production.
Environment	4	5	323.6	10.1	Application of existing technologies to air, sea and water problems. Leading to new public investment.
Others	9	12.5	160.5	5	New applications in the fields of energy, gas and construction. Leading to new products and means of production.
Total	72	100	3207.5	100	

Projects approved in the Eureka conferences at Hanover (November 1985) and London (June 1986). Elaboration on project descriptions. Some of the cost estimates refer only to the feasibility study or to the first year budget. Average length of the projects is five years.

With the European participation in SDI, such a strategy has already scored some success in directing European R&D towards the same military technologies that dominate US innovative efforts. Once it has accepted this field as the ground for international competition at the technological frontier, along with the US rules and institutional procedures, European industry can hardly hope to be more successful than its established US competitors. This is the kind of technological race that the US is certain to win.

The dangers of the US 'Technological Star Wars' strategy have been so evident to Europe and Japan that both have developed major high technology programmes in response to SDI, the European Eureka and the Japanese Human Frontiers Science Program. These are examined in the next two sections.

5. The European Eureka programme

The launch of SDI and the US offer to its allies to join the research programme sparked new debates and initiatives in Europe. Three weeks after the US offer in March 1985, the French government proposed to respond to the SDI challenge with a European civilian high technology programme, Eureka (European Research Coordination Action), with the objective of strengthening European technology in microelectronics, computers, telecommunications, robots, materials and biotechnologies.[52]

Eureka rapidly obtained the support and participation of the 12 EC countries, and of Austria, Norway, Sweden, Switzerland; later also Finland, Iceland and Turkey joined in some research projects.

The programme is directed by the Conference of Ministers of Foreign Affairs, Research, and Technology of the participating countries. A network of High Level Representatives is in charge of coordinating the projects, with the help of a small secretariat in Brussels that is independent from the Commission of the European Communities. The projects are proposed by a consortium of at least two firms of different countries, which have to provide half of the funding. That is then matched by their national governments on a project-by-project basis. Closer integration among European firms and research institutions is a major aim of Eureka, contributing also to a progressive unification of the European market, technical standards and regulatory system. While firms have a key role in selecting the areas of research and have full control over the formulation of the research projects, the governments have the more limited role of assessing and helping to fund the projects.

In 1987 the number of approved Eureka projects was 109, with a total funding of $4,200 million over a five-year average time scale, an amount of resources similar to the R&D budget of the EC. The largest share of funds has come from France, with 30%; Italy follows with 26% of the costs, while the Federal Republic of Germany and Britain contributed smaller shares. These are not, however, *additional* funds for R&D; most governments have redirected towards Eureka funds that were already appropriated for R&D budgets, while the effect on the R&D effort by private firms is not yet clear.[53]

Detailed descriptions of the projects were available only for the first 72 approved in the Eureka meetings of Hanover (November 1985) and London (June 1986).[54] In the Stockholm meeting of December 1986, 37 more projects were approved. Table 8 describes the nature and composition of the first 72 Eureka projects.

Microelectronics and computers account for 14 projects, with a cost of $443 million. They are designed to develop new industrial processes for semiconductor production, new supercomputers and gallium arsenide chips. The latter two areas have particularly important military applications. Only two projects consider the production of a final marketable good, a minicomputer.

Software and information technology are the object of eight Eureka projects, all aiming at process innovations, with a cost of $578 million. In telecommunications there are four projects, costing $477 million, that focus on the needs of the European communication network. The common nature of these projects is the application of advanced technologies to the process of production and information management, in the direction of capital-intensive 'rationalization'.

Many Eureka projects are devoted to manufacturing technology, including robots and lasers (14 projects costing $650 million), and to new materials (7 projects costing $143 million). Their objective is the automation of mass industrial production, focusing on metalworking and autos, where most of the materials research is concentrated. Again, capital-intensive 'rationalization' is the model inspiring these projects, and again a few of them have clear military applications, such as the two projects of mobile intelligent robots for security tasks.

Transportation technology (five projects and $272 million) aims at both process innovations in rail transport, and advancing the traffic management system and the infrastructure network. Existing technologies are being applied to the transportation system, offering new solutions to the needs in this area. Health and biotechnologies (eight projects and $159 million), include research both in biological processes for pharmaceuticals and agriculture, and in the development of new diagnostic systems. Environmental problems are the object of four projects costing $324 million; they consider the use of existing technologies to monitor and clean up air, water and sea in new programmes of public investment. Other projects, nine in all funded at $160 million, address problems in energy, gas technology, and construction. Some are new applications of known technologies, while others can be described again as capital-intensive 'rationalization'.

Eureka has provided the largest European firms, especially in the electronics, telecommunications and auto industries, with a major opportunity for undertaking, with government support, the R&D needed for a process of restructuring towards increasingly automated, computerized and capital-intensive production systems. While the original aim of Eureka was the development of final marketable products, of the total 109 projects only one in eight falls into this category. Less than 10% are related to public programmes and almost 80% focus on process innovations and intermediate goods.[55] This high technology restructuring of European industry is the obvious result of a programme that leaves all control in the hands of the large firms dominating Eureka. This is likely to be the direction taken by the race for 'competitiveness' sparked by the proliferation of high technology programmes.

Furthermore, many of the Eureka projects have important military applications; while the military use of Eureka is rarely discussed,[56] many of the same large firms have actively sought SDI contracts from the US Defense Department, and some Eureka projects look similar and complementary to Star Wars research.[57]

In this way the initial image of Eureka as the European civilian response to SDI has rapidly faded and now many European governments and companies have agreed to participate in both.[58]

The issue of European participation in SDI and Eureka has explicitly put European governments and corporations before the problem of the direction of technological progress. The decisions taken so far and the projects that are being developed show that the US technological strategy has already succeeded, to a certain extent, in shaping the policy agenda and innovative programmes in Europe.

6. The Japanese Human Frontier Science Program

The Japanese response to the US Strategic Defense Initiative has been a high technology programme of radically different nature from both SDI and Eureka, the Human Frontier Science Program that focuses on human biological functions and on their artificial applications.

While the Japanese government had started to discuss the programme in 1985, two years have been taken up by the preparation of preliminary plans and by discussion with the US and the European countries that are expected to join the project. Designed as a large international collaboration, the programme includes research carried out both in Japan and abroad. In charge of the Human Frontier Research Program is the Ministry of International Trade and Industry (MITI) and the Science and Technology Agency (STA), the two major institutions controlling technological policies in Japan.

The Japanese government has committed $1.4 million in fiscal year 1987 for a preliminary study and has proposed a twenty-year programme with an annual budget of $250 million.[59]

The official statements emphasize again the need for Japan to break new ground in basic science after its long effort to develop applications

FIGURE 1. Areas of research of the Japanese Human Frontier Science Program/Research subjects of the program

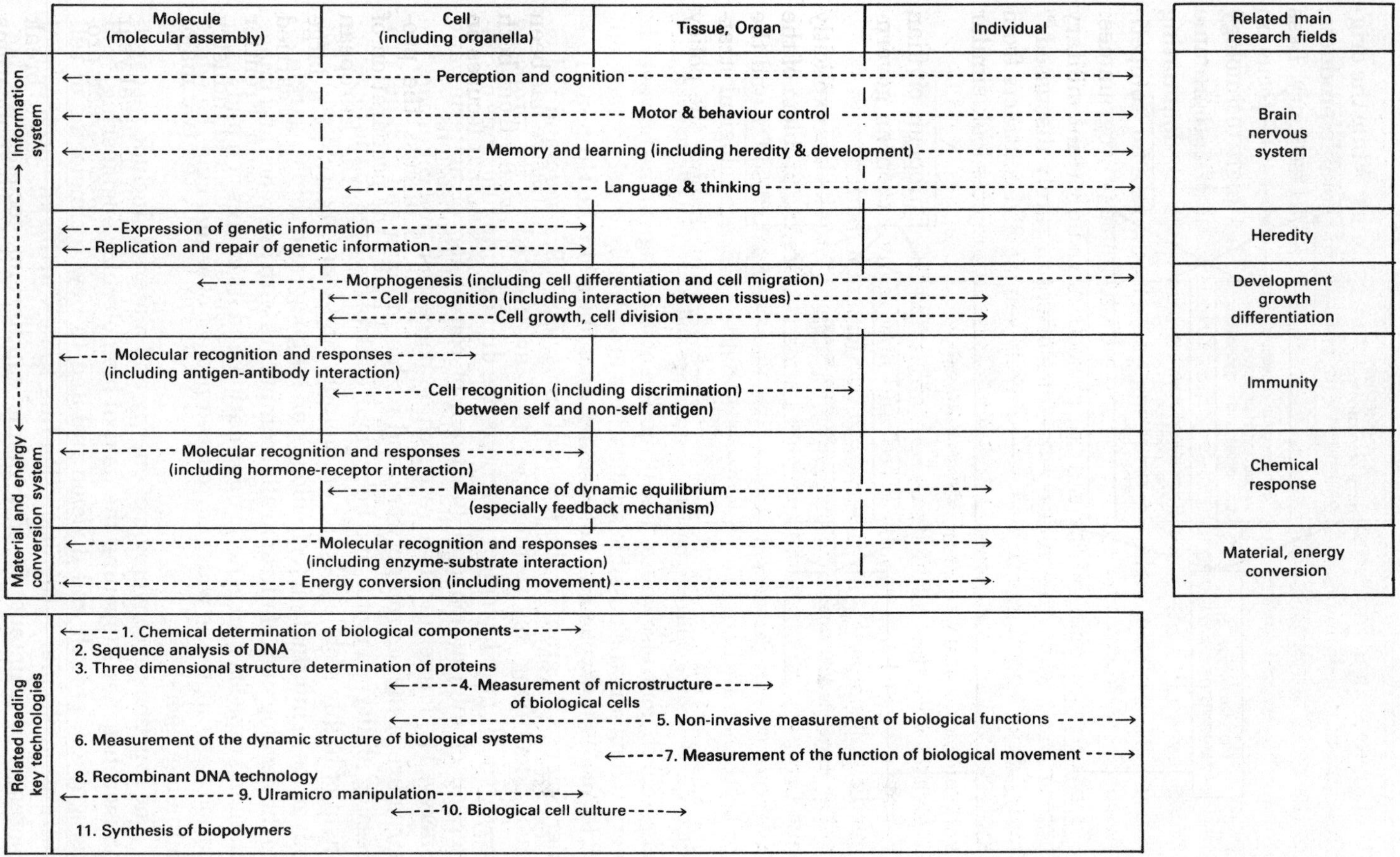
Molecule (molecular assembly)
Cell (including organella)
Tissue, Organ
Individual
Related main research fields
Information system
Material and energy conversion system
Perception and cognition
Motor & behaviour control
Memory and learning (including heredity & development)
Language & thinking
Brain nervous system
Expression of genetic information
Replication and repair of genetic information
Heredity
Morphogenesis (including cell differentiation and cell migration)
Cell recognition (including interaction between tissues)
Cell growth, cell division
Development growth differentiation
Molecular recognition and responses (including antigen-antibody interaction)
Cell recognition (including discrimination) between self and non-self antigen)
Immunity
Molecular recognition and responses (including hormone-receptor interaction)
Maintenance of dynamic equilibrium (especially feedback mechanism)
Chemical response
Molecular recognition and responses (including enzyme-substrate interaction)
Energy conversion (including movement)
Material, energy conversion
Related leading key technologies
1. Chemical determination of biological components
2. Sequence analysis of DNA
3. Three dimensional structure determination of proteins
4. Measurement of microstructure of biological cells
5. Non-invasive measurement of biological functions
6. Measurement of the dynamic structure of biological systems
7. Measurement of the function of biological movement
8. Recombinant DNA technology
9. Ulramicro manipulation
10. Biological cell culture
11. Synthesis of biopolymers

From: MITI-STA, *Current Development in Research in Relation to the Principal Biological Functions and Future Focal Points*, Tokyo, April 1987, p. 87.

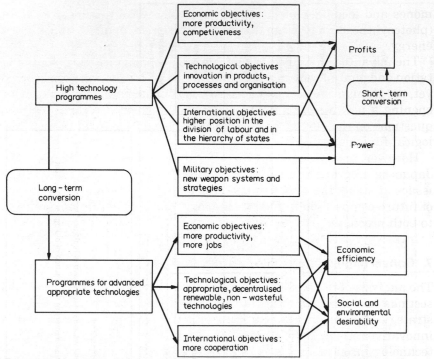

FIGURE 2. Objectives of high technology programmes and conversion alternatives

of research done elsewhere. The direction of the programme however is very strong and the possible applications are already widely discussed.

Figure 1 shows the areas of research considered in the Human Frontier Science Program at the levels of molecule, cell, tissue and individual, identifying key technologies that are related to the proposed research. Human biological functions are divided into functions of conversion of information and functions of conversion of material and energy. The former includes research on perception and cognition, the structure of the neuron network and its hierarchical and parallel processing ability; on motor and behaviour control (related to the development of highly mobile robots); on memory and learning (related to the advances in information technology); on language and thinking (related to the development of ultraparallel computers with inference and image thinking capacity); on genetic information and its expression and replication (leading to the widely discussed project of sequencing the whole human genome).[60]

The functions of conversion of energy and materials include research on morphogenesis (opening the field of biomolecular engineering); cell recognition, growth and division (related to new technologies of cell culture); molecular recognition (leading to new artificial vaccines and biosensors); maintenance of dynamic equilibrium, focusing on hormones and feed-back mechanisms; and energy conversion from light (photosynthesis) and other sources, to electric, chemical and kinetic energy.

The advances envisaged in biotechnologies, diagnostics, instrumentation and pharmaceuticals are clear. While no project has been started yet, the Human Frontier Science Program appears as a major initiative opening a new direction for research, although it also raises serious questions on the desirability of efforts to develop artificial human biological functions.

However, as a response to the US Strategic Defense Initiative, the Japanese programme has shown a much better understanding of the issues at stake; the direction of technological change and the grounds of future competition in high technology, offering an original solution to both problems.

7. Converting high technology programmes

The analysis of the major high technology programmes in the previous sections has shown the increasingly important role they play in the strategy of governments and firms and the growing concentration of innovative resources they control in all advanced countries. While high technology programmes are widely different in their institutional form, sectors of intervention and logic of operation, they all share a common nature and rationale rooted in the attempt to shape the future structure of economic and military systems. This makes high technology programmes crucial elements in directing the restructuring of advanced countries. It is therefore important to understand their specific objectives and outcomes, the criteria of their operation and their impact on the economy, technology and society.

Figure 2 shows that high technology programmes can be described in terms of four major objectives. The economic aim is to increase productivity and competitiveness of the national economy. The technological objective is to foster innovation and the development of new products, processes and forms of organization. The international objective is to improve a country's position in the international division of labour and in the hierarchy of states. The military objective is to develop new weapons systems and strategies. They all aim to increase capital accumulation in the domestic economy and to increase national power.

Obviously these four objectives are closely related to each other. Technological innovation is a condition for economic competitiveness; that in turn improves a country's international position, which is also strengthened by the development of new military technologies. But the high technology programmes previously analyzed have shown the different weight of each of these aims. In the US, the emphasis is on military programmes. In Japan, the focus is on technological objectives, with a long-term effort to open new areas of research. In Europe, a search for more short-term economic gains has led to a less selective approach and a broader range of initiatives. The lesson is that at the technological frontier many alternatives exist for advancing knowledge, stimulating innovations and extending their applications; the direction taken by each country is the result of different institutional systems and technological styles as well as of political choices and national strategies.

The case of Japan is perhaps the best example of a consistent strategy to develop new high technology areas with imaginative long-term projects such as the Fifth Generation Computer and the Human Frontier Science Program, tied at the same time to large potential markets. This is the result of a clear priority given to the goal of economic efficiency with little room for military and power considerations.

The opposite case is that of the United States where even the economic aspects of new technologies are seen in a national security perspective. A 1986 report of the US National Security Council on the importance of microelectronics for industries such as autos, computers, automation, telecommunications, defence and aerospace argued that:

> If the United States loses competitive advantage in these industries, its productivity, living standards, and growth will suffer severely. Moreover, these industries are dominated by a few nations and firms so that competitive advantage brings significant economic profits and political influence. Thus if the United States becomes a net importer and a technically inferior producer, it would also become a less independent, less influential and less secure nation.[61]

In the same way a study for the American Enterprise Institute by Richard Nelson noted that

> what is new in the current context is that the technological threats we see may come more from our allies than from the Soviet Union and may appear in the form of commercial products rather than that of weaponry . . . If the Japanese can build a fifth-generation computer before an American firm can, confidence that we are at the top of the field for military application surely will be undermined . . . For all these reasons, our policies in support of high-technology industries will continue to be intertwined with national security objectives.[62]

While military, political and economic objectives are clearly linked, and reinforce each other in a country's strategy for international leadership, high technology programmes cannot pursue all objectives at the same time. Furthermore at the domestic level, the allocation of limited national R&D resources raises difficult problems of choice that may lead to major contradictions, especially between the economic and military requirements.

This conflict goes well beyond the simple issue of resource distribution. The criteria for the development of military technologies, the performance requirements and the nature of demand have a strong effect on the technological outcomes in ways that have reduced efficiency, slowed down civilian applications and distorted the overall direction of technical change.[63]

The distorting effect of military technology can be seen in the case of the Strategic Computing Program; the DARPA report stated that 'the intelligent functions will be implemented in advanced architectures and fabricated in microelectronics to meet application performance requirements. Thus the applications serve to focus and stimulate or "pull" the creation of the technological base'.[64] In other words, the military requirements will shape the new technological outcomes from the beginning of the programme, leaving little scope for broader applications in non-military fields.

In the case of the Strategic Defense Initiative, the conflict between military and economic criteria is shown by the lack of participation in the programme of the large corporations with important commercial markets. A study by IBM, on the first 350 SDI contracts in 1983-1984, found that 'these contracts are not of any value to the civilian industry' and similar conclusions have been reached by studies of the French Foreign Ministry and the West German Ministry for Research and Technology.[65]

Oddly enough, this conflict is officially denied in the statements of the European technology policy. The European Community Framework Programme argued that the current situation is marked by an acceleration of innovation, the diffusion of new technologies in all fields, the internationalization of production and technology, the growing service sector, and

> lastly and perhaps above all . . . the growth in *defence* programmes and their repercussions as regards the world system of research, science and technology. Since the traditional frontier between civilian and military research is in fact dissolving, major defence programmes are beginning to have a dual scientific and technological purpose.[66]

Such an approach insists on combining economic and military objectives in the European high technology programmes, where the goals of power and profit are still closely intertwined, leading to an emphasis on 'hard' technologies, such as nuclear power that figures prominently in the European R&D activities and is closely related to the French nuclear weapons programme.

These ambiguities are shared also by the Eureka programme that started as the European civilian response to SDI and ended without any clear set of priorities, leaving to the large European firms the control over the direction of innovation, with projects that are sometimes similar to Star Wars research. While the Japanese Human Frontier Science Program has proposed an entirely new direction for research, Eureka has in fact accepted the arena for high technology competition set by the US with SDI.[67]

7.1. Preventive conversion: from the military to the economy

In this context, it is important to see high technology programmes not as the inevitable road to progress, but as part of the advances at the technological frontier that can take many alternative directions. The more clear and immediate alternative is between programmes designed to expand military power and programmes strengthening the economy.

The previous analysis has documented the extent of the current militarization of high technology. Arguing for a different direction of high technology can help to prevent a further spread of military projects that not only fuel the arms race, but lead also to a distortion of technical change.

A conversion strategy can be developed here, addressing in the short term the conflict between the military and economic direction of high technology programmes. As these large R&D projects lay the basis for the production systems of tomorrow, a *preventive* conversion strategy can be particularly effective in questioning the direction of innovation and investment *before* new laboratories, factories and weapons systems are actually built, increasing even more the military dependency of the advanced economies. In such a strategy, domestic economic interests, of business, trade unions and political forces, and efforts to increase social control over technology can have a strong weight in directing national technology policy towards economic rather than military objectives.

The case for such a conversion strategy can be made on technological grounds, as the current trend distorts the direction of progress towards increasingly expensive and exotic technologies, embodied in centralized, capital-intensive systems, with little room for commercial applications. In economic terms, conversion helps to prevent the polarization of the economic structure between an increasingly militarized high technology sector, with extensive automation and little employment, largely dependent on government contracts and, on the other hand, a mass of low-paid, de-skilled workers in the rest of the economy. At the international level, a conversion strategy for high technology programmes can lead to greater cooperation. It may help to prevent the growing conflict between the US, Europe and Japan in the area of high technology, associated with the rise of technological nationalism.[68]

In a strategy for converting high technology programmes the experience of Japan is a good example of a highly successful effort to develop civilian technologies. Lessons can also be learned from the European programmes aiming at the restructuring of the economy and from some Eureka projects in the areas of transportation, health and the environment. Much more can be done in these fields, on problems such as urban public transport, public health, AIDS and cancer, renewable energy, acid rain, toxic and nuclear waste, just to mention a few of the most serious and urgent problems of advanced countries.

A major programme for advancing medical research, the 'Strategic Health Initiative', has been proposed in Britain. It suggests medical applications of artificial intelligence, advancing the expert systems already developed in the areas of bacterial infections, glaucoma, internal medicine, intensive care, respiratory conditions, and cancer.[69]

Education and training are also issues of major importance for the development of new technologies. Many studies are under way in this area, including proposals for educational uses of advanced computers, language learning and translation, software writing, office work, financial modelling, design, engineering, and maintenance systems.[70] The list of alternative projects can continue at great length. It includes also much of the useful research in various areas that are currently underfunded due to the priority given to the development of military and hard technologies.

The R&D communities in these sectors represent a major constituency for a campaign of conversion of high technology. Large sectors of business and industry, especially those more exposed to international competition, have a vital interest in using new technology for improving economic performance. Together with political forces and peace movements, a coalition could develop with all sectors of society—education, health, local government, professional associations, environmental groups, trade unions, minorities—that would benefit from a reorientation of technology programmes away from the military.[71]

Such a broad spectrum of forces could seriously question government policy and budget allocations in all advanced countries, putting the conversion of high technology on the national agenda, mounting political pressure, and opposing major decisions of firms or universities to embark on large military programmes.

7.2. Conversion in the long term: new directions for technical change

The current proliferation of high technology programmes also raises fundamental questions on the direction and criteria of technical change and on the priorities of technology policy. In place of the indiscriminate pursuit of high technology, the case can be made for the development of advanced appropriate technologies, following criteria that put economic efficiency and social and environmental desirability in the place of power and profits.

The second part of Figure 2 outlines a more radical departure from the model of high technology programmes, with a reorientation of their nature and aims. In this perspective, the economic objective would combine increasing productivity and job creation. The technological objective would avoid labour-saving technologies that displace workers and centralize control. The international objective would stress cooperation and interdependence, rather than national economic and political power. The military objective would disappear from high technology programmes, as the need for security can be more properly met by political means in a common security framework, rather than with a continuing, technology-led arms race.

These changes would lead to projects that put less emphasis on hard technology, reversing the trend towards an ever-increasing capital- and research-intensity. As to the institutional setting, high technology programmes do not necessarily mean projects that have to be centralized in the hands of powerful government agencies or large multinational corporations. Quite the opposite, both in the US and in Europe the greatest innovative potential is often found in small research groups and firms.

In such a framework new appropriate technologies can be developed, advancing the technological frontier in the direction of responsible and desirable innovations. They may help to meet human needs, provide employment with equal opportunities in meaningful and fulfilling jobs, encouraging the creativity and ingenuity of people, in a flexible and decentralized economy where appropriate technology can contribute to changing the economic structure and social relations. A large-scale programme for a new generation of public infrastructure can provide the necessary demand directing the efforts of firms and R&D institutions towards the unsolved problems of housing, cities, transportation, environment, natural resources, besides the already mentioned issues of public health and education. Across national borders, new forms of international cooperation can be developed, emphasizing common needs and interests rather than competition and conflict.

The economic benefits of such a redirection of technological strategy would be immediate. New energies and resources for innovation would be liberated, with a general upgrading of the educational and technological level; the diffusion of new technologies, and their applications in other fields would accelerate; the economy would show rising employment, productivity and quality of life.

The constraints posed by the logic of capital accumulation and by the bloc system of military alliances make such an alternative appear to be a long way off. But many small immediate steps can put such a conversion strategy in motion, changing the direction and quality of innovation from 'hard' to 'soft' technologies, and moving from the creation of new means of death and control, to new tools for life and empowerment.

NOTES AND REFERENCES

1. The decline in US technological leadership is analyzed in M. Pianta, *New Technologies Across the Atlantic: US Leadership or European Autonomy?* Brighton: Wheatsheaf, 1988; see also N. Rosenberg, *Inside the Black Box: Technology and Economics*, Cambridge: Cambridge University Press, 1982; and A. Patel and K. Pavitt, *Measuring Europe's Technological Performance: Results and Prospects*, University of Sussex: Science Policy Research Unit, 1985.
2. Also in the Soviet bloc a wide-ranging high technology programme was agreed in December 1985 by a special session of COMECON, the 'Framework programme for scientific and technological progress of COMECON countries until the year 2000'. See Commission of the European Communities, *The Science and Technology Community. Guidelines for a new Community Framework Programme of Technological Research and Development 1987-1991*, Brussels, 17 March 1986, p. 13. A more specific plan has been developed in the area of information technology by the Soviet Commission for Computer Engineering of the Academy of Sciences, for research in VLSI, parallel and multiprocessor computer architecture, intelligent databases, software methodologies and logical programming. An important role in this research is played by the Hungarian Institute for Computer Coordination (SZKI) in Budapest. See R. Ennals, *Star Wars: A Question of Initiative*, Chichester: Wiley and Sons, 1986.
3. DARPA, *Strategic Computing*, Arlington, 1983, p. VII.
4. A. Din, 'Strategic Computing', *SIPRI Yearbook 1986*, p. 182; and R. Ennals, op. cit., p. 16.
5. DARPA, *Strategic Computing. Second Annual Report*, Arlington, 1986, p. 1.
6. The Strategic Computing Program is not the only US government project in advanced computing. Within the Defense Department there are projects sponsored by the Army, the Navy, the Air Force and by the Supercomputing Research Center that in 1983-85 have spent a total of $154 million for 'Federal investment in basic research and exploratory development for advanced computer research'. See US House of Representatives, *Federal Supercomputer Programs and Policies*, Hearings of the Committee on Science and Technology, June 1985, p. 694. Other US government agencies—NASA, the National Science Foundation, the Departments of Commerce and Energy—spent in 1983-85 in the same area $269 million (ibid.). In the related field of 'Federal investment in basic research and exploratory development for very-high performance computer research', Defense Department agencies (DARPA excluded) spent in the same period $55.8 million and the other US government institutions spent 74.2 million (ibid., p. 695).
7. *The Economist*, 23 August 1986, p. 13.
8. A. Din, op. cit., p. 182.
9. S. Woods, *Western Europe: Technology and the Future*, The Atlantic Institute for International Affairs: Atlantic Paper 63, 1987, p. 72.
10. D. Noble, *Forces of Production*, New York: Knopf, 1984; J. Tirman, (ed.), *The Militarization of High Technology*, Cambridge: Ballinger, 1984.
11. DARPA projects have increasingly taken the form of high technology programmes. Besides the Strategic Computing Program, the other major projects by DARPA include the National Aerospace Plane programme, developed by the Defense Department and NASA (the cost is shared 80%-20%) for an aeroplane able to fly at hypersonic velocity and to become a launch vehicle into orbit; the Submarine Laser Communication project, using new technologies developed in connection with SDI; the Armor/Anti-Armor research; and the University Research initiative. See DARPA, *Fiscal Year 1987 Research and Development Program*, Arlington, 1986.

12. T. Hayes, 'New MCC Chief's Strategy: To Speed Payoffs on Research', *The New York Times*, 24 June 1987, p. D6.
13. Ibid.; see also R. Brainard and J. Madden, *Science and Technology Policy Outlook*, Paris: OECD, 1985, p. 64; *Financial Times*, 27 January 1986.
14. *The Economist*, 23 August 1986, p. 13.
15. After years of rapid internationalization of the semiconductor industry, in March 1987 the US government prevented the takeover of Fairchild by Fujitsu for reasons of 'national security'. Later, arguing that Japan failed to comply with the market sharing agreement of July 1986, the US government imposed unprecedented trade sanctions against Japanese electronic goods. In February 1987 a report by the US Defense Science Board criticized the 'unacceptable' reliance of US military on foreign semiconductors and proposed a $2 billion programme to support American producers. See R. Reich, 'The Rise of Techno-Nationalism', *The Atlantic Monthly*, May 1987.
16. *Business Week*, 20 April 1987, p. 63.
17. Commission of the European Communities, *Towards a European Technology Community*, Brussels, 25 June 1985, p. 4.
18. Commission of the European Communities, *The Science and Technology Community*, 1986, op. cit., p. iii; *Gazzetta Ufficiale delle Comunitá Europee*, 24 October 1987, p. 302 (Italian edition).
19. Ibid.
20. Ibid.
21. Ibid.
22. R. Brainard and J. Madden, *Science and Technology Policy Outlook*, op. cit., p. 65.
23. Other EC projects aim to develop services that integrate information technologies and telecommunications for applications in learning (DELTA); road safety (DRIVE); medical informatics (BICEPS); laboratory technology and productivity (PERT); financial technology (DIME). See Commission of the European Communities, 1986, op. cit., p. 64. Programmes similar to ESPRIT have been developed also in individual European countries. The most important one is the British Alvey programme, launched in 1983, that focuses on VLSI, software engineering, man-machine interface and intelligent, knowledge-based systems. See R. Ennals, op. cit., p. 14. In Europe also private firms have pooled their resources in a project similar to the American MCC. The German Siemens, the French Bull and the British ICL have formed the European Computer Industry Research Centre (ECRC), with 50 researchers in Munich, to bring in the same laboratory research already undertaken separately in the ESPRIT projects (ibid, p. 28).
24. Commission of European Communities, 1986, op. cit., p. 63.
25. Ibid., p. 79.
26. *The Economist*, 24 August 1986, p. 13.
27. R. Ennals, op. cit., p. 5.
28. Ibid., pp. 8-9.
29. RIKEN, *Frontier Research Programs*, Tokyo, 1987.
30. Ibid., p. 4.
31. A OECD report stressed the similarities between the R&D programmes of the US Defense Department and those of the Japanese Ministry for International Trade and Industry (MITI). Besides the Fifth-Generation Computers, in Very Large Integrated Circuits (VLSI), one-third of the development costs in Japan has been funded by MITI, while in the US the Defense Department has a $300 million project. In fibre optics, MITI spends $30 million a year and the Defense Department spends 40 million. In manufacturing, they both have $200 million programmes, MITI for industrial robots and flexible manufacturing and the Defense Department for industrial automation. See R. Brainard and J. Madden, op. cit., pp. 59-60.
32. On the strategic and feasibility problems of SDI, see Office of Technology Assessment, *The Strategic Defense Initiative*, Washington D.C.: US Congress OTA, 1985; D. Parnas, 'Software Aspects of Strategic Defense Systems', *American Scientist*, Vol. 73, September-October 1985; E. P. Thompson, ed., *Star Wars*, Harmondsworth: Penguin, 1985; Waller et al., *SDI: Progress and Challenges*, Staff report submitted to

Senator William Proxmire, Senator J. Bennett Johnston and Senator Lawton Chiles, US Senate, 17 March 1986; R. Ennals, op. cit.

33. *Nature*, 21 May 1987, p. 175.
34. J. Pike, *The Strategic Defense Initiative: Areas of Concern*, Washington D.C.: Federation of American Scientists, 1985, p. 4.
35. Ibid., p. 12. Until the 1990s SDI is 'only' a research programme. Estimates on the costs to produce and put in place a strategic defence system vary, but are always enormous. SDIO director, General James Abrahamson, told the Appropriations Committee of the US Senate, on 15 May 1984, that a complete system of strategic defence may cost between 400 and 800 billion dollars (DeGrasse and Dagget, *An Economic Analysis of the President's Strategic Defense Initiative*, New York: Council on Economic Priorities, 1984, p. 17). The magazine *Aviation Week and Space Technology* put the total cost at a trillion dollars, with the system operational by the year 2000 (2 April 1984). According to estimates by former military officials and other analysts, 'the total cost could reach anywhere from 500 billion to 2 trillion dollars, with still more needed to maintain and modernize it'—F. Kaplan, '4 of 5 Top US Scientists Oppose "Star Wars", Poll Finds', *The Boston Globe*, 31 October 1986.

An example of the costs of putting SDI in place is offered by the launching into space of the hardware. A congressional report to Senator Proxmire noted that 'presently, it costs 1,500 to 3,000 dollars to lift a pound of material into orbit . . . The Phase I architecture studies predicted that anywhere from 20 to 200 million pounds of SDI material would have to be put in space. That would conceivably mean 600 to 5,000 shuttle flights whose launch costs could run anywhere from 30 to 600 billion dollars at today's prices'—Waller et al., op. cit., p. 56.

36. Council on Economic Priorities (CEP), *Star Wars: The Economic Fallout*, Cambridge: Ballinger-Harper & Row, 1987. It is remarkable that the largest contracts for missile defence have gone to the same companies that are major producers of US nuclear weapons: the MX missile (Rockwell, TRW, Avco, Martin Marietta), the B-1 bomber (Rockwell, Avco, Boeing, LTV), the Pershing (Martin Marietta), the Trident (Lockheed), Cruise Missiles (Boeing, Litton).—Hartung et al., *The Strategic Defense Initiative: Costs, Contractors and Consequences*, New York: Council on Economic Priorities, 1984, p. 24—It is hard to imagine how companies with a major interest in the production of nuclear (attack) weapons could be the agent of a strategic transformation that would make such weapons, in President Reagan's words, 'impotent and obsolete'.
37. CEP, 1987, op. cit.
38. *The Economist*, 15 November 1986, p. 23.
39. J. Cushman, 'Europeans Given US Missile-defense Contracts', *The New York Times*, 5 December 1986.
40. J, Pike, *Barriers to European Participation in the Strategic Defense Initiative*, Statement to the Subcommittee on Economic Stabilization, House of Representatives, 10 December 1985, pp. 3-4; *The Economist*, 15 November 1986, p. 23.
41. Ibid.
42. CEP Newsletter, January 1986.
43. Ibid.
44. US universities increased the share of their funds coming from the Defense Department from 10% in 1980 to 16% in 1985. The peaks are in the areas of astronautical engineering (82%), electrical engineering (56%), aeronautical engineering (54%), metallurgy and material engineering (48%) (*CEP Newsletter*, January, 1986). For the restrictions related to SDI research, see V. Kistiakowsky, 'Should University Researchers Accept SDI Funding?' *Technology Review*, 1 January 1986. The US academic world has however remained opposed to Star Wars. A Cornell University study on 451 physicists, engineers, chemists and mathematicians in the National Academy of Sciences showed that 80% are opposed to SDI and only 10% support the current research programme (Kaplan, op. cit.). Furthermore, 60% of those polled think that funds for SDI should remain below $1.5 billion a year, about the same amount that was already spent on missile defence projects before the launch of Star Wars in 1983 (ibid.). Opposition to SDI research has also been explicit: 'Some 6,700 scientists and

engineers signed a pledge not to accept SDI money: these include more than half the faculty members in 110 university physics and engineering departments. Another 1,600 researchers at government and industrial laboratories appealed to Congress last June to reduce SDI financing because of a lack of technical scrutiny', *The Economist*, 15 November 1986, p. 23.

45. A. Markusen, 'The Militarized Economy', *World Policy Journal*, Summer 1986; J. Stowsky, 'Competing with the Pentagon', *World Policy Journal*, Fall 1986.
46. N. Rosenberg, *Civilian 'Spillovers' from Military R&D Spending: The American Experience Since World War II*, Stanford University, September 1986, p. 30.
47. *CEP Newsletter*, January 1986, p.6.
48. A. Markusen, op. cit., p. 506.
49. Council for Science and Society, *UK Military R&D*, Oxford: Oxford University Press, 1986, p. 46.
50. N. Rosenberg, 1986, op. cit., pp. 30 and 32. The same point has been made by John Pike, of the Federation of American Scientists. In a testimony before a congressional committee, he argued that 'the specific economic benefits that have been claimed for SDI are greatly exaggerated. To begin with, the SDI will stress the development of performance parameters that have limited relevance to the civilian world. Star Wars computers must be able to survive the effects of nuclear explosions, and so the SDI is putting money into research on radiation-hardened gallium-arsenide computer chips. But banks and insurance companies don't need computers that can continue working during World War III. Directed energy systems can also have industrial and medical uses. But the military needs weapons with power outputs of many millions of watts that will operate for a few minutes, whereas civilian tools must operate for months or years at powers of only a few watts. X-ray lasers could be used in medical research or the production of computer chips, but the SDI is working on X-rays powered by nuclear explosions, and no hospital or factory is going to detonate atomic bombs in its basement on a regular basis'.—J. Pike, *Barriers to European Participation*, op. cit., p. 10.
51. M. Pianta, 'Star War Economics', paper for the conference 'The State of the Star Wars', Transnational Institute, Amsterdam, 23-24 January 1987, M. Pianta, *New Technologies Across the Atlantic . . .*', op. cit., 1988.
52. Republique Française, *Eureka: la renaissance technologique de l'Europe, Propositions françaises*. Paris, June 1985.
53. C. Mancini, *Eureka e la partecipazione italiana*, Rome, 1987.
54. Eureka, *Eureka Projects*, Rome: Documentazione Enea, 1986.
55. C. Mancini, op. cit.
56. After the initial emphasis on the civilian nature of Eureka, the possibility of military projects as 'spin-offs' from Eureka R&D has been increasingly discussed. Many European experts and officials stress that 'there are no boundaries between civilian and military in high technology application', 'Eureka-Europe. La renaissance technologique', *Sciences et Techniques*, No. 19, October 1985, p. 27; and Skons reported 'some interest in military applications among the countries taking part in the discussions' on Eureka—E. Skons, 'The SDI Programme and International Research Cooperation', *SIPRI Yearbook 1986*, p. 290. Especially in the Federal Republic of Germany, politicians and strategists have proposed to link Eureka to plans for a European anti-missile system complementary to SDI—L. Dechamps, *The SDI and European Security Interests*, The Atlantic Institute for International Affairs, Atlantic Paper 62, 1987, p. 47.
57. See *Science and Techniques*, 1985, op. cit.; and L. Dechamps, op. cit., p. 40.
58. This attitude is epitomized by the Christian Democrat Chancellor of the Federal Republic of Germany, Helmut Kohl who, shortly before signing the agreement on SDI with the US, in September 1985, gave his support also to Eureka, arguing that 'the common security interests of Europe and the US also demand a comparable state of the respective economic and technological developments. If we want to strengthen the European pillar of the trans-Atlantic bridge, it also presupposes that we must increase the technological and industrial efficiency in Europe' (quoted in S. Wells, 'Technology Transfer between US, its NATO Allies and Japan as it Relates to the

Present Strategic Defense Initiative,' Testimony before the Committee on Foreign Affairs, US House of Representatives, 10 December 1985, p. 7). See also M. Lucas, 'SDI and Europe', *World Policy Journal*, Vol. 1, Spring 1986.

59. *Nature*, 5 March 1987, p. 8.
60. The sequencing of the human genome is an area of growing interest in many countries. In Japan the Science and Technology Agency has been developing for many years with Seiko and Fuji Film an automatic DNA-sequencing machine, and a separate STA programme has started in 1987 in this area, while the work for sequencing machines will be part of the Human Frontier Science Program, *Nature*, 26 March 1987, p. 323.

    At the same time the US Department of Energy has proposed a seven-year, $1,000 million project for the mapping and sequencing of the human genome. The Department is already sponsoring a $10 million a year research at the Los Alamos and Lawrence Livermore laboratories on chromosomes 16 and 19. A major role is also played by the National Institutes of Health, which already spends almost $300 million a year for related research, *Nature*, 19 February 1987, p. 651; 2 April 1987, p. 429.
61. Quoted in R. Reich, 'The Rise of Techno-Nationalism', *The Atlantic Monthly*, May 1987, p. 65.
62. R. Nelson, *High Technology Policies: A Five-Nations Comparison*, Washington D.C.: The American Enterprise Institute, 1984, p. 79.
63. See M. Kaldor, *The Baroque Arsenal*, London: Deutsch, 1981; S. Melman, *Profits Without Production*, New York: Knopf, 1983; J. Tirman, ed., *The Militarization of High Technology*, op. cit; M. Thee, *Military Technology, Military Strategy and the Arms Race*, London: Croom Helm and New York: St. Martin's Press, 1986.
64. DARPA, *Strategic Computing*, op. cit.
65. E. Skons, *The SDI Programme . . .*, op. cit., p. 282.
66. Commission of European Communities, *The Science and Technology Community*, op. cit., p. 6.
67. See M. Pianta, *Star War Economics*, op. cit., and M. Pianta, *New Technologies . . .*, op. cit.
68. Cf. R. Brainard and J. Madden, *Science and Technology Policy . . .*, op. cit.; R. Reich, *The Rise of Techno-Nationalism*, op. cit.
69. R. Ennals, *Star Wars . . .*, op. cit., pp. 122 and 129.
70. Ibid., p. 93.
71. The political problems of a conversion strategy are addressed in S. Melman, *A Road Map, Not a Stop Sign: Politics of Peace*, New York: Columbia University, 1986; and S. Melman, *An Economic Alternative to the Arms Race*, New York: Columbia University, 1986.

IV. Scandinavian Studies

Conversion from Military to Civil Production in Sweden*

INGA THORSSON

1. The international background

Sweden and the other Nordic countries proposed in 1977 that the United Nations examine the relationship between disarmament and development. One important purpose of the UN study which grew out of this proposal was to expand the awareness in the Member States of the consequences of the arms race and of the possibilities that exist for reallocating resources should the superpowers begin to disarm.

Following the report by the Group of Governmental Experts in 1981, Member States were urged at the 37th Session of the General Assembly in 1982 to adopt measures in line with the Group's recommendations.

The national measures envisaged by the UN recommendations were of two sorts:

- *first*, description and analysis of the resources devoted to the military sector and of the economic and social consequences of the current pattern of resource allocation,
- *second*, decisions concerning preparations and planning for conversion, that is, the transfer of human and material resources from the military to the civil sector and the simultaneous increase in development cooperation with the Third World.

Viewed from a wider, global perspective, there are persuasive reasons to reflect more closely upon the role played by the armament process in

---

* Shortened version of 'Apprisals and Recommendations' from *In Pursuit of Disarmament—Conversion from military to civil production in Sweden*, Report by the Special Expert Inga Thorsson, Stockholm 1984, Vol. 1B, pp. 43-57. This study has been undertaken as part of Sweden's active participation in efforts designed to promote international disarmament. Sweden and the other Nordic countries proposed in 1977 that the United Nations examine the relationship between disarmament and development. The UN General Assembly accepted this proposal in its first Special Session on Disarmament in 1978. In 1982 the General Assembly requested Member States to take further steps on the national level to follow up the UN report prepared by a group of governmental experts in the years 1978-1981. Sweden was the first country to respond to these recommendations. In September 1983, Inga Thorsson was commissioned by the Swedish Foreign Minister to carry out, as a Special Expert, such a national case study for Sweden.

today's society and its likely future effects. It is particularly important to ponder two aspects:
- *first*, the implications of the arms build-up for the security of nations and individual human beings,
- *second*, the effect of the armament process on employment, economic stability and socio-economic development.

The assumption that security can be reinforced by the acquisition of a greater number of more sophisticated weapons has increasingly begun to be questioned in both East and West. Armaments have become an onerous economic burden, not least for the superpowers.

At the same time, North-South negotiations for a more just economic world order have become deadlocked. The world clearly stands at a crossroads. The global situation may deteriorate even more and lead to confrontation and chaos. Alternatively, an attempt can be made to build a more secure and just world, where greater trust and cooperation would replace the rivalry and the use of gun-boat diplomacy which currently prevail.

Up to 100 million people are dependent for their livelihood on the defence sector. Disarmament must not be seen as a threat to the future of these individuals. By emphasizing civil projects and by expanding the service sector, a large number of people will benefit and new jobs will be created as military orders decrease. Reducing their military expenditures would enable the industrialized countries to allocate more resources to the Third World. Such an increase of transfers would enhance the awareness of the interaction between disarmament, security and development. It ought to be in the enlightened self-interest of all countries to implement a policy which would result in more rational utilization of resources.

2. General considerations

Given the Special Expert's view that disarmament must not be allowed to increase unemployment, it is necessary that the process of adapting the economy to reductions in defence outlays begin now. From the point of view both of the overall health of Swedish industry and of employment, a diversification into the civil sector is clearly warranted. If the current trend towards greater industrial automation continues, all resources—including those in the defence-industrial sector—must be used in a productive manner in order to maintain employment.

Reducing the dependence of the defence industry on military orders is a long-term proposition. If international disarmament and a subsequent Swedish disarmament are not to result in increased unemployment, the defence industry must continually expand its capacity to produce for the civil market. Resources and knowledge currently used for military-related purposes ought increasingly to be directed to civil projects in both the defence and the civil sectors.

3. Conclusions

With this general background in mind, some of the conclusions reached by the Special Expert will be summarized here.

- The financial resources absorbed by the Swedish defence sector exceed the annual budget allocation for total defence. The largest extra-budgetary categories which must be included in any calculation of the social cost of the Swedish defence sector are *first* the reduction in the growth rate which can be attributed to defence expenditures, *second* the production losses which result from the operation of the conscript system, and *third* the defence-related portion of subsidies to agriculture and other sectors of the economy.

- Sweden possesses a domestic defence industry which is as broad and as technologically advanced as the defence industries of other larger Western European countries. This industrial capacity enables the Swedish armed forces to give a special, Swedish profile to defence materiel. The ability to do this both underlines Sweden's determination to defend itself and reduces the effectiveness against Sweden of the weapons and countermeasures employed by NATO and the WTO. A study carried out within the project has shown that in Sweden the defence industry has on average a higher research intensity than comparable firms which produce entirely for the civil market. Over 20% of publicly funded research in Sweden is at present defence-related.

- However desirable nuclear-weapon disarmament may be, not least in terms of relations between the superpowers themselves, its attainment would not influence Swedish defence planning in any decisive manner. In the disarmament scenarios submitted in this study, it has been assumed that reductions in the Swedish defence effort would be possible if a balanced reduction took place in the conventional forces possessed by NATO and the WTO. In line with the terms of reference of this study, disarmament scenarios have been elaborated which can reasonably be expected to occur under *favourable conditions*. A precondition for these scenarios is a considerable improvement in the international relations. Disarmament will occur only if the superpowers display greater mutual consideration and increased trust. If NATO and the WTO were to cut their total military forces by half, including a sharper reduction of their clearly offensive units, the Special Expert is of the opinion that Sweden could also reduce its defence effort by 50% without renouncing its security-policy goal of maintaining independence and security.

- This disarmament process involves a progressive reduction in military efforts over a 25-year period (1990 to 2015), which implies a gradual cut in the Swedish military-defence budget from 20 to 10 billion SEK in current prices ($2.5 billion to $1.25 billion). This would have considerable impact on both the wartime and the peacetime organizations. A large number of units would have to be demobilized. It would be necessary to cut the size of the armed forces by about 870 full-time employees per year. It should be pointed out, however, that this reduction in personnel is somewhat smaller than current or already planned reductions due to rationalization. It is military personnel who would be most affected by these changes because the opportunities for transferring personnel to new jobs within the armed forces would be sharply limited during a period of disarmament.

- The number of defence-industry employees would in all likelihood be reduced to an even greater extent. Between 1990 and 2015 about two-thirds (14,000 workers) of those currently employed in the production of defence equipment would have to find jobs in the civil sector. The ability to convert production successfully will vary from company to company. Some companies are heavily specialized in military production while others have already established an expanding civil-sector manufacturing base alongside their military capability. An emphasis on high-technology products and a low level of dependence on military-related exports will presumably facilitate the conversion process.

- There is reason to believe that the effects of disarmament would be manageable. A precondition is, however, that defence-sector conversion (including the defence industry) be well planned and carried out gradually. Government, defence producers and unions should be actively involved in this process, adopting a long-term perspective. If these requirements were met, the disarmament scenarios sketched out in this report would not lead to increased unemployment.

- If the conversion of existing production facilities were to prove impossible and alternative employment could not be found in the same community, some defence-industry personnel might be affected. Where such consequences cannot be prevented, it would be necessary to draw on the existing system of unemployment measures.

- The Swedish economy as a whole would undoubtedly benefit from disarmament. Resources released from the defence sector could be used not only to improve economic and social conditions in Sweden but also to increase international development cooperation with the

Third World above and beyond the present Swedish goal of devoting 1% of the GNP to development assistance.

4. Recommendations for facilitating the conversion process

4.1. Motives

Disarmament must not under any circumstances lead to increased unemployment. Therefore the Special Expert has concluded that it is necessary to monitor closely developments within the armed forces and the defence-industrial sector in those regions and communities whose economies are heavily dependent on the defence sector. At both the national and the local levels it is important to investigate the possibilities that exist for expanding civil production within the defence firms. One other measure to be taken is to emphasize the public procurement of technology for civil markets.

A concrete programme of action should be worked out in cooperation with the defence producers. Mechanisms must also be created which would enable the progressive implementation of conversion programmes. It is important to take such actions immediately. To wait until disarmament is in progress before taking any action might cause considerable difficulties when conversion is finally attempted. As an earlier examination by the so-called Defence Industry Committee has emphasized, it is too late to start when defence procurement has already begun to decline.

It is up to the Government to help set the conversion process in motion as soon as possible and in a more forceful, more organized fashion than hitherto. The problems currently facing the Swedish defence industry, caused by declining orders, demonstrate that financial support from the Government is necessary even today. Experience has shown that conversion to civil production cannot take place overnight. It is a time-consuming and costly process. It is not unusual for new civil products to need up to ten years before becoming profitable. The Special Expert thus believes that there is every reason to intensify cooperation between state agencies and the defence industry. Institutionalized cooperation does not have to lead to unnecessary bureaucratization. Instead it should facilitate cordinated and well-planned actions which would promote the use of defence-sector resources for civil-sector production.

Access to financial resources should facilitate the process of restructuring the defence industry. Changes in this sector would be further facilitated by the creation of an institution which would guide and assist in the task of planning and coordinating conversion programmes at both national and local levels. In the view of the Special Expert, there are clear industrial and employment motives for the state to coordinate the restructuring of the defence-industrial sector and to provide financial assistance where needed.

The Government is also by far the largest purchaser of defence materiel and plans the acquisition of new materiel together with the defence producers. The state thus has a special responsibility for the human and technical resources which have been built up in order to produce equipment for the Swedish armed forces. The Defence Materiel Administration (Försvarets materielvert, FMV) normally provides firms with considerable advance notice of anticipated reductions in defence orders, whether these are temporary or long-term in nature. Hence, firms should be able to adapt to a smaller volume of orders. While primary responsibility for restructuring production thus rests with the firms themselves, there is good cause for the Government to help ease the conversion process.

In addition to these economic and social reasons, the Government has strong foreign-policy motives for involvement in conversion. The special characteristics of the defence companies would be even more evident if a sharp decline in defence orders occurred as a result of Government decisions on disarmament. Such an essentially political step would radically alter the economic situation of the defence-industrial sector. The Government would thus have a definite responsibility to help to resolve emerging industrial and employment problems. The Swedish study shows that a reduction in military expenditure can release valuable resources which could be put to better use both within Sweden and in the form of development assistance to Third World countries. It is also suggested that Sweden should be prepared to go one step further and show that by planning and implementing specific measures, defence-industry conversion can be carried out without any serious employment problems arising.

If every country possessing a sizable defence-industrial sector were to attempt to reduce the dependence of arms producers on military orders, this would certainly favourably influence attempts to set in motion a genuine process of disarmament.

4.2. Proposals

Against this background, the Special Expert proposes that the Government:
- establish a Council for Disarmament and Conversion,
- set up a central conversion fund, linked to this Council,
- promote the creation of local conversion funds within each defence company.

The tasks of the Council should be to:

- follow developments within the armed forces and the defence-industrial sector, especially in those regions and communities which are heavily dependent on the defence sector;
- keep itself informed about and systematically up-date knowledge of particular aspects of the disarmament-development relationship (military expenditure, weapons production, arms trade, conversion projects, economic and social effects of the defence sector and disarmament, among other aspects);
- examine the possibilities of increasing civil-sector employment, for example by placing greater emphasis on public procurement of civil-sector technology;
- develop a programme of action in conjunction with relevant defence producers and unions, which would be designed to resolve conversion problems through the application of existing industrial, regional development and employment species;
- act as administrator of the central conversion fund and allocate resources from that fund to projects promoting civil-sector production within the defence industry as well as to research projects studying issues related to disarmament and conversion.

In the view of the Special Expert, the proposed *central conversion fund* should be sufficiently large to enable it to play a significant role in the conversion process.

Once disarmament is well under way, the fund might normally be financed by allocations from the savings realized through reductions in the defence budget. Before disarmament has actually begun, however, it would be necessary to devise another method of *financing*. Various solutions are possible.

One such possibility would be to put a surcharge on the payments made by FMV to defence producers financed from the Ministry of Defence budget. A second possible means of financing the fund in the initial stage would be for the Ministry of Industry to make special conversion payments to the defence producers. A third method would be to use money already in the budget for promoting employment policies. The fund could use this money to retrain the work force and implement and other measures designed to help firms adapt to reduced defence orders. None of these three Ministries should, however, have to bear the entire financial responsibility of the central fund.

A fourth method of financing the fund would be to put a special levy on the export of war materiel. This alternative would place the financial burden of the fund on the defence producers or on the foreign purchasers of weapons. In the opinion of the Special Expert, this alternative, *a levy on the export of war materiel*, has considerable budgetary, political and economic advantages over the others suggested above. A levy on war-materiel exports would create a separate source of income to cover most of the cost associated with the proposed Council and central fund.

The Special Expert also believes that attempts on the part of the defence industry to increase its civil-sector activities ought to be promoted by contributions from *local conversion funds* situated within each defence company. It is suggested that these be financed by a state conversion supplement placed at 1% of the value of contracts concluded between FMV and Swedish defence companies. This method of financing is essentially in line with what has been suggested by the Defence Industry Committee. In order for companies to receive this supplement, however, they should be required to match its value with their own funds.

It is the need for local conversion funds which will determine whether they are set up within individual defence companies. If management and unions are interested in establishing such a fund, it would be best if it were administered by a joint leadership group and regulated through a negotiated agreement. This group should continually survey and discuss conversion issues of current interest. It should also decide how the fund's money could be used to support new civil-sector projects within the company.

4.3. Political aspects

The measures proposed here may seem unnecessary since the Swedish defence sector encompasses a relatively small portion of the economy. Compared with past and present conversion in, for example, the ship-building and steel industries, it may seem surprising that the defence-industrial sector could not cope by itself with conversion over a 25-year period. There, are, however, important reasons why the defence sector should receive special consideration.

- The 30–40,000 persons who would have to find alternative employment must not look upon disarmament as an imminent threat. Rather, they should feel that society is determined to use their competence and know-how in other, more productive activities.
- The defence-industrial sector must not be allowed to find itself in as difficult a conversion situation as the Swedish shipyards did. The Government can avoid having to present the taxpayer with a multi-billion crown bill for defence-industry conversion by engaging in advance, long-term planning with the defence firms.
- Sweden's experience of conversion shows that the unions have played an important role in instigating change. The Special Expert has been able to observe that there are many ideas and suggestions for civil projects in the defence sector which ought to be exploited. The ship-yards' decision to produce oil-rigs and the diversification of the aero-

space industry into the civil sector—both of which have proven to be profitable over the long term—owe much to strong pressure from the unions.

- Finally, but not least important, Sweden should adopt specific measures in order to fulfil the United Nations disarmament recommendations since disarmament is an area in which Sweden has long been active diplomatically. This would give increased strength and credibility to Sweden's activities in this area.

As was shown both in the UN Report on the Relationship between Disarmament and Development and in this paper, it is important, particularly for political reasons, to attempt to connect disarmament and development by transferring resources from the global military sector to development assistance. This would create more favourable conditions for the promotion of development in the poorest parts of the world and for the attainment of a more just distribution of the world's resources.

The Special Expert believes that the establishment of such a link would be facilitated by the creation of an International Disarmament Fund for Development within the UN system.

Conversion: Global, National and Local Effects. A Case Study of Norway*

NILS PETTER GLEDITSCH
OLAV BJERKHOLT
ÅDNE CAPPELEN

1. Disarmament and development

A number of UN studies have linked the two objectives of disarmament and development. For example this relationship was analyzed by a UN Group of Governmental Experts which based its analysis and recommendations on no less than 40 commissioned research reports (United Nations, 1981). The basic aim of the study was to analyze how resources released from the arms race might be used to accelerate the process of development. Such reallocation of resources from arms to development we shall call *conversion*.[1]

The main potential positive economic effect of conversion is to increase the standard of living in developing countries. Various studies have confirmed this, and have provided some more precise and reliable evidence. The most obvious negative economic effect of conversion is the adjustment required in the industrialized countries. The magnitude and duration of the adjustment problems and how they may be overcome are the main subjects of this article. In the longer run, conversion may well lead to positive effects for the industrialized countries as well as for the developing countries. This perspective has been explored in the UN report, but is barely touched upon here. Of course, conversion is likely to have social and political effects—particularly important are the effects on national security and the danger of war. These non-economic effects are only briefly discussed in the UN report, and not at all within our project.

* Revised version of 'Conversation: Global, National and Local Effects: A Case Study of Norway' by Gleditsch et al., in *Cooperation and Conflict*, Vol. XVIII (1983), No. 3, published by Norwegian University Press (Universitetsforlaget), Oslo. This paper is in large part a summary of a larger report prepared for the Norwegian Government's Advisory Committee on Arms Control and Disarmament as part of the research programme on disarmament and development initiated by the United Nations.

231

2. Three levels of conversion

The economic effects of conversion may be analyzed at three different levels: the global, the national, and the local. The *national* and *global* levels are both important as decision-making units. One can imagine disarmament and increased transfers to developing countries as a result of a purely unilateral decision. More in line with the conventional wisdom is a scenario in which conversion follows a series of international events, such as decisions in the United Nations and other international bodies. The framework provided by the UN Group of Governmental Experts, which was instrumental in the initiation of this and several other research projects, was obviously that of a global effort towards disarmament and development. Even in this latter case, however, the nations are crucial as decision-making units.

The global level is also important as a *context* for any national decisions. Regardless of whether decisions to convert are coordinated internationally, the national effects of conversion in an open economy depend on the interaction between the national economy and the global economy. Disarmament in any arms-importing country affects the export industry in one or several others. Increased global development aid will also be beneficial to industrial countries which can exploit the increased purchasing power of the Third World.

The *local* level is important because it is here that the effects on employment and living conditions will be spelled out most clearly. Will arms factories go out of business? Will a municipality suffer because a military base is closed down? Decisions about disarmament are not reached at this level—although local involvement in discussions about the arms race is increasing in many countries, with towns and regions declaring themselves 'nuclear-free'. On the other hand, fear of losing employment or tax income in several smaller communities may serve to block national decisions. The macroeconomic analysis of disarmament at the national level tends to assume a highly mobile labour force, ignoring political and social costs in local communities.

The present study on Norway is primarily concerned with the national economic effects of Norwegian disarmament and increased transfers to developing countries. However, within the framework of this project, we have also made some attempt to calculate the effects of global conversion, using the World Model developed by Leontief et al.[2] We will also report some calculations of the likely effects of global conversion on the Norwegian economy. Finally, there will be a brief discussion of local employment effects.

The results for Norway are not representative of all other countries. Norway is a small country with a very small arms industry.[3] However, we believe that the results may have some relevance for other small

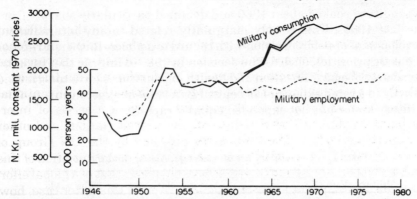

FIGURE I. Absolute size of the Norwegian military establishment, 1946-79

Sources: Data from Tables A.1 and A.3 in Appendix A of Bjerkholt et al. (1980).[4] The discontinuity in the curve for military consumption is due to changed definitions in the national accounts. Military consumption is defined in the national accounts as the value of real resources used for military purposes by state and local (municipal) authorities. The more common term *military expenditure* is defined as the amount actually *budgeted* or *spent* each year. For 1978 Norway's budgeted military expenditure exceeded military consumption by about 10%, mainly due to the advance payments on the F-16 fighter aircraft. A detailed explanation of the differences between the various measures of military spending can be found in Appendix A of Bjerkholt et al. (1980). For most of the results reported here it makes little if any difference whether one or the other measure is used: we therefore frequently use the more general (and not as precisely defined) term *military spending*.

Western European countries. In addition, we hope that some aspects of the study may serve as a model for conversion studies in other countries.

3. The Norwegian military sector

Between independence in 1905 and the German invasion in April 1940, Norway pursued a policy of neutrality. During the German occupation in World War II the Norwegian government in exile in London became very closely allied with the Western powers. In 1949 Norway became a founding member of NATO. Military spending rose sharply, particularly after the outbreak of the Korean War. The duration of military service was successively lengthened from 1948 through 1952.

The development of the absolute size of the Norwegian military establishment is shown in Figure 1. The curve for *military consumption* shows clearly the period of immediate postwar disarmament, followed by a short period of stability—at a higher level than the prewar military establishment—and finally, strong rearmament in the early 1950s. Following the 'détente' after the end of the Korean War, military consumption decreased. It has increased again from the late 1950s until today, although less steeply than in the early 1950s and with some minor ups and downs. Military expenditure in percent of central government expenditure peaked about 1960 and declined particularly sharply from the late 1960s. This is only marginally related to any international development or policy decision with regard to defence. Rather, it reflects domestic priorities, such as the decision in 1966 to initiate the National Pensions Scheme. Education and health expenditures have contributed heavily to a rapid expansion of central government expenditure and the military sector has not expanded equally rapidly.

TABLE 1.   *The military use of resources, Norway and the world*

Military share of	Norway	The world
Gross Domestic Product	3%	6%
Central Government expenditure	12%	22%
Population	1%	1.25%
Labour force	0.3%	4%
Land area	0.3%	0.3–0.5%
Research expenditure	3%	25%

Source: The global data are from the final report of the UN Group of Governmental Experts.[5] The Norwegian data are from our first report[6] as well as from public research statistics and from SIPRI's study of the use of land resources.[7] The global data are naturally subject to considerable error, as the UN report discusses at length.

The curve for *military employment* shows a stable pattern after the rearmament period in the first half of the 1950s. Along with other industrial nations Norway has acquired a number of technologically advanced weapons systems during recent years. This might have been expected to lead to a less labour intensive military sector. On the other hand, Norway has maintained universal male conscription throughout the postwar period, and this has served to maintain labour intensiveness. The net effect is that military employment has remained roughly constant. Conscripts are paid less than their market value and constitute 40% of military employment. Unlike the case of civilian government spending, the share of wages and salaries in the total military spending has not increased over the past 25 years. Nevertheless, salaries still represent about two-fifths of military expenditure and slightly over half of military consumption.

From 1951 to 1970 Norway received very substantial military assistance in kind from the United States, estimated at about 20% of the domestic military spending from 1951 to 1970. After the military assistance programme was terminated, a part of the military establishment continued to be funded by external sources, but in 1978 the published figure for such transfers was less than 2% of the defence budget. Thus, although it would be necessary to take into account the transfers to Norway to get a correct picture of Norwegian armament in the postwar period, we can ignore this factor in a study of conversion in the 1970s or 1980s.

In Table 1 Norway's use of resources for military purposes is compared with the world total. Judging from these indicators, Norway's economy can be said to be somewhat less militarized than the average for the world as a whole.

3.1. Disarmament scenarios

To study conversion, we first need scenarios for the disarmament of Norway. Such scenarios can be based on global or regional disarmament plans, Norwegian political alternatives, more or less arbitrary percentage cuts in defence spending, or comparisons with other countries. Of these, *percentage cuts* are by far the simplest and most flexible. The main disadvantage of this approach is that the scenarios are not linked to politically meaningful alternative policies either at the national or the international level. However, we have found little help in developing such scenarios in current global or regional disarmament plans, in current negotiations for arms control, or in the Norwegian discussion about defence. Therefore, we have chosen to use fairly arbitrary percentage cuts for our disarmament scenarios, and we assume the cuts to be equal for all resource inputs to the military sector.

We have selected one *moderate alternative* (reduction of military spending to about 85% of its current (1978) level), one *radical alternative* (reduction to the average military spending levels of Austria and Finland, called *two neutrals* for easy identification), and finally *complete disarmament*. The first alternative was suggested by the Norwegian member of the UN group and has been referred to, for short, as the *expert group* alternative. As a baseline for the other alternatives, we have included in all calculations one alternative which is not a disarmament scenario, but precisely the opposite. This corresponds to the decision of the NATO Council of Ministers in 1978 to increase real military spending by 3% per year.[8] Since an overall growth rate of 3% in the economy will be assumed throughout, this baseline implies that military spending retains a fixed share of the national product.

The disarmament scenarios were originally developed with a view to stretching out the conversion over a twelve-year period. For various reasons we have reasoned for the most part as if conversion took place in 1978. Using the 1978 version of the Norwegian model for national economic planning (MODIS IV),[9] we obtained the following results for complete disarmament: reduction in total employment 5.6%, in GDP 3.8%, and in total imports 3.1%. The results are very close to those found in previous studies of the economic effects of disarmament in Norway by Bjerkholt and Andreassen.[10] Before discussing the implications of these results for conversion, we must briefly examine the question of development policy.

4. Norwegian official development assistance

Norway has no recent history of colonial expansion and thus her development aid has no historical basis in colonial ties and practices. The official—and very widely accepted—policy governing Norwegian development aid has been as follows:

—to raise public development assistance to one percent of the national product
—to provide the assistance as gifts, not as loans
—to allocate half of the assistance multilaterally through the UN and other international organizations, and the other half bilaterally
—to concentrate the assistance geographically to a small number of countries where its effect can be greater than if spread over a larger group of recipients
—to adjust the assistance to local development programmes
—to make the ordinary man and woman the main beneficiaries of the assistance
—to select recipient countries where the governments conduct a development-oriented and socially just policy.[11]

By 1978 total official assistance had reached 0.9% of GDP, with loans not counted as part of the aid. Multilateral activities represented 46%, as close as is practicable to an even split. The aid has been geographically concentrated, with East Africa and South Asia as particularly important target areas. There has been a deliberate effort to channel aid to countries with 'development oriented regimes', even though it remains politically very controversial to determine which countries qualify for this label. Finally, there have been some attempts to reach 'ordinary people', but such efforts meet with obvious bureaucratic obstacles along the way and their effectiveness is hard to evaluate. Over the years there has been a modest tendency in the direction of less emphasis on capital project financing and more on programme assistance and contributions in kind. This has probably resulted in a more extensive use of Norwegian resources (labour and commodities). Thus, a larger part of the aid is channelled back into the Norwegian economy. However, this is by no means a large share. Most bilateral assistance still consists of capital project financing and programme assistance, both of which have a strong component of financial transfers.

Data for the OECD countries indicate that Norway has moved over the last two decades to the front rank with regard to development aid as a share of GNP—only The Netherlands, Norway, and Sweden exceeded 0.8% in 1978. Relative to most countries outside Scandinavia, Norway also gives aid that is less tied and more multilateral. This policy is now linked to strong Norwegian support for the demands of developing countries for a New International Economic Order, but it has roots back to before the goal of an NIEO was formulated.

4.1. Transfer policies

In order to analyze the quantitative economic consequences of conversion, we require some specific assumptions concerning the *kind* of development aid that will be given. Instead of trying to predict the most probable composition of development aid in the next decade, we have decided to study the economic consequences of several transfer policies. Unlike the disarmament scenarios defined in the previous sections, these policies are not simply percentage variations in the quantity of aid. Rather, our five transfer policies given below span some important political alternatives for the years to come. The greatest weakness is the lack of any policy alternative involving structural change in the world economy. Actual policies may, of course, be a mix of our scenarios, but the effect of such mixes can easily be judged on the basis of the results from our five policy alternatives.

The five transfer policies are:

(A) Financial transfers

By financial transfers we mean *gifts* given either bilaterally or through the UN. We assume that gifts have no effect on domestic production or employment.

(B) Exports/gifts of commodities in which Norway has excess production

In recent years there have been increasing demands from various Norwegian industries to promote new export markets by using subsidies or cheap credit financed through the development aid budget. Because of the crisis in the shipbuilding and fisheries industries, this transfer policy involves exports or gifts of new ships.

(C) Exports/gifts of commodities the developing countries think they need

This scenario is meant to mirror the subjective view of the needs of the developing countries as seen by their decision-making elites. The development aid is used to finance imports of goods and services from Norway. We assume that the commodity mix of exports resulting from this increased aid is equal to the existing export pattern from Norway to the developing countries in 1977.

(D) Exports/gifts of commodities that Norway thinks the developing countries need

This policy reflects Norwegian policy statements about what is needed in the developing countries, and particularly the idea of 'aid for self-reliance'. We have specified it to mean aid in the form of fishing technology; machinery for agriculture; machinery for mining, manufacturing, and construction; machinery for hydro-electric power plants; and equipment and experts for education and health services.

(E) Increased aid with unchanged aid composition

This policy involves additional aid with the same composition as that given in 1978. A high proportion of the aid consists of financial transfers.

TABLE 2. *Effects on employment of pure conversion in 1978 (%)*

Disarmament scenario	Transfer policy				
	Financial transfers (A)	Commodity transfers			Current aid composition (E)
		(B)	(C)	(D)	
(1) Expert group	−0.8	−0.3	−0.3	−0.3	−0.6
(2) Two neutrals	−3.9	−1.5	−1.6	−1.3	−2.9
(3) Complete disarmament	−5.6	−2.1	−2.3	−1.8	−4.2

Total employment excluding self-employed in 1978: 1,444,000 person-years.

5. Conversion

As indicators of the possible economic dislocations resulting from conversion we have used *employment, GDP, imports*, and *balance of payments*. In the first set of calculations—which we call *pure conversion*—we look at the effect on the first two of these indicators for all 15 combinations of disarmament scenarios and transfer policies. In all combinations the transfers are scaled to match the *ex ante* fiscal implications of the corresponding level of disarmament.

5.1. Pure conversion

In Tables 2 and 3 the disarmament scenarios are listed vertically in increasing degree of disarmament. The transfer policies are listed horizontally in the order discussed in section 4. The results are calculated as if full conversion had taken place in 1978. Both tables give *relative effects* (percentage changes).

Transfer policy A (financial transfers) has no employment effect on the domestic economy. Therefore the results in the first column in both tables reflect purely the effect of reduced military consumption. The employment effects vary from a decline in employment of 5.6% for the case of complete disarmament and transfer policy A, to a decline of 0.3% for the case of disarmament scenario 1 and transfer policy D. The results also confirm that the three alternative commodity transfer compositions yield results of the same level of magnitude, while current aid composition has employment effects between those of financial transfers and the three commodity transfer policies.

TABLE 3. *Effects on GDP of pure conversion in 1978 (%)*

Disarmament scenario	Transfer policy				
	Financial transfers (A)	Commodity transfers			Current aid composition (E)
		(B)	(C)	(D)	
(1) Expert group	−0.6	−0.1	−0.1	−0.1	−0.4
(2) Two neutrals	−2.6	−0.7	−0.7	−0.6	−1.9
(3) Complete disarmament	−3.8	−1.0	−0.8	−0.8	−2.7

Gross domestic product in 1978: N.Kr. 213,079 million.

It may not be intuitively obvious that a shift in expenditure from armaments to commodities for development transfers implies a net result of *less* employment. An important part of the explanation is the labour intensiveness of military spending. The total effect on GDP is very small in each case. Transfer policy D (exports/gifts of products Norway thinks the developing countries need) is the most favourable alternative in terms of *employment* and *production*. However, the effects on *imports* and the *balance of payments*—not presented here— are not so favourable as for transfer policies B and C. From a macroeconomic point of view, policy D nevertheless seems preferable for the Norwegian government. This is somewhat surprising, since it was policy B that we formulated with Norwegian interests directly in mind. However, these interests were not chiefly of a macroeconomic nature— the main object was to secure continued employment in the shipyards.

Both transfer policies A and E include financial transfers (in fact, policy A is nothing else). The import requirements of these policies are correspondingly lower. On the other hand, financial transfers have a direct and negative effect on the balance of payments.

5.2. Conversion with countermeasures

Although the economic dislocation of the pure conversion scenario is not very large, it is sufficiently large to present a political problem—particularly with regard to employment. Various domestic counter-measures may be suggested to compensate for the employment-reducing effects of pure conversion. In general, a suitable countermeasure should:

—be highly labour-intensive
—give a good geographical spread of employment
—tap a labour reserve (previously unused or liberated by disarmament)
—fill an unmet societal demand
—be popular and visible
—be publicly financed already (or a natural candidate for public financing)
—be relatively independent of other scarce or slowly developing resources (such as city land or trained manpower)
—have no other major adverse effects (e.g., a negative effect on female employment).

We have selected social home-help services for the old and the sick as a programme that does well on all the criteria. Essentially, this programme functions as an alternative to the institutionalization of the old and the sick in hospitals, nursing-homes, or retirement homes. The programme is highly labour-intensive; it extends to all Norwegian municipalities; it taps to some extent a labour reserve of experienced housewives; potential demand is enormous; the programme can actually affect every family and is therefore quite visible and popular and probably would contribute to public acceptance of the conversion package as a whole; the programme is already largely publicly financed; there are no other major bottlenecks except financing; and finally the programme has a favourable rather than negative effect on employment for women and no other important known adverse effect. Public financing is shared by state and local council budgets. However, in order to offset possible negative effects on local council finances, the percentage of state financing can easily be adjusted. It can also, if necessary, be adjusted differentially on a regional basis if one wants to compensate for military employment in Northern Norway.

A comparison—not presented here—of the economic effects of a number of compensatory measures, including social home-help programmes, reductions in personal income taxes, increases in government investment, increases in private investment, and increases in general central government expenditure, shows that government expenditure in general is a good countermeasure from the point of view of our economic indicators. But social home-help services is the only programme which does better than or as well as military expenditure on all four.

TABLE 4. *Effects on GDP of conversion with countermeasures 1978 (%)*

Disarmament scenario	Transfer policy				
	Financial transfers (A)	Commodity transfers			Current aid composition (E)
		(B)	(C)	(D)	
(1) Expert group	−0.02	−0.01	−0.01	−0.01	−0.02
(2) Two neutrals	−0.04	−0.01	−0.01	−0.01	−0.04
(3) Complete disarmament	−0.05	−0.02	−0.01	−0.02	−0.05
Conversion index:	23%	45%	42%	48%	28%

The conversion index is the proportion of the financial value of the resources released through disarmament which is allocated to development aid. Transfer policy A, for instance, implies that 23% of the reduction in military spending would be allocated to development aid, and 77% to domestic countermeasures.

In Table 4 the three disarmament scenarios are combined with a *mix* of increased transfers and increased social home-help services, *which keeps overall employment exactly constant.*[12] This means that the proportion of released resources allocated to development will vary between the transfer policies. For each transfer policy the percentage allocated to increased development aid is reported as the *conversion index*. These results should be read as an illustrative example of a *possible* conversion, rather than as a politically viable alternative.

Column 1 shows the joint effect of disarmament, increased development transfers (corresponding to 23% of the reduction in military consumption), and increase in home-help services (the remaining 77%). Because the purely financial transfers in policy A have no effect on employment, a large part of the resources released by disarmament is used domestically to keep employment unchanged. The effects on the Gross National Product are now scarcely noticeable. The three commodity transfer policies (B, C, D) yield very similar results in this case as in the case of pure conversion. About 55% of the reduction in military consumption is used domestically under these three transfer policies. The effects on the economy are now so small that it is not even possible to show clearly the difference between the disarmament scenarios. In the case of transfers with the present composition (policy E) only 28% of the reduction in military consumption is converted to aid. The results are very similar to transfer scenario A because spending on home-help services dominates the effects.

5.3. Conversion in a global context

As noted earlier, the results of the various conversion scenarios could be interpreted as the outcome of unilateral Norwegian political decisions or as the result for Norway of a multinational or even world-wide agreement on conversion of military expenditures. If conversion takes place within a regional or global setting the policy changes in other countries will obviously have some effects for Norway. Decreased demand for military products and increased transfers to development aid may have negative and positive implications for the exports of Norwegian products and thus for employment and other key economic variables. It is not obvious without detailed empirical study whether the negative will outweigh the positive effects or vice versa.

It seems very likely that effects of conversion in other countries will be much smaller than the effects of domestic conversion. However, the value of Norway's exports and imports in 1978 corresponded to 44% and 42%, respectively, of the Gross Domestic Product. Therefore, changes in the world demand for products in which Norway trades heavily may have more than a negligible impact on the domestic economy.

In principle such external effects can be modelled in the same way as the effects of domestic policy changes. However, until recently there has been no economic model to permit us to do this with even approximately the same kind of forecasting accuracy as the national budget model provides for the domestic economy.

Leontief and his associates have developed a world input-output model which can be used to simulate the cross-national effects of conversion.[13] The model does not have individual states as units, except the Soviet Union. The world economy is divided into 15 regions (including the Soviet Union as a separate region). Norway is one of 17 countries in the region called 'High Income Western Europe'. The effects for Norway can be assessed from the World Model and the trade pattern of the Norwegian economy. Each region is described in terms of 45 sectors of economic activity. This is considerably less than in the Norwegian model, which divides domestic production into about 150 industries.[14] Nevertheless, the Leontief model is undoubtedly the most successful attempt at extending the flexible and comprehensive input-output approach to the world economy.

The World Model was originally developed to study international development policies in connection with the Second United Nations Development Decade. More recently it has been extended to include specifications of military expenditure categories. This version of the model has been used in reports submitted to the UN Group of Governmental Experts and to the US Arms Control and Disarmament Agency on various global scenarios for conversion.[15]

Leontief and Duchin have used scenarios which implied a *reduction in the increase in* military spending, but not disarmament in the sense of *reduced levels* of military spending. In our own application of the World Model[16] we have used disarmament scenarios which reduce military expenditure to 85% and 70% in 1990, compared to 1980, and twice that reduction in 2000. If one assumes that development aid increases correspondingly, the GDP of the receiving regions can be increased by 50% or 100% by 1990, depending on the degree of disarmament. This is achieved without any loss in the Gross Domestic Product or personal consumption within the donor countries.

The World Model assumes that employment in developed countries is equal to the estimated labour force. This assumption, which seems less reasonable now than when it was originally made, implies that one cannot calculate the effects of conversion on global employment in the same way that we earlier reported the employment effects of conversion in Norway. However, we have calculated the employment effects for Norway of global conversion on the assumption of full worldwide employment. Because Norway has such insubstantial arms exports, this effect is positive and cancels out about three-quarters of the loss in employment resulting from Norwegian national conversion. We have also used the Norwegian national growth model (MSG-4) to study the long-term effects of conversion. Given the same disarmament scenarios, the results for 1990 and 2000 are hardly discernible from the projections in the government's long-term programme, which of course do not assume any disarmament. Most of the slight changes are in a favourable direction according to conventional economic indicators (increased production, increased private consumption, etc.). Thus, the national economic effect of this scenario for global conversion acts as a 'countermeasure' for the Norwegian economy, comparable in its favourable effects even to the social home-help services described above.

5.4. Local Effects of Conversion

Military employment in Norway varies by region from 1.6% in the south and southwest to 9.1% in the north. If the same proportion between direct and indirect military employment held at the regional as at the national level, complete disarmament without countermeasures would lead to a total reduction in employment of 17% in this region. However, this figure represents an upper limit, since 'import leakage' is much higher in northern Norway than in the rest of the country. Therefore a larger part of the indirect effects of military employment occurs outside the region. 17% would be an unacceptably high figure.

For some *municipalities*, the actual figure for direct military employment is even higher than 17%. The only previous study of local effects (made by Tormod Andreassen) does not give directly comparable figures for the total military employment, but reports that in 1969, 18% of the local taxes in Porsanger municipality in Finnmark (population 3,861 in 1970) were paid by personnel of the armed forces.[17] He also estimates that in the two municipalities of Bardu and Målselv in Troms (population 3,896 and 7,937) close to 40% of the retail trade was due to demand from military personnel. Even municipalities in southern Norway may experience considerable conversion problems. The percentage of military production in the two large publicly owned arms factories, Kongsberg Våpenfabrikk and Raufoss Ammunisjonsfabrikker (RA), hover slightly below 50% and their production plants are located in a small number of locations.[18] In Raufoss, for instance, the total employment of the RA in 1970 was 2,483 and military employment can be estimated at 1,018. This was 19% of that year's total employment in that municipality. Considerations of local employment were said to have played a role in a Cabinet decision in 1958 to permit the export of small arms from the RA to Cuba, and in more recent decisions to modernize certain smaller military systems rather than scrapping them. They have also played a role in the public debate about major arms acquisitions, such as fighter aircraft (the F-16 purchase), submarines, and air-defence missiles. In times of rising unemployment, the possibility that such considerations might affect a conversion programme cannot be excluded.

6. Conclusions and recommendations

The concept of conversion—disarming and using the money saved for development aid—may have an intuitive appeal, but it is superficial from a more basic economic viewpoint. Disarmament will release *resources*, and these resources may be used for other purposes. The extent and time-phasing of conversion will have to depend upon the amount, composition, and mobility of resources released. The fiscal consequences are of second-order importance only, serving as a possible constraint on measures taken to put conversion into effect. In this connection, *labour* is the most important resource to bear in mind: both because of the political importance of full employment in Norway and because of the constraints on labour supply even in a medium to long-term setting. Low regional mobility of labour can be a severe constraint on this type of conversion. Such low regional mobility reflects a stable regional pattern of production, in itself a goal of economic policy in Norway.

For a rich country with 3% of its resources devoted to military purposes, a shift in the composition of demand away from armaments may be analyzed as a marginal change in the economy which does not upset the economic structure or the functioning of the economy at large. The impact for particular industries and smaller regional areas may be considerable. But the overall extent of the problem strongly suggests that from a macroeconomic viewpoint a smooth transition is perfectly possible, if appropriate measures are taken to maintain external and internal balance in the economy. The adjustment required is, of course, of a different order of magnitude than that involved in conversion from a war economy to a peace economy or vice versa. For example, Britain spent about 60% of its GNP on the war effort during World War II and the US reached 40%.[19] We have no directly comparable figure for Norway. However, some interesting calculations have been made as to the total costs of the war and the German occupation for the Norwegian economy.[20] The national income declined by 15–20% during the war, while the prewar trend was an annual increase of 2%. Goods and services amounting to slightly above one-third of the national income during the period 1940-45 were confiscated by the German occupation forces. The national income at the disposal of the Norwegian population (average for 1940-45) was thus only 58% of the 1939 level. In order to keep the standard of living closer to the prewar level, there was increased consumption from stocks, increased wear and tear on the means of production, etc. As a result, the national capital is estimated to have declined by about one-sixth during the war. Taking account of these various factors, including the loss of growth because of the war, the war cost about 45% of the expected national income for the war years. This, of course, was the result of a situation which was forced on Norway, not a political choice. But the example shows that in economic terms, conversion is a very minor event compared to the last war. And of course the costs of a future war, particularly a nuclear one, are likely to be vastly greater.

The suggestion that the relatively minor adjustment involved in conversion can be undertaken without major problems has been supported by several empirical studies in the 1960s and 1970s, including the earlier studies of Norway by Bjerkholt and Andreassen. This study confirms the earlier findings for Norway. Norwegian experience in the immediate postwar period after 1945 also supports this conclusion. In response to a large and abrupt increase in the labour supply the level of employment increased sharply and the unemployment rate in 1947–1950 was lower than ever before or after. It was widely believed at the time that large-scale unemployment due to shortages and the need reallocations was inevitable.[21]

Nevertheless, the present results are not trivial. The earlier studies did not couple disarmament with increased transfers to developing countries. In Bjerkholt's 1965 study, for example, the author was free to devise a set of countermeasures which would reduce the problems of transition to complete disarmament. In this study we have imposed the additional restraint that at least a significant portion of the released resources should be made available for increased transfers. From a domestic economic point of view this is clearly a less advantageous starting-point: 63% of the Norwegian development aid in 1978 consisted of financial transfers. Since Norway is a small part of the world economy, increased financial transfers from Norway alone are unlikely to have any significant feedback effect on the Norwegian economy. Therefore, expansion of Norway's aid programme with the current profile is strictly a burden from a domestic economic point of view: it adds little to the national product, provides practically no employment, and makes a negative contribution to the balance of payments.

From the national part of this study four strategies emerge for dealing with any negative effects of the extreme case of pure conversion to financial transfers within one year:

I. Disarm less *(change of disarmament scenario)*
II. Disarm more slowly *(extended conversion)*
III. Select a type of development aid which in itself counteracts some of the transition problems *(change of transfer policy)*
IV. Use some of the resources for domestic programmes which counteract the negative effects of conversion, particularly unemployment *(conversion with countermeasures)*.

Our study provides data which can shed some light on all of these four strategies. Table 5 takes as a baseline the 'extreme case' of complete disarmament and pure conversion to financial transfers. This is the worst case from the point of view of the domestic economic transition problems. Table 5 also contains examples of results for the four strategies to counteract the transition problems. Strategy I is illustrated by the most modest disarmament model—the expert group alternative. For Strategy II we have selected the effects of the first year of extended conversion (complete disarmament in 1990). To illustrate Strategy III we have selected the commodity transfer policy which gives the most advantageous effects on the four indicators. And finally Strategy IV is exemplified by the case of conversion with countermeasures, i.e., social home-help services. The table shows some effects of the extreme case that are probably politically unacceptable—at least the 5.6% reduction in employment. At the same time any one of the four strategies I-IV will significantly reduce the problems. As the two final columns of the table indicate, this can happen either at the cost of reducing what we have called the conversion ratio, i.e., make a lesser part available for increased transfers (strategies I, II, and IV) or by changing the form of transfers to a variety of tied aid (a commodity transfer). Both of these have disadvantages, and the relative weight of the disadvantages will be evaluated differently by different people. Our own preference would be to retain the principle that most if not all of the aid should be given on an untied basis, i.e., as financial transfers.[22] But Table 5 should give the reader a better basis on which to make his or her own choice.

TABLE 5. *Strategies to decrease the negative effects of conversion*

	Effect in 1978 on					
	Employment (%)	GDP (%)	Imports (%)	Balance of payments (% of GDP)	Conversion ratio (%)	Type of transfer
Extreme case—Complete disarmament, pure conversion, financial transfers (Scenario A-3 in one year)	−5.6	−3.8	−3.1	−2.0	100	Financial
I. Less disarmament (Scenario A-3 in one year)	−0.8	−0.6	−0.5	−0.3	15	Financial
II. Extended conversion first year (Scenario A-3 in 12 years)	−0.4	−0.3	−0.2	−0.2	8	Financial
III. 'Best transfer policy (Scenario D-3) in one year)	−1.8	−0.8	+1.2	−0.4	100	Commodity
IV. Countermeasures (Scenario A-3 in one year with countermeasures)	0	−0.1	−0.1	−0.0	23	Financial

Source: Tables 4.2–4.5, 4.12–4.14, and Tables B.1–B.9 in Bjerkholt et al. (1980).
(Note that a negative figure means a negative impact in columns 1, 2, and 4, but a positive impact in column 3.)
The *conversion ratio* is the proportion of 1978 military consumption converted to transfers to developing countries, i.e., it is not identical to the *conversion index* reported in Table 4.

In addition, our work on the World Model indicates that global conversion detracts from the adjustment problems created by national conversion in Norway. For instance, unilateral conversion of 15% of military expenditure in one year and with no countermeasures involves a loss of 0.8% of total employment. This loss is reduced to 0.2% in the multilateral case, without employing any of the other three strategies of Table 5. In a sense, therefore, the multilateralization of conversion in itself works as a 'countermeasure' for Norway, although not one that can be considered a national policy instrument.

As mentioned earlier, this study may have some relevance for other countries in its methodology and to some extent its results. Most West European countries at least have military establishments which occupy roughly the same place in the economy as Norway's. It seems quite reasonable to assume that the adjustment problems can be alleviated using various countermeasures such as those described in the Norwegian case. Some countries are likely to experience somewhat more serious conversion problems, because they have a peacetime economy which is more geared to military production, or because military bases make up a high proportion of the employment in certain areas. On the other hand, some countries may also have an export structure which permits them to take better advantage of the increased aid transfers. Obviously, all countries cannot—like Norway—obtain an increase in employment as a result of global conversion if global employment is assumed to remain constant. In general, only a separate empirical study can determine for a given country the size of the positive and negative effects.

NOTES AND REFERENCES

1. The term *conversion* is frequently used to describe the process whereby a person, a firm, or an industry retools from 'swords to ploughshares'. Our own analysis is confined to examining economic effects at the macro-level, rather than at the micro-level. In our usage conversion means retooling the economic structure of the country or the international system as a whole. But we have no objection to readers mentally replacing conversion by *reallocation* and reserving conversion for the process at the micro-level.
2. Wassily Leontief et al., *The Future of the World Economy. A United Nations Study*, New York: Oxford University Press, 1977.
3. The arms exports are very small relative to the Norwegian economy or Norwegian total exports. However, SIPRI statistics indicate that Norway ranked as high as no. 7 in the *absolute* export value of major weapons systems in the late seventies. *World Armaments and Disarmament, SIPRI Yearbook 1981*, London: Taylor & Francis, 1981, p. 188.
4. Olav Bjerkholt, Ådne Cappelen, Nils Petter Gleditsch and Knut Moum, 'Disarmament and Development: A Study of Conversion in Norway', PRIO publication S-7/80, Oslo, 1980.
5. United Nations, 'Review of the implementation of the recommendations and decisions adopted by the General Assembly at its tenth special session. Development and international economic cooperation. Study on the relationship between disarmament and development.' *Report to the Secretary-General*, A/36/356, 1981, Ch. III.
6. Bjerkholt et al. op. cit., Ch. 2 and Appendices.
7. Malvern Lumsden, 'The Use of Raw Materials, Land, and Water for Armament and War', in Wendy Barnaby, ed., *War and Environment*, Stockholm: Liber Förlag for the Environment Advisory Council, 1981, p. 42.
8. This was also the policy of the Labour government which left office in October 1981. The new Conservative government is committed to a 4% real increase over the next few years.

9. MOdel of a DISaggregated type. Cf. Olav Bjerkholt and Svein Longva, 'MODIS IV— A model for National Economic Planning', *Samfunnsøkonomiske studier*, No. 43, Oslo, 1979.
10. Olav Bjerkholt, 'An Analysis of the Economic Consequences of Disarmament in Norway', in Emile Benoit, ed., *Disarmament and World Economic Interdependence*, Oslo: Norwegian Universities Press, 1967, 'Økonomiske konsekvenser av nedrustning i Norge' (Economic Consequences of Disarmament in Norway), *Tidsskrift for Samfunnsforskning*, Vol. 6, 1965, No. 4, pp 249–267; and Tormod Andraessen, 'Forsvarets virkninger på norsk økonomi' (The Impact of the Defense on the Norwegian Economy), *Samfunnsøkonomiske studier*, No. 22, Oslo, 1972.
11. Cf. the government's *Report to the Storting*, No. 94, 1974/75. A good secondary source of policy statements is Olav Stokke, *Norsk utviklingsbistand* (Norwegian development assistance), Wennergren-Cappelen, Oslo/Uppsala, 1975.
12. We could have performed these computations instead under the restraint that GDP or balance of payments or imports was to remain unchanged under conversion. Our choice of employment reflects the view that a potential negative effect on employment is the politically most sensitive issue in conversion.
13. Leonteif et al. 1977, op. cit.
14. Bjerkholt and Longva, op. cit.
15. Wassily Leonteif and Faye Duchin, *Worldwide Economic Implication of a Limitation on Military Spending*, Institute for Economic Analysis, New York University, for Center for Disarmament, New York: United Nations, 1980; and Leontief and Duchin, *Worldwide Implications of Hypothetical Changes in Military Spending (an Input-Output Approach)*, Institute for Economic Analysis, New York University, for US Arms Control and Disarmament Agency, New York, 1980.
16. Ådne Cappelen, Olav Bjerkholt and Nils Petter Gleditsch, 'Global Conversion from Arms to Development Aid: Macroeconomic Effects in Norway', PRIO publication S-9/82, Oslo, 1982.
17. Andreassen, op. cit., p. 124.
18. For more detailed figures, see Magne Barth, 'Military Integration—the Case of Norway and West Germany', PRIO publications S-18/81, Oslo, 1981, Ch. 3.
19. Cf. Laurence Martin, *The Management of Defense*, New York: St. Martin's, 1976.
20. Cf. Odd Aukrust and Petter Jacob Bjerve, *Hva krigen kostet Norge?* (What the war cost Norway), Oslo: Dreyer, 1945, particularly pp. 41–49.
21. Central Bureau of Statistics, 'Norges økonomi etter krigen' (The Norwegian postwar economy), *Samfunnsøkonomiske studier*, No. 12. Oslo, 1965. pp. 91–94.
22. That aid be given as financial transfers is a *necessary* but not *sufficient* condition for its being untied. In fact, all Norwegian bilateral aid is politically tied in the sense that countries with development-oriented policies are given priority. Nevertheless, the high proportion of multilateral aid ensures that Norwegian aid remains largely untied.

V. Conclusion

The Promise of Economic Conversion

LLOYD J. DUMAS

1. Conversion and addiction

Many centuries ago, the Roman military analyst Vegetius proclaimed, 'Let him who wants peace, prepare for war.' A few decades ago, one of the most brilliant creative minds of modern times, Albert Einstein, said, 'You cannot simultaneously prepare for and prevent war.' The long stretch of history since the time of Vegetius has been filled with attempts to deter aggression through military strength, to preserve peace by building and threatening to use powerful military forces. It has also been filled with war. The twentieth century alone has seen over 200 wars.[1] They continue even in the face of the overwhelming threat of nuclear holocaust. Perhaps it is time for us to stop listening to Vegetius and give Einstein a chance.

The paradigm of domination as a model for human relationships—personal, local, national and international—has held us captive throughout much of human history. Violence and the threat of violence has become the accustomed means of trying to control the behaviour of other peoples or to prevent them from controlling us. The present worldwide conventional and nuclear arms race is the logical result of this pattern. It lies at the end of a long, sad road. And make no mistake about it, it is the end of the road.

The arms race cannot be indefinitely continued and controlled. We are racing in the dark towards the edge of a crumbling cliff. There is no doubt that we will sooner or later go over the edge if we continue. Even the best of intentions and the best of controls will not stop it. Whether ultimately brought about by arrogance, misunderstanding, miscalculation or accident, the holocaust we most fear lies at the end of this path. The only way it can be prevented is to stop, carefully turn around and move in the other direction. If we succeed, we will not only remove the present threat to our future, but will also make great progress towards finally relegating the 'era of arms races' to the ash heap of history.

Economic conversion has a key role to play in the process of reversing our direction, of abandoning our obsession with the bankrupt idea that

253

security comes only from the barrel of a gun. Advanced planning for conversion is critical to preparing for peace. It is an important part of moving away from the failed advice of Vegetius toward a more Einsteinian view of the world.

If all of this appears a bit too visionary and grand, there are much more ordinary yet compelling reasons why the pressure for arms reduction is bound to grow. It has become abundantly clear, and apparently accepted at the highest levels of government, that the economic burden of the arms race is an important part of what is preventing the Soviet Union from improving the relatively low material standard of living of its people. The forces of economic reform in the USSR, recently grown much stronger, are of necessity being partially translated into forces for a degree of demilitarization of the economy. While there appears to be much more resistance to recognizing the obvious fact that the arms race has also seriously undermined economic efficiency in the United States, the federal government is nevertheless faced with a budgetary crisis that has already begun to create considerable pressure for some reductions in military spending.

The enormous budget deficits that the US government has been running have more than doubled its national debt in only six years (1981–86), adding more than one trillion dollars ($1,000,000,000,000) of borrowed money on which interest must be paid. This debt, accumulated largely in the service of a huge military build-up, has risen so high that interest payments alone now absorb a substantial fraction of federal tax revenues. Income taxes account for the largest part—some 85%—of discretionary federal revenues.[2] In 1986, nearly 40% of all income taxes collected from individuals and families in the US was required to meet interest payments on the national debt.[3] In fact, in 1986, interest payments on the national debt and the military budget combined, absorbed *all* of the federal income taxes paid by all individuals, families *and* corporations in the US.[4] It is thus going to be very difficult to bring the US federal budget into anything remotely resembling balance without some reductions in military spending.

Government recognition of the growing economic damage of the arms race and tightening fiscal constraints varies among the nations of Western Europe, and among the other more developed and less developed nations of the world who have been caught up in the international arms race. But the handwriting is on the wall. For budgetary and economic reasons, the case for reducing military expenditures grows stronger every day. And heavily militarized economies have little chance of smoothly and painlessly demilitarizing without paying attention to the various aspects of economic conversion raised by the analysts who have contributed to this volume. This issue is thus bound to grow in importance.

Military spending is as dangerously addictive to an economy as drugs can be to an individual. Like a drug, it is seductive because it creates a feeling of well-being in the short run, by temporarily stimulating jobs and income. And like a drug, continued overuse destroys the health of the user, by diverting critical resources from activities that directly increase economic well-being or enhance the economy's capacity to produce efficiently. Because it undermines the ability of the economy to function, as time goes by larger and larger doses are required to achieve the same short term 'high'. Yet even after it becomes clear that the addiction is doing great damage, it is very difficult to get the user to stop, because simply stopping will cause a great deal of pain and suffering during the transition.

Planned economic conversion is an antidote for such an addiction, a kind of detoxification programme for military addicted economies. By smoothly and efficiently rechannelling resources, the pain of transition is greatly eased or completely eliminated. It therefore can be expected to reduce the political resistance to arms reduction and more productive economic policy that arises from the fear of military dependent individuals and communities that they will be subject to serious economic dislocation.

2. The common threads

There are significant differences of opinion and emphasis in the various chapters of this book. That is not surprising. Thoughtful people bring differing perspectives to any issue of concern. There is little to be gained by attempting to homogenize their thinking. Yet there are clearly some common threads that emerge when this collection of analyses is viewed as a whole.

Among the most important are two basic pieces of wisdom about economic conversion. The first is that conversion is not that easy. It requires a thorough understanding of the considerable difference between the worlds of military-oriented and civilian-serving production. There is no magic—of the market system or the central planning committee—that will quickly and effectively reconnect people, equipment and facilities displaced from military-oriented activity to the civilian economy without special attention to the problems of this peculiar transition. There are no switches to flip, no wands to wave that can turn tank factories and missile plants into efficient producers of appliances, mass transit vehicles and the like overnight.

The second piece of wisdom about conversion is that it is not that difficult. Planning for economic conversion is a useful, down-to-earth strategy for effectively organizing even very large-scale redirections of people, equipment and facilities from military to civilian work. Different economic and political systems may require different approaches to the planning process. But given a proper understanding of the differing military and civilian worlds of research, design and production, a degree of patience *and* a serious political commitment to easing the transition, there is every reason to believe that conversion can be accomplished smoothly and well.

Conversion will take time. Even the planning process is likely to be a lengthy one. Nearly half a century ago, the Vice-President of General Electric Company, David Prince, argued this point in a letter written to the War Production Board, calling for the US to begin reconversion planning prior to the end of World War II. Prince wrote,

> . . . there is a very great inclination to underestimate the length of time it takes to proceed from the conception stage to the tooling stage for any product.
> The very least time during which a new product can be conceived, models made and tested and pilot plant production initiated is on the order of two years.
> . . . priorities of the very highest order must be given to a very limited amount of work for long-range things. I am probably talking about a great deal less than 1/10 of 1 percent in terms of the effort of the country, but that 1/10 of 1 percent will make the difference of . . . anything up to two years in making the conversion back from war to peace in those industries affected.[5]

The substantial divergence between military and civilian research and production activity that has taken place since 1945 makes the argument even stronger today. The planning at least can be done in advance on a contingency basis, and that will save years of confusion and disruption. There is no point in waiting for arms reductions before we begin to take conversion seriously. We have delayed far too long already in paying attention to this critical problem.

3. The future of conversion research and practice

The essential problem of conversion is by now fairly well understood. This understanding has unfortunately not been disseminated widely enough to have yet become a major part of public and political debate. It is hoped that this book will help in the vital process of widening public exposure to the nature and importance of this problem. Yet there is still a considerable need for more research to strengthen and refine our base of knowledge about conversion and to fashion more effective strategies for carrying it out.

One especially glaring omission from the body of conversion research is the lack of systematic analysis of the psychological and sociological dimension of this particular form of transition. Not only might significant changes in organizational structure result from conversion, but there may also be significant alterations in the nature of social relationships in the workplace and beyond. Changes of this sort are likely to have substantial psychological effects as well. For that matter, the change in the nature of the product itself may also have meaningful psychological impact.

It is ordinarily assumed (at least by economists and engineers) that workers are indifferent to the kind of product they are producing. This is almost certainly untrue. To assume it is true to assume workers are less than full human beings. Are we not all to some degree aware of and affected by the consequences of that to which we contribute our efforts? If not, why is it that volunteer work—where there is no financial reward or compulsion—is almost invariably done for 'helping' organizations (such as shelters for the homeless) or for organizations advocating a cause in which we believe (such as environmental or peace groups)? Is it not because we believe these organizations are producing 'socially useful' products? It is certainly not simply because these organizations may be poorly funded. After all, there are many small businesses in dire financial straits, yet they do not typically attract volunteers. And voluntary work is common at hospitals with enormous financial resources. At the very least, there is sufficient reason to suspect that workers may be affected by the nature of the output they produce. It is therefore not legitimate to blithely assume this possibility away without serious examination.

More research is also needed to more accurately estimate the extent and structural depth of dependence on military-oriented activity. For example, much of what has been discussed in various of the preceding chapters would be given greater clarity if it were possible to develop more accurate and more detailed information on the size and shape of the military's pre-emption of economically productive resources. For example, just how large a fraction of the national or global pool of engineering and scientific talent is engaged in military R&D? How does this break down by discipline, level of training, geographic location and sector of employment (i.e., industry, university or government laboratory)? What about the drain of capital resources? How much industrial machinery and other fixed productive capital has been taken in the service of the military? What fraction of the national tax potential has been absorbed?

And on the other side of the issue, how much of what kinds of capital and labour are required to carry out politically attractive projects, public and private, that would attend to strongly felt needs not currently being adequately addressed? Infrastructure creation and renewal, housing, health care, etc., are a few of many possibilities. Such analysis, which could be called 'social needs research', looks at the conversion from the other direction by considering some of the places where resources freed from the military sector might usefully be put to work.

At present, we are working with only the roughest of estimates of the nature and extent on resource drain into the military sector and social needs resource requirements. It would be a great advantage in the business of developing practical conversion strategies if the quality of the estimates were considerably improved. And of course, more accurate and complete estimates of the quantity and type of resources required to carry out the conversion process itself (e.g., faculty and facilities needed to retrain military engineering staffs) become possible once better estimates of the current resource drain and potential resource destination are available.

The unavailability of more accurate, detailed and reliable estimates is at least in part the result of problems created by the way in which the relevant data are collected and reported. To begin with, the secrecy with which most nations feel compelled to shroud their military-related activities creates a strong inclination to hide data on military resource use in confusing aggregates or suppress it entirely. Furthermore, relatively few economic analysts today recognize the peculiar, non-economic nature of military-oriented activity (though that apparently seemed clear enough to Adam Smith, for example, two centuries ago). Consequently, there is little pressure on governments from that quarter to collect data on economic resources and production in ways that highlight the role of the military sector.

The Soviet Union, for example, officially reported their military budget at some 17 billion rubles for many years. No one took that official figure seriously, or even believed that the level of the USSR's military spending remained constant, whatever it actually was. With so much distortion in such a basic datum, it is not surprising that meaningful estimates of data at lower levels of aggregation, e.g., number of engineers and scientists employed in the military sector, were simply not available. Perhaps now, as both *glasnost* and *perestroika* proceed, at least civilian analysts in the Soviet Union will be able to obtain data sufficient in quality and quantity to make real progress in studying the nature of the conversion problem there. It is to be hoped that the results of such studies, as well as the data on which they are based, will eventually become available to outside analysts as well. There is, after all, little or nothing in those data that could realistically compromise the security of the USSR.

Nor has the US been as forthcoming in these matters as one might expect. There is little question that the US has been relatively open about such matters. Though it has been estimated that the Pentagon's highly secretive 'black budget' has more than tripled since 1981,[6] a great deal of data on US military expenditures, numbers of military-oriented facilities and even characteristics of specific weapons systems are publicly available. Still there has been considerable obfuscation of certain key pieces of information. For example, according to data provided for 1981 in the Defense Economic Impact Modeling System (DEIMS) of the Department of Defense, only about 12% of the nation's engineers and scientists are included in 'defense induced' employment. However, the methodology used in DEIMS excludes from the 'defense-induced' category employment related to arms exports, programs for nuclear weapons research design, testing and production . . . and the military-oriented part of the space program. Perhaps even more significantly, the methodology assumes that the percentage of engineers and scientists in any given industry is the same in the military-serving part of the industry as in the civilian-oriented part. Yet is is clear that the technological intensity of the labor force in the military-oriented segments of industry is much greater.[7]

Nevertheless, at least in those countries where relevant data are more available, it should be possible to penetrate some of the fog. With concentrated effort and a measure of methodological creativity, substantial improvements should be possible in the accuracy of key estimates. This will clarify and deepen our understanding of the extent of military diversion of productive economic resources, the economic impact of that diversion, and the requirements for successful conversion. Perhaps work along these lines will create pressure for recategorization of published data in forms more appropriate to the study of these critical problems, along with generally greater openness.

Much more research is required on case studies of conversion. Even the great post-World War II demobilization and 'reconversion' has been insufficiently researched and analyzed. There have been a great many conversions of military bases. One publication of the US Department of Defense, for example, cites 94 conversions of military bases in the US between 1961 and 1981.[8] A few of these 'conversions' turn out to be shifts from military base activities to military production activities, hardly what could be called real economic conversion. But many are legitimate exercises in military-to-civilian conversion. Systematic and detailed study of these American cases, as well as base conversions in other nations, would be extremely useful. It would help to expose problems that might well be encountered elsewhere, and to highlight workable solutions.

In the past few years, the People's Republic of China claims to have demobilized in the order of one million soldiers and converted various military-producing facilities to civilian production.[9] To this date, the information on this extremely important development remains very slim and largely anecdotal. If a substantial amount of conversion has actually occurred and continues in China, it would be a great contribution to the well-being of the international community of nations for serious studies of this conversion experience to be undertaken and made available.

Unlike base conversion, there are few if any real cases of the conversion of production facilities over the past few decades. A number of military-serving companies in the US, for example, have attempted to produce civilian products without going through the extensive retraining and reorientation required for effective conversion. The results in terms of both technical performance and cost were predictable. The products were invariably excessively complex and did not perform well under normal conditions of civilian use. They were also intolerably expensive. Again, this was not real conversion.

Some military-serving companies have reduced their dependence on military product lines through diversification, i.e., the financial acquisition of civilian producing facilities or entire companies. Diversification is an implicit recognition of the wisdom of moving away from dependence on military markets, but it is *not* conversion. While diversification affords financial protection to the company, it does nothing for the workforce or communities involved in the company's military divisions. Planning for conversion, on the other hand, protects the workers, military dependent communities *and* the company.

It is very important to have case studies of actual conversions of military production, research and design facilities. No matter how well thought out any process is, no matter how good it looks on paper, there is no substitute for the experience, insight and understanding that accompanies actually doing it. Conversion is no exception. The building and testing of product prototypes is common engineering practice, as is the construction of pilot plants when contemplating putting an entirely new process into production. That is the result of many decades of accumulated design experiences which has taught us that some of what looks good on the drawing board works fine in practice, and some does not.

If there are insufficient existing present day examples of real conversion to study in depth, then we will simply have to create some. Governments or companies must be convinced that conversion pilot projects are critical to testing and refining our knowledge of conversion, which is in turn crucial to avoiding serious and painful economic dislocation as military budgets are reduced. And it makes no sense to delay such projects until substantial military cutbacks have already occurred. They should be undertaken now.

4. Conclusions

Developing the capacity for smooth and effective conversion is a key part of the process of achieving peace by preparing for it. It is not a strategy for handling the transition of nations that have given up the reins of power and influence to a position of weakness. Quite the opposite, conversion holds great promise for easing and encouraging the kind of transition that is capable of simultaneously increasing the security and economic wellbeing of nations that have the confidence and foresight to turn away from failed policies and find new productive directions.

In his study, *The Rise and Fall of the Great Powers*, in which he looked at the past 500 years in excruciating detail, Yale historian Paul Kennedy came to the conclusion that,

> If . . . too large a proportion of the state's resources is diverted from wealth creation and allocated instead to military purposes, then that is likely to lead to a weakening of national power over the longer term.[10]

> Great Powers in relative decline instinctively respond by spending more on 'security' and thereby divert potential resources from 'investment' and compound their long term dilemma.[11]

Furthermore, substantial improvement in the level of economic development of the world's less developed countries (LDCs) is a prerequisite to real improvements in world security, stability and prosperity. The United Nations' Study on the Relationship between Disarmament and Development (partially reproduced in this volume) has made the power of the connection between those two processes abundantly clear. One of the most productive uses, both in terms of economic well-being and security, of some of the resources freed from the service of the world's militaries is precisely to provide the wherewithall to move the development of the Third World dramatically forward.

It is important to note that this connection is not simply a matter of the more developed nations making use of resources freed by disarmament to increase their aid to the Third World. The less developed nations themselves have diverted many of their own critical resources to military-oriented activity, interfering with their internal capacity to achieve significant development gains. The share of world military expenditures undertaken by the LDCs has essentially doubled since the early 1960s. As a rough indication of the magnitude and potential of just the diversion of financial resources, if the LDC's share of world military spending in the six years previous to 1982 had been the same as their share in the early 1960s, they would have saved enough money as a group from this one source alone to finance repayment of nearly two-thirds of the Third World debt outstanding at that time (a saving of more than $400 billion).[12]

Nearly all of the more than 100 wars fought since the end of World War II have been fought in the LDCs. That should not be surprising. The conditions of poverty, frustration and foreign domination which afflict so much of the Third World breed the discontent and desperation that so often explode into violence. Real development would do a great deal to mitigate these problems, but real development will be exceedingly difficult if not impossible to achieve without throwing off the terrible economic burden of rampant global militarism.

We must no longer blindly accept the validity of the assumptions that have brought us to this condition—that preparing for war guarantees peace, that security depends almost exclusively on military power, that stronger nations achieve the greatest possible gains by dominating and exploiting weaker nations. We must reject this conventional wisdom to seek new definitions of security and more productive strategies for achieving it. In this process of restructuring, economic conversion has a key role to play.

The persistence of vastly overblown military spending is not only undermining our economies, it is distorting our societies. Militarism is inherently authoritarian. It is permeated by a hierarchical worldview that emphasizes obedience and conformity, that discourages individuality and creativity. Perhaps most damaging, militarism encourages compulsion rather than persuasion. It is time for us to grow up and learn, as children do, that the use of force is not acceptable in settling disputes. In short, we need to demilitarize our minds and our societies, not just our economies.

Here too conversion, properly done, has something to offer. It pushes us to think creatively and positively about alternatives. It encourages us to seek the cooperation and advice of the parties at interest. It can help to begin a great debate on the nature of the economy and society we want to create as we refocus our attention and energy.

Economic conversion is not a solution. It is a mechanism for effectively rechannelling our efforts. We have the power to choose our own direction. Let us hope we choose well.

NOTES AND REFERENCES

1. R. L. Sivard, *World Military and Social Expenditures: 1986*, Washington D.C.: World Priorities, 1986, p.26.
2. *Economic Report of the President (January 1987)*, Washington D.C.: US Government Printing Office, 1987, Table B-74, p.333.
3. Ibid.
4. Ibid.
5. D. Prince, Vice-President of General Electric Company, Schenectady, New York, Letter to Ernest Kanzler of the War Production Board, Washington D.C. (28 April 1943).
6. T. Weiner, 'The Pentagon's Secret Cache: A Growing "Black Budget" Pays for Secret Weapons, Covert Wars', *The Philadelphia Inquirer*, 8 February 1987.
7. L. J. Dumas, *The Overburdened Economy: Uncovering the Causes of Chronic Unemployment, Inflation and National Decline*, Berkeley, California: University of California Press, 1986, pp.209–10.
8. Office of Economic Adjustment, *Summary of Completed Military Base Economic Adjustment Projects, 1961–1981: 20 Years of Civilian Reuse*, Washington D.C.: The Pentagon, November 1981.

9. B. Hu, 'Noodles and Nukes: China Recasts Army Upgrading with Economic Growth', *Far Eastern Economic Review*, January, 1988.
10. P. Kennedy, *The Rise and Fall of the Great Powers: Economic Change and Military Conflict from 1500 to 2000*, New York: Random House, 1987, p.xvi.
11. Ibid., p.xxiii.
12. Dumas, op. cit., p.244.

Appendix

United Nations Study on the Relationship between Disarmament and Development*

The terms conversion and redeployment describe the process of change whereby real human and material resources shift from the production of one set of goods and services to the production of another. The specific concern here is the shift of resources from the production of commodities and services for military purposes to goods and services that can contribute to economic and social development. More particularly, we are concerned with conversion and redeployment of the resources involved in the production of commodities used or consumed by the military and which have little or no civilian utility. A significant part of military demand is directed at goods and services that are essentially identical to those consumed in the civilian sector. In this case, the problem is the relatively minor one of ensuring that civilian demand fills the gap left by cutbacks in military spending. This is not the case with nuclear and chemical weapons, combat aircraft, missiles, warships, tanks and so on. The resources involved in producing these items are likely, in varying degrees, to be unsuited for the production of civilian goods, so that explicit consideration must be given to how their capabilities can be altered to permit the smoothest possible transition to the production of socially useful goods and services.

The groups involved in the development and production of modern weaponry and military equipment are conscious of their specialization and of the uncertainties they might encounter in the civilian arena. Disarmament measures are therefore viewed as a threat to both their means of livelihood and to established structures of power and influence. In the present economic and social settings, the existence of large groups dedicated to and uniquely specialized in meeting military requirements will inevitably translate into strong political and bureaucratic pressures to preserve the *status quo*. The political obstacles to

* *The Relationship between Disarmament and Development*, United Nations, New York, 1982, Study Series 5 (Study chaired by Inga Thorsson). Excerpts from Chapters V and VII related to problems of conversion and redeployment of resources released from military purposes through disarmament measures to economic and social development purposes.

disarmament are formidable enough without the added difficulty of opposition to it, direct or indirect, from groups acting in their perceived economic or bureaucratic interests. Simply stated, one major purpose of planning and preparing for conversion is to minimize opposition to disarmament measures emanating from these economic and bureaucratic considerations.

At one time it was thought that the issue of doing away with the military sector in modern industrial market economies would threaten the viability of the entire system. This hypothesis was usually based on the tendency in market economies towards under-consumption or for productive capacity to outrun effective demand, resulting in unemployment and excess capacity. This systemic tendency necessitates the injection of additional demand from outside the market system and, it was alleged, the capitalist system displayed a propensity to use arms production in this role. This view has been repudiated and it is now believed that whatever reputation arms expenditures had as a stimulant for market economies was quite undeserved. Moreover, in the industrialized countries, the focus of concern in economic policies has switched from a lack of demand to supply capacity limitation, whereas in the developing countries the concern continues to be inadequate supply with which to satisfy major unmet needs . . . the opportunity cost of the contemporary arms race is extremely high for all participants, irrespective of the type of economic and social system and of the level of development. The perceived requirements of national defence under contemporary conditions necessitate the investment of time, funds and manpower that, at best, will be of only modest benefit to other industrial sectors and that, over the long term, contribute significantly but indirectly to a variety of economic maladies. Thus, while this chapter is concerned specifically with the conversion of real resources from military to non-military uses, in a wider context, this issue can be seen as one of the more concrete dimensions of the conversion to a more balanced and realistic approach to national and international security, an approach that recognizes that military security has been overstressed to the detriment, in particular, of economic security.

Conversion and redeployment is not a phenomenon associated uniquely with disarmament. Any form of economic and social development represents a continuous process of conversion. Particularly in modern industrial economies, the factors of production must respond continuously to the development of new products and the phasing-out of old ones and to the introduction of new production techniques. Indeed, the pace of technological change and the extraordinary mobility of capital in recent decades has led most countries to undertake measures to facilitate necessary changes in the structure of industry and to adopt legislation to provide some protection for workers affected by such changes. The point here is to stress that modern industrial economies including, in particular, the economies with the largest military establishments, have a considerable inbuilt capacity to convert resources from one activity to another. The conversion from arms to production for civilian purposes will be, at the level of execution, merely one aspect of this process. Furthermore, as we shall argue below, any process of conversion and redeployment associated with disarmament measures if developed in the context of even more far-reaching structural adjustments and modifications of national economies and of the international economic system, could be productively integrated with these wider changes.

From the standpoint of placing the problems of conversion in perspective, a second important point to bear in mind would be that the process of disarmament is almost certain to be quite gradual. In other words, it is quite unrealistic to portray the conversion problem as involving, in a single step, the need to replace $500 billion of demand or absorb tens of millions of persons into the civilian work-force. In practical terms, the scale of the conversion problem stemming from disarmament measures will be orders of magnitude smaller than this at any given point in the process. Indeed, it is far more likely that the rate of disarmament agreed upon will lag behind conversion capabilities or, to state the matter less pessimistically, there should be no difficulty in gearing the rate of disarmament to the rate at which the resources involved can move smoothly to alternative activities.

Defence industry characteristics

The conversion problems associated with disarmament are rightly considered to be concentrated in the industries that develop and manufacture weapons and military equipment. This is the component of the military sector as a whole where one is most likely to find the resources—personnel, plant and equipment—unsuited to satisfying civilian demands because of a high degree of specialization for military work. In order to anticipate the nature of the problems that a conversion process will have to address, it is instructive to look in as much detail as possible at the characteristics of defence industries. While one can expect to find significant differences depending on the economic and social environment in which these industries are located, there will also be important uniformities imposed by the very nature of military production. For this reason we have elected to arrange the following discussion by characteristic rather than by country.

. . . globally, this is an 'industry' that directly employs perhaps 4 million persons in the production of goods and services specialized for military purposes. A very approximate estimate of the value of the output of this industry in 1980 was $127 billion. This industry is, of course, highly concentrated geographically.

The distribution of workers directly engaged in military production must, of course, closely parallel the distribution of output. As explained earlier, it is very important in gauging the probable magnitude of the conversion problem in particular countries to distinguish between direct and indirect employment and between specialized and non-specialized military demand. Such problems as will arise will be heavily concentrated in the labour force directly engaged in meeting the military demand for specialized goods and services. Unfortunately, the available data is neither comprehensive nor sufficiently disaggregated to permit making these distinctions.

A second important characteristic of the global defence industry is its high degree of concentration in specific sectors. Modern armed forces are structured around costly major weapon systems—aircraft, missiles, warships and tanks—and the bulk of procurement expenditures are directed at the industries that supply these items. In addition, modern weapons and supporting equipment make extensive use of electronics. In that group of the important arms-producing countries where data is available, military demand accounts for shares of between 40 and 80 per cent of total production and employment in the aerospace sector, which is thus probably the sector most heavily engaged in military business. In the electronics sector of these countries, the shares of production and employment accounted for by military work currently appear to range between 20 and 30 per cent. These are wide ranges within which substantial national variations can be traced in the sources identified. Regrettably, because only a limited group of countries publish such data, it is impossible for the Group to generalize confidently on the degree of concentration in other important arms-producing countries, as should be done to judge the full extent of potential redeployment problems and opportunities.

The converse of the concentration of military demand in specific industries is the dependence of these industries on military contracts. In this regard, it is often observed that, particularly in the aerospace and electronics industries, the statistics cited above, in so far as they do not already include the R&D element, probably understate the degree of dependence as military orders may actually account for a disproportionately large share of the industry's research and development expenditure. To some extent new technologies developed for military purposes can be transferred to civilian products, usually with a considerable time-lag. The more important factor, however, is that military demand enables these industries to assemble and maintain the scientific and engineering teams that perform research and development.

Another dimension of concentration is that, within the industrial sectors most heavily involved in military work, a relatively small number of firms win a major portion of defence contracts. This concentration is not, in itself, unusual, but the unique characteristics of the military market and the enormous size of individual contracts have made it particularly conspicuous in the military sector.

The degree to which individual firms depend on military contracts is often illustrated by comparing the value of contracts received in a given year with total sales for that year, at least in the United States where the appropriate information is available. This is a misleading procedure because military contracts awarded normally cover work to be performed over a period of years. To illustrate, in 1978 General Dynamics was awarded military contracts valued at 129 per cent of the company's total sales for that year. In fact, if this procedure is properly applied, the degree of dependence of the major United States defence contractors on military business has declined quite sharply. The top 25 defence contractors went from nearly 40 per cent of their business in the defence area in 1958 to under 10 per cent by 1975. On the other hand, a distinction must be drawn between diversification and conversion, and the fact is that this decline in dependence on military business has been accomplished through expansion and mergers. The defence divisions of these large corporations remain almost exclusively dependent on military contracts but the fact of diversification will make it easier for these major contractors to cope with a decline in their military contracts.

Very little information is available on the defence industry in the Soviet Union but, as one would expect, such indications as are available suggest a high degree of concentration of military production in specific industrial sectors. Most military production would take place in the machine-building and metal-working sector of industry. Of the 20 ministries that comprise this sector, it is evident from the titles that military production is concentrated in nine of them, suggesting, at least in selected ministries, levels of dependence on military contracts comparable to those found in the major Western arms-producing countries. Similarly, the technological pressures promoting specialization and the geographic concentration of the defence industry are also evident in the Soviet Union.

A third distinguishing feature of defence industries is the composition of the work-force. The post-war period has witnessed an extraordinary focus on the accomplishment of scientific and technological advances deemed to be relevant to weapons and warfare and on translating such advances as quickly as possible into operational hardware. The defence industry is constantly working with concepts, processes, techniques, materials and so on that, by civilian standards, are esoteric, and attempting to incorporate these things in products that will function in the harsh environment of the modern battlefield. Accordingly, one would expect that defence industries spend disproportionately large sums on R&D and employ disproportionately large numbers of scientists, engineers, technicians and skilled workers. Moreover, while the most specific data is available for the United States and France, it is reasonable to assume that defence industries everywhere exhibit similar characteristics. For the United States in 1978, R&D expenditure as a percentage of sales was 3 per cent on the average for all industries, 6.6 per cent for electronic components and 12.4 per cent for aircraft and missiles. Similarly, the all-industry average of scientists and engineers per 1,000 employees was 27, compared to 54 in electronic components and 80 in aircraft and missiles. For France in 1973, 7.9 per cent of the work-force in the defence industries were engineers compared to the all-industry average of 1.4 per cent. The same relationships for technicians and skilled workers were 19.8 per cent against 4.2 per cent and 42.1 per cent against 25.6 per cent respectively.

A fourth characteristic with potential ramifications for the conversion process is the degree of dependence of the defence industries of some countries on exports. . . . despite the limited utility of the available data, the international trade in arms now takes place on a scale that is undeniably of economic significance. The estimates generated in . . . [Chapter 3 of the UN Study] suggest that exports account for at least 20 per cent of the global production of goods and services specialized for military purposes. At the global level, armaments constitute less than 2 per cent of the goods and services traded internationally, but the picture changes quite drastically if the level of analysis is reduced to the four major arms suppliers and to particular sectors of the defence industry within these countries. It should be recalled that the estimated value of arms transfers is computed indirectly on the basis of observed deliveries of weapons and equipment and that these estimates have been roughly expanded to include such things as construction and technical assistance contracted for by a foreign military establishment. Similarly, the estimates do not necessarily reflect the value of the financial or commodity payments made for arms. Nevertheless, there is ample supplementary evidence for individual countries and firms that fully bears out the critical importance of arms exports for the defence industries of the major arms producers.

For a variety of reasons—including the technological imperative, the periodic nature of major orders for the national forces and a desire for a surge capacity in the event of war—the defence industry is prone to chronic excess capacity and most arms producers have sought exports to ameliorate this condition as well as for other reasons. Once again data are available only on a limited number of major arms-producing countries and the extrapolation to this category in general would be extremely hazardous. This reservation is doubly important in the case of arms exports because volumes tend to fluctuate widely in response to particular situations as well as the availability of military goods for export. The discernible range of export-shares in military goods production for selected industries has been between 40 and 70 per cent for particular years. If such patterns have any wider applicability to arms-exporting countries in general they clearly have major implications for conversion possibilities.

The degree to which the State is in direct control of military industry is a fifth characteristic of direct relevance to the problem of conversion. In the Soviet Union and other centrally-planned arms-producing countries, state control of the defence industries is, of course, complete. But even in market-economy countries, the defence sector is, of course, dominated by the purchasing power and influence of the State and is frequently State-owned. In France, in 1980, more than one half of the workers directly engaged in military production were employed in state establishments or nationalized enterprises and much the same has probably been true in the United Kingdom, given the heavy government stake in the two dominant concerns, British Aerospace and Rolls Royce. The degree and type of state involvement in such countries varies with the policies of the Government of the day. On balance, direct ownership or heavy financial involvement by the State is characteristic of defence industries in nearly all countries, including developing countries. Only in the United States is private enterprise seemingly dominant but even here, in the aircraft industry, for example, approximately one third of plant space, a significant share of manufacturing equipment and all military maintenance and repair depots are Government-owned. Government-owned facilities and equipment are also of critical importance in other sectors of the defence industry.

Increasing government involvement in the defence industry, even in market economies, has been essentially unavoidable. For all practical purposes the Government is the major market for the products of the industrial sectors supplying military goods, and doing business in this market is very different from the commercial world. The first concern in developing and producing military products is not cost or price but that their performance be better or at least as good as those of potential adversaries. As is well known, this imperative, coupled with the commitment of enormous resources to military R&D, has resulted in an extraordinarily rapid rate of growth in the cost of developing and producing weapon systems. The development of a major weapons system now typically involves hundreds of millions or even billions of dollars, with billions more for production. No private concern can marshall resources on this scale and even if it could it would not commit them to a single product whose marketability was subject to so many factors outside the firm's control. The Government, therefore, assumes all the financial risks. Development and production take place only after a sale has been made and contracts signed. Buyer and seller collaborate in specifying the product and, to a reasonable approximation, price is established subsequently on the basis of the cost of meeting the specifications.

Bearing these various considerations in mind, one can attempt to list the characteristics of defence industries from the standpoint of the problems that these industries would encounter if conversion to non-military production became necessary. As regards labour, the emphasis on quality and performance in specialized branches of the military sector has led to the acquisition of skills and, more particularly, to the adoption of attitudes towards design and production that would be out of place in most commercial fields where high production rates and increased efficiency compete with quality as goals. This applies especially to the scientific and engineering labour that constitutes, as pointed out, a large fraction of the military industrial work-force. The skills required of the management personnel of military industrial enterprises are also quite unique to this field. On the one hand, few if any production activities in the commercial field rival the military sector in terms of the technical complexity of the product and the number of suppliers of parts and components involved. The experience that the military prime contractors have accumulated in systems management is one of the main reasons why Governments in the major Western arms-producing countries are so reluctant to see any of these concerns go under. On the other hand, dealing with the Government as a buyer is a unique challenge in marketing, requiring the adoption of special accounting procedures and conforming in general with government regulations. Familiarity with government red tape is no small matter and requires extensive background and experience. Indeed, surveys in the United States have revealed this to be one of the main reasons why some private concerns are reluctant to become involved in defence-related production.

Secondly, much of the capital equipment used in some branches of defence production is highly specialized and lacks the flexibility for application to civilian output. In sharp contrast to the Second World War, when civilian industry undertook to produce war materiel and then reconverted to production for the commercial market, the present situation is the product of a 30-year period during which military and civil technologies evolved partly on separate and divergent paths. A proportion of military industrial production takes place in facilities that are used exclusively for this purpose. Apart from the fact that a massive and sustained military R&D effort has yielded military industrial capacities that operate on a technological plateau considerably higher than the bulk of civilian industry, extremely demanding (or just different) military standards and specifications and the desire to have capacity available for mobilization also contribute to the separation of military from civilian industry. One of the more conspicuous results of this is that the defence industry tends to have a lot of excess capacity ranging, in the United States, from over 90 per cent of the munitions industry to between 30 per cent and 50 per cent in most other segments of the industry.

There are several other features of the defence industry that tend to make the companies of enterprises involved apprehensive about disarmament measures and the prospect of having to convert to civilian production. For example, most defence-work is paid for on a continuous basis providing a very favourable cash-flow situation, particularly for financially weak companies. Similarly, companies accustomed to performing low-risk military R&D will be understandably nervous at the prospect of committing their own resources to the development and production of commodities for the uncertain and competitive civilian market. These concerns will be amplified by the fact that companies specializing in military work will have legitimate fears regarding their competitiveness in the civilian sphere owing to large overhead costs—because the work-force is dominated by managerial, scientific and engineering personnel—and because they lack skill or experience in the marketing of civil products. Furthermore, given the financial magnitude or military contracts and the long periods involved in development and production, the major contractors will, at any given point, have a substantial backlog of military work for both national and foreign military forces to complicate the process of conversion to non-military work.

Finally, there is the question of profit. The evidence here is inconclusive: depending on how the rate of profit is computed, whether this is done for large or small defence contractors and for prime contractors or subcontractors, it is possible to show that the rate of profit in military industry is both high and low compared to civilian industry. On the other hand, once a military contract has been secured the rate of profit is at least fairly certain owing to cost-plus pricing. Moreover, the magnitude of the profit that can be earned on a single military contract is often very large indeed and this can serve important corporate objectives even if the rate of profit is relatively low. It can also be mentioned that, at least in the United States, foreign military sales are significantly more profitable then domestic sales.

It is clear that these various characteristics will be present to varying degrees varying on where military industry is located. Profits, for example, are not a significant force in the Soviet Union, motivating industrial concerns to enter or to remain in the military sector. Similarly, the managers of Soviet military industrial enterprises will not be concerned at their lack of experience in marketing civil productions, since this function would be performed by the central planning authorities. On the other hand, the evidence suggests that, owing to the high priority accorded to defence, managerial personnel in the Soviet military industrial sector are relatively insulated from the foremost managerial problem in the rest of the economy, namely, securing the supply of needed personnel and materials.

As regards the retraining of labour, it is often assumed that the workers engaged in the development and production of modern sophisticated weapon systems possess uniquely specialized qualifications and skills. In fact, the professional skills needed in this field are linked in most cases with production techniques that are identical or comparable with these for civil products. Some reorientation and retraining may be required for certain specialized occupations and skills, particularly in respect of R&D personnel. Informed judgement in the Soviet Union suggests that retraining for a period of up to one year for scientists and up to two years for certain engineers is needed for a successful transition to civilian work. An additional problem is that a significant part of the stock of knowledge possessed by scientists and engineers in certain specialized branches of the military sector is classified and would be wasted unless restrictions on its use were lifted.

Specialized capital equipment presents less of a problem. Where such equipment is owned by private concerns a variety of indirect measures can be adopted to make it attractive for them to divest themselves of this equipment and reinvest for civilian production. And where this equipment is owned or controlled by the State quite direct measures can be used. Since it is quite unrealistic, at least for an extended interim period, to expect States to totally demolish their military industrial capabilities, it would be highly desirable to reduce the gap between military and civilian industrial requirements. If military and civil production took place side by side at the plant level, all dimensions of the conversion problem would be minimized. To accomplish this, it would be necessary to curb the military appetite for performance and technological excellence which, in itself, would make an enormous contribution to slowing down the arms race and facilitate the achievement of arms control and disarmament measures. Since it has proved impossible, to date, to control the pace and direction of military technology, it is important to note that, in the United States, even those who are concerned about the adequacy of the military industrial base consider that more integration of civil and military production is feasible and advantageous. Labour unions constitute another powerful constituency supporting greater integration of civil and military production, since, under present circumstances, employment stability in the United States defence industry is low and, to avoid unemployment, workers must be prepared to move from one concern to another depending on who wins the major contracts.

Military research and development

Notwithstanding that defence industry almost everywhere draws on results of R&D for non-military purposes, the human and material resources devoted to R&D for military purposes are to a significant extent located in the defence industry. At the same time, however, an amount of work on R&D for military purposes is performed in specialized laboratories, both public and privately owned, and in universities. In the Soviet Union, it appears that military R&D is quite rigorously separated from the production of weapons and equipment. In other words it is worth while to examine briefly the potential difficulties that the scientific community would face in the event of a significant reduction in military R&D.

It was pointed out in chapter III [of the UN Study] that an estimated 500,000 scientists and engineers are engaged in military R&D world wide, approximately 20 per cent of all the manpower devoted to research and development. In so far as there is a consensus of opinion on the capacity of these men and women to redirect their efforts to non-military ends it is that the problems encountered will be relatively minor. The military R&D effort is very broadly based; few areas of scientific enquiry are considered to have no potential military applications. Furthermore, scientific and technological advances, at least up to the point of their accomplishment, are neutral in the sense that they can be used for military or civilian purpose. In other words, it is widely felt that the problem of converting to peaceful purposes the human resources now devoted to military R&D is, in essence, one of the governmental decisions concerning the financing and orientation of scientific research.

This issue cannot, however, be so lightly dismissed. Reference was made in the previous section to the evidence that some of the personnel engaged in military R&D acquire attitudes towards scientific and technical problems that would have to be changed in essential ways to be useful in the civilian sphere. Moreover, some parts of the military R&D community will be engaged in areas and/or at levels that have little immediate civilian utility. In a similar vein, it is quite possible that the composition of the military R&D community in terms of scientific discipline is such that the adoption of a science policy that places greater stress on economic and social needs will render significant numbers of scientists and engineers in particular disciplines redundant. The military R&D community itself will certainly be conscious of these possibilities, and their support for disarmament and conversion will clearly

depend on evidence that the nature and magnitude of potential dislocations have been realistically assessed and that credible arrangements have been made to smooth the transition.

Uniformed military personnel

The conversion of uniformed military personnel is a separate problem,
both quantitatively and qualitatively. Since the global figure for personnel in the armed forces is at least 25 million, even agreement on modest
force-level reductions could involve the demobilization of millions of
persons. Furthermore, since the civilian economy, to a reasonable
approximation, already provides for the consumption needs of military
personnel, their demobilization will constitute an addition to the labour
market.

Reference [has been] made in [previous chapters of this report] to the
wide variety and growing level of skills required of military personnel.
In broad terms, this will clearly ease the transition to civilian work, but
the available evidence suggests that significant problems can still be
anticipated. In the late 1960s, it was estimated that 80 per cent of the
military jobs held by enlisted men in the United States armed forces
corresponded to only about 10 per cent of those held by male civilian
workers. This fact, of course, suggests that vocational and educational
training prior to demobilization will play a major role in easing the
transition. Similarly, it will obviously be advantageous to ensure at
least an approximate correspondence between the skills acquired before
demobilization and employment opportunities in the civilian economy.
And since the latter will be influenced by the conversion strategies
implemented in the military industrial sector, it will be necessary to coordinate and integrate the conversion measures adopted in the various
parts of the military sector.

It is worth while pointing out that the majority of countries will have
some experience in transferring manpower from the military to the
civilian sector. Conscription remains the most widespread arrangement
for securing military manpower and this involves the continuous acquisition and release of labour resources. Of even greater relevance would
be the experience with the flow-through of regular or career military
personnel. In the Federal Republic of Germany, for instance, nearly 10
per cent of all uniformed military personnel are demobilized annually,
mostly draftees but also regulars completing longer tours of duty. In
addition, several of the major military powers have had more or less
recent experience with significant reductions in military manpower, for
example, the Soviet Union in the late 1950s and the United States
in the early 1970s. Project Transition, initiated by the United States
Department of Defense in 1967, provided training and/or job counsel-

ling six months prior to discharge and actively involved both private industry and other government agencies in locating employment opportunities and preparing servicemen to meet the skill requirements. As broad evidence that this project was quite successful, it can be pointed out that total defence-related employment as a percentage of the labour force declined from 10 per cent to 9 per cent between 1967 and 1969, while the over-all rate of unemployment decreased from 4 per cent to 3.5 per cent. Subsequently, between 1971 and 1973, over-all unemployment in the United States economy fell from 6 per cent to 5 per cent, while defence-related employment continued to decline, from 7 per cent to less than 6 per cent of the labour force.

Regional and subregional effects

Given that military industrial activity is heavily concentrated in a few industries, that a few major concerns dominate the market and that a relatively small number of major weapons systems account for a disproportionately large fraction of total expenditure, it is inevitable that the economic impact of military activities is particularly heavy in selected regions and communities within the arms-producing countries. Major military bases, often located in remote areas for strategic and security reasons, similarly provide the dominant rationale for economic activity in the surrounding region. For such subnational regions and communities—for example, Southern California in the United States and perhaps the region around the White Sea in the Soviet Union—the conversion issue will have to be addressed in a particularly thorough and imaginatve fashion, since it will extend beyond finding alternative products and retraining workers to replacing a significant portion of the entire economic and social fabric of the region. In some cases, this will doubtless prove unfeasible so that workers and their families will have to be deployed to other regions.

In order to tackle this particular dimension of the conversion problem, an essential requirement is the preparation of comprehensive and detailed information on how military expenditure works its way through the economy, with the objective of determining with a high degree of accuracy the direct and indirect employment effects in particular subnational regions and communities. Needless to say, this is not a simple undertaking. The pattern of effects will be different for different categories of military expenditure, for particular types of major weapons systems and will change over time as the mix of weapons in production changes. In the complex and interdependent economies of the major arms-producing countries the regional distribution of defence-related employment has been shown to be a wide-reaching amalgam of primary, secondary and higher-order linkages as well as direct and indirect effects. The same will be true in other industrialized and developing countries with significant defence industries, although in the latter case many of the industrial linkages will extend overseas, particularly to the main industrialized arms suppliers.

Fortunately, all Governments have the capacity to assemble the relevant data, and analytical tools are available to process this information in the manner necessary to provide a solid basis for planning for conversion. Information on the primary regional distribution of military spending, coupled with inter-industry input-output models and data on industry and plant location can provide highly accurate estimates of the regional employment effects of general or specific disarmament measures. A considerable amount of illuminating work has already been done, particularly in the United States but also in the United Kingdom, the Federal Republic of Germany, Canada, Norway, Sweden and other countries. Most of the analysts involved reported being constrained by data limitations—the data was either not available, inappropriate or insufficiently detailed—so that this experience can serve as a guide to gaps in the existing data base.

As regards the particular issue of military base closures, there is also considerable experience on which to draw. For reasons of economy and because of shifting tactical and strategic requirements, many countries have closed down or relocated military bases. In the United States, between 1961 and 1973, there were 1,387 such closures and the Office of Economic Adjustment (OEA) in the Department of Defense has acquired considerable experience and expertise in helping the affected communities to organize and plan the adjustment, particularly in terms of acquainting community officials with the various Federal and state programmes available for manpower retraining, loans and grants for redevelopment and so on. While the OEA contribution has been significant, it has had no authority and no resources of its own to streamline and accelerate the adjustment process. Many of the affected communities ultimately benefited from the shift to a more stable and diversified economic base, but the transition period was long and painful. For this reason, proposed based closures, both in the United States and elsewhere—in Sweden, for example—continue to be vigorously opposed. On the whole, the experience with base closures, while providing invaluable material on which to draw, illustrates once again the need for elaborate and thoughtful preparation for conversion to non-military activities rather than *ad hoc* assistance after the fact.

Measures to minimize the problems of transition

The foregoing discussion has, in passing, identified many of the policies and measures that could be adopted to facilitate the conversion process.

An important conclusion that emerges is the need for planning. At all levels, from the central Government to the individual munitions factory and the military-dependent community, the question of doing without all or some military activity must be thought through to determine the character and magnitude of the difficulties that will arise and to evaluate the effectiveness and feasibility of possible solutions. In this fashion, it would be possible to develop a comprehensive strategy for conversion that addressed the specific concerns of the various groups that would be affected and allocated responsibility for the various aspects and phases of the process in the most efficient manner.

Primary responsibility for conversion, in an overall sense, will inevitably fall on the central government. This follows from the nature of the relationship between the Government and the military sector and is particularly true in regard to initiating preparations for a conversion process. The Government should take the lead, but the process of acquiring detailed knowledge on the nature and probable magnitude of the adjustment problems and devising measures and arrangements to overcome them would be a joint endeavour with industry, trade unions and officials in the most military-dependent regions and communities.

The nature and extent of government involvement, following disarmament measures, in the process of conversion itself will vary from country to country, depending in large part on the type of economic system but also on many other factors. Each State, within its particular context, could take maximum advantage of the variety of resource allocation mechanisms available, ranging from central or indicative planning and budget allocations at the federal, state and local government level through the open market to direct negotiations between the management and workers of military industrial concerns and consumer groups, such as the innovative efforts undertaken in the United Kingdom by the shop-stewards of the Lucas Aerospace Company.

It should also be emphasized, however, that the achievement of disarmament measures would represent a strategic opportunity to use the flexibility thus gained to address major economic and social problems, both at home and abroad. Governments in all States should be prepared to take maximum advantage of this opportunity through establishing broad priorities—both domestically and internationally—and taking appropriate steps at the macro and micro levels to ensure that the conversion process contributes, as far as is possible, to a pattern of resource use that reflects these priorities.

Governments in all countries can be broadly confident—at least over the medium and long terms—in their capacity to play a major role in maintaining the general level of economic activity in the event of significant reductions in military expenditure. On the key issue of employment, there is, as we have seen, persuasive evidence that virtually all possible alternatives to military expenditure and production will result in at least as many and, in most cases, more jobs being created. In planned economies, of course, the government has direct and comprehensive authority to accomplish this and in market economies, there exists a diversified arsenal of fiscal and monetary measures to complement the market system. In all cases, however, the Government must carefully dovetail disarmament with the time required to accomplish the conversion of the resources thus released so as not to overtax adjustment capabilities. The basic considerations determining the transition period are identifying new markets, developing new products, retooling to produce them and retraining management and production workers. In market economy countries, an additional important consideration will be the timing of compensatory fiscal and monetary policies to ensure that the stimulating effects coincide with military cutbacks. While the mix of compensatory programmes is of little consequence in the long run, it is very important in the short run owing to the varying time lags associated with different measures. For example, increases in non-military government spending will have direct and immediate effects while the full effects of a tax cut will not be felt for several years.

It is a widely held belief that the opportunity to apply science and technology more directly and systematically to economic and social problems is the most significant dividend that disarmament would bring. A nation's military, scientific and technical resources comprise manpower (scientists, engineers, technicians and technical management), facilities and equipment, and scientific and technical information. Each of these components requires separate attention for conversion purposes. The formulation of a national science policy that reflects economic and social priorities both domestically and internationally would be extremely useful in order to give direction and focus to the conversion effort. The specific requirements for adapting personnel in military R&D will vary considerably among and within the different categories of personnel involved. Determining the probable requirements for retraining, re-education and redeployment will require detailed knowledge of the composition of the military R&D community. Thought must be given to how and where retraining and re-education is to be done and who would pay for it.

As regards facilities and equipment, it would be necessary to compile a detailed national inventory as a basis on which to assess its adaptability to civilian R&D. Similarly, the stock of military, scientific and technical information can be declassified and systematically canvassed for possible civilian applications. An important complementary measure would be to encourage civilian industry to be more receptive to R&D. This could boost productivity and also generate a demand for management personnel with knowledge and experience in the effective use of R&D resources, that is, the type of management personnel employed in disproportionately large numbers in the defence industry.

The ambition—and the need—to make science and technology more responsive to economic and social requirements will not be realized in a straightforward fashion. It is true that such sectors as civil aerospace, research into alternative sources of energy, further development of nuclear energy technologies so as to make them safer for civilian use, or the design of remotely-controlled underwater devices for the extraction of raw materials are similar to the highly specialized technologies in some areas of the armaments sector. On the other hand, such issues as coping with pollution, improving the effectiveness and availability of education and increasing agricultural productivity in the developing countries are enormously different from and far more complex than the technical problems confronted in transporting a man to the moon or delivering a nuclear warhead accurately to a target 5,000 miles away. It is perhaps no exaggeration to say that we are still quite ignorant as to how to apply R&D resources to such problems. Developing new methods, techniques and approaches for applying scientific and technical resources effectively toward the resolution of economic and social problems will require a great deal of thought and experiment.

The general approach to conversion just outlined with regard to military R&D can also be applied to military industry. The first order of business is to determine as accurately as possible which industries in which locations depend to a significant degree on military demand, the characteristics of the work-force involved and the type of plant and equipment used. Where plant, equipment and manpower—and by implication, the product—are not unduly specialized for military purposes, the Government can determine whether general compensatory monetary and fiscal policy, together with market forces, will suffice to maintain demand and employment or whether more specific measures would be desirable. Input-output models can be employed to anticipate the extent to which the pattern of demand associated with compensatory policies might differ from that associated with military outlays. Where the mismatch is significant, more industry-specific measures could be prepared for possible implementation.

At the other extreme—represented by the munition plans and the prime military contractors in aerospace, electronics and shipbuilding—the problems are rather formidable. The Government, in conjunction with management and unions in the industry, must determine what alternative uses for these resources are feasible and desirable, with the feasible alternatives clearly more important in the short run. Once these strategic judgements have been made, the requirements for retraining, re-education and redeployment can be gauged and programmes developed to satisfy them. Similarly, the data base and a

broad strategy for the alternative use of military industrial resources
are essential elements for determining the nature, extent and duration
of specific measures—tax concessions, investment incentives and the
like—needed to accomplish the transition. At least in market economies, the State would not have to concern itself with specifying alternative products in any detail or determining how they will be
manufactured. Nor should it attempt to do so. Its role should be to guide
and facilitate conversion and to alleviate to hardships imposed on the
manpower resources displaced in the process. Nevertheless, to perform
this role effectively the State must be well informed of the difficulties
associated with developing and producing a new product and the time
required to accomplish it. Similarly, it must be prepared to eliminate
any unreasonable barriers to entry to the civilian markets that the
former suppliers of military equipment hope to penetrate. It should be
stressed again, however, that this central dimension of the conversion
issue—the resources directly employed in meeting the military demand
for specialized goods and services—is not overwhelmingly large even in
the most heavily armed States. Moreover, a process of disarmament
will be gradual rather than abrupt and this will further diminish the
magnitude of the problem at any particular time.

One question that will have to be considered with particular care is
whether the prime military contractors can convert to civilian production and still retain broadly the same structure. It was pointed out
above that these concerns have developed unique capabilities in scientific and systems management, that their work-force is markedly top
heavy with scientists, engineers and technical management personnel
and that their marketing skills are oriented exclusively towards government procurement. Some analysts feel that conversion to civilian production will probably require that these large-scale units be broken
up. Others, however, while granting the need to change habits and
attitudes acquired in the military environment, argue that many important requirements in the civilian arena closely resemble large military
projects in terms of scientific and technical input and requirements
for strong capabilities in systems management. Examples here would
include new sources of energy, exploiting the resources of the ocean,
environmental protection and new systems for major cities in such
areas as transportation and sanitation.

In addition to requiring that military industry prepare and periodically review plans for conversion, a number of other preparatory steps
can be taken to minimize the scale of the problems that will arise when
disarmament measures are actually implemented. As mentioned
above, it is considered possible and desirable, at least in the United
States, to reverse the trend of increasing separation of military and
civilian business. Measures to encourage this integration could include

adopting commercial standards and business practices for military procurement and permitting defence contractors to charge research and development in preparation for conversion against military work. The objective would be to reduce the extent to which individual companies and plants were dependent on military work. Similarly, steps can be taken to gradually diversify the economic base of those regions and communities now heavily dependent on military contracts.

It is worth reiterating at this point that this discussion is directed specifically at the resources—human and material—specialized in and wholly concerned with meeting the military demand for goods and services. These are the resources that accomplish the final manufacture and assembly of specialized military products. The industries in which these resources are located – primarily aerospace, electronics and shipbuilding—serve both the military and civilian markets, and as one moves down the manufacturing chain from the level of the prime military contractor there is increasing scope for meeting both demands from the same production facilities. In the Soviet Union, for example, it was stated in 1971 that 41 per cent of the output of military industry consisted of civilian products and the current five-year plan (1981-1985) provides for a considerable expansion of such production. Similarly, it is estimated that about 60 per cent of the output of military industry in the United States in 1978 was for the civilian market.

An excellent example of the scope and content of a strategy for conversion is provided by a bill (S.1031) introduced in the United States Senate in 1979. The purpose of S.1031 is to facilitate the economic adjustment of communities, industries and workers to civilian-oriented activities in the event of reductions in military business. It provided for the establishment of a Defence Economic Adjustment Council composed of representatives of the major Federal Government departments, private industry and the labour unions. The Council would be supported by a professional staff of specialists in such fields as marketing and production engineering and would be authorized to secure whatever data and information it needed from any government or government-affiliated body. The duties of the Council would include the preparation and distribution of a Conversion Guidelines Handbook on such issues as the retraining and reorientation of managerial, professional and technical personnel and the redirection of physical plants to civilian production.

The bill further provided for the establishment of separate management and labour Alternative Use Committees at every defence facility employing more than 100 persons. These committees would be required—subject to penalties—to develop and keep up to date plans to permit complete conversion to civilian work within a period of two years, to identify the civilian personnel that would have to be released in the process and to make provision for their occupational retraining as necessary. Thirdly, the bill provided for the establishment of a special Workers Economic Adjustment Reserve Trust Fund to be financed from budgetary savings resulting from military cutbacks (10 per cent of the computer savings) and from earnings in industry associated with military contracts (1.25 per cent of a contractor's annual gross revenue from sales to the Department of Defense). Other provisions in the bill offer income maintenance guidelines for the workers involved in retraining and redeployment. Finally, the bill gave the Defense Economic Adjustment Council authority to earmark for communities seriously affected by military cutbacks an adequate portion of the economic development funds administered by various Federal agencies.

Alternative work

. . . experiences during the 1970s reaffirmed in a quite spectacular fashion that resources are indeed limited, even from a global perspective. The massive requirements for development so forcibly articulated in the context of a new international economic order; the oil crisis; mounting concern over access to other non-renewable raw materials; and the complex, synergistic relationships between pollution of the air, water and land environment have produced an impressively long list of national and international economic and social problems that require solution on a more or less urgent basis. In other words, identifying economic and social requirements that could use the resources now devoted to the arms race does not present the slightest problem. Indeed, the problem would once again be one of choice, of establishing priorities, since even disarmament would not eliminate the over-all scarcity of resources relative to demand. Significant disarmament could, however, provide a flying start, particularly as such a development would almost certainly provoke a more generalized rationalization in the allocation of resources.

In the long run all resources are perfectly malleable. The conversion to socially useful purposes of the resources now employed in the military sector is a somewhat more constrained operation since it is not practicable to reduce a 45-year-old aeronautical engineer to a high-school graduate or a missile assembly plant to scrapmetal and refashion them in the desired manner. Nevertheless, there is an overwhelming consensus, based on solid experience, that the resources employed for military purposes can, over a period extending up to about two years, be adequately 'refashioned' to work effectively towards meeting civilian needs. Finding civilian products to replace the military ones can best be done within the company itself, making use of the competence existing in the company. Past investigations into the conversion issue have identified a broad range of civilian activities to which military resources could be shifted, particularly, of course, within States with a large and diversified military sector but also in the context of international development. The latter perspective is of special interest in the present context and will be discussed separately below.

The national perspective: alternative work in the industrialized countries

As pointed out in earlier chapters, many of the major industrialized countries have in recent years experienced unusually high rates of inflation and unemployment and declining productivity growth. Some of them have severe pollution problems, decaying cities, declining standards in education and health care and increasing numbers of people who live at or near the poverty line. Particularly urgent problems in these countries are those surrounding energy. The development of commercially viable renewable sources of energy is an urgent priority and one to which military R&D resources could effectively be applied. Reverting to a greater reliance on coal seems virtually inevitable in the short run, but even here there are major research requirements to mitigate adverse environmental effects. There is every reason to believe that a focused and systematic research and development effort on the part of Government and industry could produce the necessary technological breakthroughs. Given the size and considerable urgency of the energy question and the common interest in providing global energy security, one could envisage an international energy agency to facilitate scientific exchange and minimize the duplication of effort.

In addition to providing alternative work for significant numbers of scientists and engineers now engaged in military R&D, one United States study has found that production workers in the military sectors could quite readily transfer their skills to solar development, production and installation. Clearly, once commercially viable solar systems had been developed, their production, installation and maintenance would be a vast undertaking with employment effects that would extend far beyond the (converted) military community. In a more general sense, the development of more energy efficient technologies for application throughout the manufacturing and transportation sectors of industry is a key requirement for so-called re-industrialization, and provides a variety of areas into which military R&D resources could be directed.

Another area urgently in need of attention is the environment. An essential prerequisite to arresting environmental degradation and repairing the damages already done is a more comprehensive understanding of the complex, synergistic relationships between the air, water and land environments. A wide variety of disciplines from both the natural and social sciences would be relevant here, including all or most of those found in the military R&D community. Housing and urban renewal offer another outlet for a range of R&D capabilities and, subsequently, for massive reconstruction programmes. Such programmes call for the development of new materials, construction techniques and tools, coupled with imaginative planning to make cities and urban concentrations more liveable.

New transportation systems are sorely needed, particularly in urban areas, and have long been regarded as a major civilian alternative for the high technology industries in the military sector. This remains the case, but experience has confirmed the importance of ensuring that criteria other than performance and technical competence are factored in during the conversion process. In the United States in particular, upgrading the system of railroads is potentially an enormous market for military R&D and production capabilities. Rail remains the most fuel-efficient means of transporting people and goods. The newest rail systems incorporate very advanced technology, require major investments in rolling-stock and in new construction, particularly the separation of passenger and freight lines on high density routes. As regards health care, the enormous advances in methods of treatment have not been matched by the organization and delivery of services at affordable cost. The military sector's skills in organization and systems management could find applications in this area. Similarly, it is widely believed that the revolution in communication technologies has major applications in the field of education. Employment opportunities could be created here for engineers from the military sector. It will be recalled that engineers are expected to pose the most difficult problem as regards re-employment because the requirements for engineers in most civilian industries, as a percentage of the total work-force, is markedly lower than in military industry.

More detailed information is available in the literature on alternative civilian work for the resources now producing specialized goods and services for the military. The previous United Nations report on disarmament and development identified more than 70 possible alternative uses for military R&D capabilities. Alternative work for military industry has been the subject of active investigations in the United Kingdom in recent years. An important feature of this work has been the direct involvement of the workers concerned, particularly those at Lucas Aerospace and Vickers. This work has also yielded long lists of civilian products relatively suited to the capabilities of the plan, equipment and labour force now manufacturing military electronic systems, naval vessels, armoured vehicles and the like. Unfortunately, this initiative has been stopped well short of the implementation stage.

A specific dimension of conversion of particular interest at the present time is the resources now devoted to the development and production of chemical warfare agents. Efforts are now being made to permit negotiations to begin on a convention that would prohibit the development, production, deployment and stockpiling of chemical weapons and the secure destruction of such stockpiles. A recent study by the Stockholm International Peace Research Institute concluded that conversion was technically feasible and would involve little or no disturbance for the work-force involved. On the one hand, it is considered technically feasible to break down stockpiled chemical warfare agents into their base materials and intermediate products and apply these to products useable for civilian purposes. Moreover, this process requires the same specially skilled scientific and technical personnel as are needed for the production of chemical warfare agents. On the other hand, it is quite feasible to produce commercial products such as pesticides, plasticizers and fire retardants in plants producing chemical warfare agents. Ironically, the very ease of conversion is a serious drawback in this case because it would be relatively easy to rededicate the facility to agent production. Unless there were to be a breakthrough on the question of on-site inspection, verification of compliance with a chemical warfare convention would probably require that the facilities be shut down and broken up.

Given the almost universal judgement that, with appropriate preparation and planning, the transitional problems associated with conversion can be readily accommodated and bearing in mind that disarmament will almost certainly be a selective and gradual process, it should be apparent that the industrialized countries, including, in particular, the major military powers, do not lack the important civilian uses for the resources now dedicated to the military.

The national perspective: alternative work in the developing countries

It will be recalled that the developing countries still account for only about 16 per cent of global military expenditure and that this sum is heavily concentrated in a relatively small number of countries, particularly those in the Middle East region. With a few important exceptions, R&D for military purposes is negligible. The production and assembly of major weapons is considerably more widespread but, again, the scale of the effort is significant in only a few countries. By and large, the labour employed in the military sector will not be uniquely specialized for military work, and technology in military industry will not be so far removed from civilian industrial technology. It is true that industry in the developing countries is generally narrowly based and less dynamic than in developed countries so that the inherent capacity for adjustment and conversion is lower. On the whole, however, the problems associated with conversion would seem to be relatively small in all but a few developing countries and the benefits from disarmament easier to realize.

At some $73 billion in 1980, military expenditures by the developing countries are by no means inconsequential. Moreover, the alternative uses to which these resources might be applied are particularly compelling so that, as in the industrialized countries, the State will have to consider very carefully how the opportunities opened up by disarmament measures can be exploited to alleviate the most urgent economic and social problems and to contribute towards placing the economy on a more sound and independent long-term path. In many developing countries, substantial disarmament would significantly ease prevailing financial constraints on the implementation of development plans. The reduction in the import of arms and spare parts and of capital goods and intermediate products for such local military production as is undertaken would release foreign exchange to alleviate bottle-necks in the programmes for industrialization and the expansion of agricultural production. The armed forces, the military bureaucracy and personnel in defence industries would provide a pool from which to reduce shortages of various types of skilled labour and of managerial personnel. Moreover, the diversion to the military of able-bodied, educated and skilled manpower from schools, universities and technical institutions could be minimized.

Reducing the incidence of hunger and malnutrition will clearly be a priority claimant on the resources released by disarmament measures both in the short term and the longer term. Education and health are two more areas which require vast resources even to make basic services and amenities available to all. In short, the developing countries will have even less difficulty than the industrialized countries in identifying beneficial alternative uses for the resources now consumed for military purposes and, on the whole, should find it easier to accomplish the transition.

The international perspective: alternative work in the context of a new international economic order

A structural transformation such as the conversion to civilian activities of the resources now employed for military purposes will be much easier to accomplish in a dynamic economic environment. Present economic difficulties may to some extent be symptoms not merely of a temporary cyclical downturn but of deeper structural problems. The saturation of major consumer markets and the emergence of serious supply-side constraints on economic growth—energy, raw materials and so on— all suggest the need in many countries for significant changes in the structure of industry, in the direction of future investment and in the pattern of consumer demand.

There is a body of opinion that holds that the industrialized nations cannot by themselves bring about world economic recovery. Specifically, it is widely and openly stated that an essential requirement is to make effective the enormous potential demands in the developing countries. The OECD countries are fully aware that their present economic situation would be significantly worse had not the demand for their exports from the developing countries remained relatively buoyant through the 1970s. There is growing support for the view that a more balanced pattern of world growth and development is strongly in the mutual interest of industrialized and developing countries for both economic and political reasons. Moreover, the expansion of international economic co-operation and the collaborative management of interdependence for mutual benefit and particularly towards the goal of diminishing prevailing assymetries in the interdependence between industrialized and developing countries, can and should be fostered to encompass East-West, East-South, South-South as well as West-South relations.

Needless to say, broad agreement on where the solution lies is a far cry from the elaboration and implementation of a strategy to reach that solution. The Declaration and the Programme of Action for a New International Economic Order adopted in 1974 (General Assembly resolutions 3201 (S-VI) and 3203 (S-VI) and their subsequent elaboration at the seventh special session of the Assembly (resolution 3362 (S-VII)) and in the International Development Strategy for the Third United Nations Development Decade (resolution 35/56) form the most comprehensive plan of action that exists at present. The broad outlines of this strategy were sketched in chapter II [of the UN Study] and will not be repeated here. Suffice it to say that the implementation of this strategy with deliberate speed is a vast undertaking, with commensurately massive requirements for resources and far-reaching implications for the structure and pattern of global economic activity. When one is speaking of new economic and social programmes requiring resources valued at several hundreds of billions of dollars the resource constraints imposed by the arms race become apparent. What is still more fundamental, one can legitimately wonder whether the adoption of such a bold and enlightened perspective is at all possible if international relations continue to be dominated by an arms race mentality.

The more specific questions to be considered here are first, in what ways could the resources now employed for military purposes contribute to accelerated economic development in the developing countries and secondly, are the transitional difficulties associated with conversion increased or lessened if the problem is cast in a framework of international co-operation? The latter question, to take it first, is an area that needs more investigation, but such indications as are available suggest that the conversion of resources from military to civilian uses would be facilitated if the process is integrated with programmes aimed at the achievement of a new international economic order. But even in the present context, it is difficult to conceive how the alternative work envisaged could be undertaken exclusively within national boundaries and even more so among developed or developing countries taken as separate groups when much work will have to be done in the global commons shared by all mankind.

As mentioned above, economic adjustments of any kind are more easily accomplished in a dynamic economic environment and it seems to be agreed that an essential requirement here is strong growth and expansion of the world economy, and, in particular, of the developing countries. In addition, however, there is evidence that imports of capital goods by developing countries could coincide to a significant extent with the productive capacities released by disarmament and conversion in Norway, for example, when increased resource transfers to developing countries were factored in as one of the options for conversion, it was found that the transfer policy least disruptive for the Norwegian economy involved goods and services that closely matched the new emphasis in developing countries on providing basic needs and promoting self-reliance; that is, agricultural machinery, fishing technology, machinery for mining, manufacturing, construction and hydropower plants and equipment and personnel for education and health programmes. Similarly, a case study of the Federal Republic of Germany found that existing development assistance programmes, even though predominantly untied, resulted in substantial business for the German economy with the benefits concentrated in the engineering, vehicle-building and metal-production sectors of industry. It will be recalled that military demand is also concentrated in these sectors so that a general expansion in the import capacity of developing countries would facilitate conversion.

As regards the first question, it would seem that the opportunities for the direct conversion of resources from military purposes to economic and social development purposes in the developing countries are most prolific in the field of R&D. The importance of science and technology for development can scarcely be overestimated. Indeed if it were not possible to be confident of the contribution that scientific and technological developments can make in solving the problems of underdevelopment these problems would seem quite hopelessly large. At present, however, the developing countries account for just 12 per cent of the scientists and engineers involved in R&D worldwide and for less than 3 per cent of global expenditures. Directing part of the military R&D

resources in the industrialized countries to the economic and social problems of developing countries would go a long way towards correcting this imbalance. Over the short and medium terms, this might be characterized as temporary access to additional R&D capacity, but it is particularly important that the effort be made in such a way as to permanently strengthen the indigenous capabilities of the developing countries. Among other things, there is need for a great deal more research into how technology is transferred and the prerequisites for technology to be adapted and to take root.

The prevailing imbalance in R&D capabilities has placed the developing countries in a position of virtually complete technological dependence on the industrialized countries. This technology is costly to acquire and, as experience has shown, more often than not unsuited to the circumstances prevailing in most developing countries. Technology transferred under these conditions has tended to result in large-scale, capital-intensive enterprises appended to the predominantly agricultural indigenous economy, facilitating the concentration of power by minority elites and reinforcing social and economic inequalities within the developing countries. It has also tended to result in the shift of environmentally destructive industrial activities to the developing countries. In other words, if military R&D capabilities in the industrialized countries are to be converted to addressing the economic and social problems of the developing countries, it is essential that it be done as if these countries themselves possessed such capabilities. Only in this way can there be reasonable assurance that the results will be maximum benefit and consistent with the development objectives and requirements of individual countries.

As with the industrialized countries, one of the foremost requirements in the developing world is for new and renewable sources of energy to supplement petroleum. While there need be no particular inhibitions about seeking high-technology solutions, the more important requirements would be that the devices be producible on a small scale and relatively easy to operate and maintain so as to permit their proliferation throughout the rural sector. Many developing countries lack even the technical and managerial resources needed to provide a base for developing an energy strategy, that is, to conduct geological and geophysical surveys of fuel minerals and other energy sources, examine conventional and new technologies and assess trends in the demand for commercial and non-commercial energy. Satellite technologies would be of great utility here.

Food production is another critical area. Under present conditions, many developing countries are projected to become more dependent on imported food over the next two decades. This is a serious hazard, both because the global balance between supply and demand could easily become quite delicate and because the real cost of food will almost certainly increase substantially so that major food import requirements will constitute an even heavier drain on foreign exchange reserves and, indirectly, on the capacity to sustain growth. There are a variety of research and development challenges in this field: the development of high-yielding varieties of staple food for the diverse soil and climatic conditions found in developing countries; pest control; methods of food storage and processing suited to local conditions; water management and irrigation technologies; and tools and equipment that use local raw materials, can be produced domestically and with low acquisition, operating and maintenance costs.

Recent advances in molecular biology hold particular promise for food-deficit developing countries. It is now considered possible to produce protein from bacteria and algae far more quickly and at considerably less cost than from animal and agricultural sources. It remains to translate this knowledge into facilities and processes suitable for application in developing countries. A recent investigation concluded that '. . . advances in enzyme engineering, microbial genetics and fermentation technology . . . point at new approaches to the development of small-scale processes that could form a logical take-off point for industrialization.'

Industrialization has been afforded central importance by the developing countries in accelerating their development in the context of a new international economic order. It has been estimated that attainment of the Lima target of increasing the share of developing countries in global manufacturing output to 25 per cent by the year 2000 requires a ninefold increase in the industrial output of the developing countries, necessitating investments of the order of $400 billion to $500 billion. Several possible foundations for an industrialization programme have already been mentioned and there can be no doubt that the military scientific and engineering capabilities in the developed countries could be applied in many other areas to provide an appropriate technological foundation for industry.

Two other areas in which the needs of the developing countries are very great and which offer considerable potential for the conversion of military R&D resources are health and education. For a variety of reasons, including, until recently, preparing for the possible use of biological weapons in warfare, the military in the industrialized countries has paid a great deal of attention to infectious diseases, food hygiene and the management of water and waste under field conditions. The knowledge acquired and the preventive capabilities developed have potentially great applications in improving health conditions in developing countries. It has also been suggested that military capabilities in the biological sciences could be readily applied to the fight against infectious diseases, particularly those in childhood, with military skills in organization and logistic planning providing essential backup to ensure the systematic and effective implementation of remedies. As mentioned previously, modern communication technologies and new media techniques offer great potential to make educational facilities more generally available in developing countries. Translating these capabilities into practical applications appears to be a fruitful alternative for the engineering and systems management capabilities of the military sector in the industrialized countries.

The reallocation of research, development and technological capacity to the information and communication networks of developing countries would be a major contribution to furthering their economic and social development. The World Administrative Radio Conference of 1979, the first of its kind in 20 years, undertook a comprehensive review of the world radio regulations dealing with the procedures governing the use of the radio frequency spectrum and the Geo-stationary Satellite Orbit (the single equatorial orbit in which a satellite has to be placed in order to remain stationary with respect to the earth's surface). Developing countries find themselves at a disadvantage in many respects, not the least being the use of frequencies by the major weapon States for military purposes in ways inconsistent with accepted procedures. This has adverse effects on the capabilities of the developing countries to make use of radio frequencies for communications. A crash programme to overcome illiteracy is another area in which, with the allocation of resources, developing countries could benefit.

This section is not exhaustive on the scope of alternative work. Mention needs to be made of the more or less predictable cycle of natural disasters and the need for vast quantities of resources to meet basic requirements for survival. These are two areas in which the international community has shown itself in recent times to be willing to assume a collective responsibility.

Similarly, no discussion of the potential alternative uses for military resources in an international framework would be complete without consideration of capital flows to developing countries. However much success the developing countries have in generating more resources internally and whatever is done in the fields of collaborative R&D, technology transfer, terms of trade and preferential access to markets in the industrialized countries, the achievement of high and sustained growth rates will require growing capital flows to fill the gap between domestic savings and investment requirements. A recent World Bank report estimated these requirements for what it called the 'high case', an optimistic projection given a generally austere economic outlook for the global economy. The projection was labelled optimistic because it presumed strong policies in all countries to adjust to high and growing energy costs; that the industrialized countries would run large deficits in the balance of payments in order to maintain their demand for imports and avoid an excessive slowdown in world trade in the early 1980s; that the industrialized countries would provide sufficient aid, particularly to low-income countries to minimize debt-servicing difficulties; and that the developing countries would continue to make determined efforts to raise investment ratios and productivity.

Clearly, the 'existing conditions' governing international capital transfers are not satisfactory in the light of the requirements for investment and growth in the developing countries. The magnitude and perceived urgency of military requirements is a strong and direct contributor to this state of affairs. Military requirements siphon off significant investible resources in the developing countries on the one hand and, on the other, seriously restrict the volume of developmental capital that the industrialized nations can provide on concessional terms. Accordingly, disarmament measures would ease the constraints at both ends. In particular, significant disarmament would permit a major increase in the share of the total foreign capital requirements of the developing countries provided in the form of grants and soft loans.

Summary, conclusions and recommendations

This investigation suggests very strongly that the world can either continue to pursue the arms race with characteristic vigour or move consciously and with deliberate speed towards a more stable and balanced social and economic development within a more sustainable international economic and political order. It cannot do both. It must be acknowledged that the arms race and development are in a competitive relationship, particularly in terms of resources but also in the vital dimension of attitudes and perceptions. The main conclusion of this report is that an effective relationship between disarmament and development can and must be established.

Economic growth and development would, of course, take place even with a continuing arms race but it would be relatively slow and highly uneven geographically. The co-operative management of interdependence, on the other hand, can be demonstrated to be in the economic and security interests of all States. But the adoption or rather the evolution of such an outlook is quite improbable if the arms race and failures to observe the principles of the United Nations Charter continue.

It would be virtually impossible to dispute the desirability of reversing the arms race in order to speed up the process of socio-economic development. But the very disappointing history of disarmament efforts on the one hand, and the less than satisfactory results so far in establishing a new international economic order on the other, have underlain the regrettable reluctance among some States to perceiving a disarmament-development relationship. Against this background, concrete measures within the framework of disarmament for development might have a psychological and political impact affecting positively the relations between developed and developing countries and thus international peace and security.

While recognizing the importance of the post-war conversion or reconversion experience, the Group has argued that the problem is now so influential and ingrained that preparing for its solution cannot be deferred until disarmament measures are agreed upon. The character of the military sector has changed dramatically over the post-war period and conversion of resources now used for military purposes will be qualitatively different from the demobilization exercises following past world conflagrations and military conflicts.

The worldwide defence industry is characterized by a high degree of geographical and sectoral concentration. It also involves a considerable degree of specialization in its work-force and a very pronounced emphasis on research and development, particularly in economies with sophisticated military sectors. This apparent exclusiveness of the defence industry should not, however, prove to be an insurmountable problem because:

(a) Conversion and redeployment is not a phenomenon uniquely associated with disarmament. Any form of economic and social change represents a continuous process of conversion. Particularly in modern industrial economies, the factors of production must respond continuously to the development of new products and the phasing-out of old ones and to the introduction of new production techniques;

(b) A significant part of military demand is directed at goods and services that are essentially identical to those consumed in the civilian sector. In this case, the problem is a relatively minor one of ensuring that civilian demand fills the gap left by cutbacks in military spending. Primary responsibility for conversion, in an over-all sense, will inevitably fall on the central Government, particularly in regard to initiating preparations for such a process. The nature and extent of government involvement, following disarmament measures, in the process of conversion itself will vary from country to country, depending in large part on the type of economic system but also on many other factors.

A relatively major problem in preparing for conversion, however, pertains to resources unsuited for the production of civilian goods such as those involved in combat aircraft, missiles, warships, tanks and so on. The primary need here would be for advance consideration of how their capabilities can be altered to permit the smoothest possible transition to the production of socially useful goods and services. A commitment to preparing for conversion will be an investment in minimizing the problems of transition. Such a commitment would entail thinking through the problems likely to be encountered by workers, industries and communities in the event of reductions in military business and devising measures and arrangements to overcome or minimize them.

The opportunity to apply science and technology more directly and systematically to economic and social problems is probably one of the most important dividends that disarmament would bring. As a potential asset for socially productive uses, the R&D component of the military outlays has the utmost significance. The previous United Nations report on disarmament and development identified more than 70 possible alternative uses for military research and development capabilities. The Group's investigations suggest that production workers in the military sectors could quite readily transfer their skills to the development, production and installation of solar energy devices. Environment is another area likely to gain from a possible rechannelling of military R&D. An essential prerequisite to arresting environmental degradation and repairing the damage already done is a more comprehensive understanding of the complex, synergistic relationships between the air, water and land environments. A wide variety of disciplines from both the natural and social sciences would be relevant here, including all or most of those found in the military R&D community. Housing and urban renewal offer still another outlet for a range of R&D capabilities and, subsequently, for massive reconstruction programmes. New transportation systems, particularly in urban areas, are sorely needed and have long been regarded as a major civilian alternative for the high technology industries in the military sector.

On the basis of its findings and conclusions, implicit in this entire report and more explicitly summarized above, the Group makes the following recommendations:

1. Most Governments have, in the past, shied away from any thorough public cost-accounting of military activities. The presumption has been that, to a first approximation, the requirements of military security must be met regardless of cost. The evidence assembled in this report suggests strongly that this attitude cannot be sustained. It is widely acknowledged that the true foundation of national security is a strong and healthy economy but the evidence is well nigh overwhelming that the contemporary military establishment significantly distorts and undermines the basis for sustained economic and social development. Furthermore, the arms race is in fact accompanied by a growing sense of national insecurity. Thus, to the extent that military expenditures do not purchase security they represent a pure waste of resources. *Accordingly, the Group recommends that all Governments, but*

particularly those of the major military Powers, should prepare assessments of the nature and magnitude of the short- and long-term economic and social costs attributable to their military preparations so that their general public be informed of them.

2. The structural changes associated with the conversion of military resources to civilian purposes and, even more so, those implied by the movement towards a new international economic order require a strong and sustained political commitment. Moral considerations will undoubtedly be influential in producing this commitment but of decisive importance is that all parties also perceive such changes to be in their own interests. In particular, the costs and benefits of moving towards a new international economic order are difficult to compare in conventional ways. The costs tend to be felt sooner than benefits are received. There can be little doubt that, especially in the long term, all societies would reap major benefits from a reduction in the economic weight of military activities and that there is a strong mutuality of interests between industrialized and developing countries in utilizing a significant fraction of the resources thus released to accelerate the economic and social development of the developing countries. *The Group recommends that Governments urgently undertake studies to identify and to publicize the benefits that would be derived from the reallocation of military resources in a balanced and verifiable manner, to address economic and social problems at the national level and to contribute towards reducing the gap in income that currently divides the industrialized nations from the developing world and establishing a new international economic order . . .*

3. The actual conversion of resources now employed for military purposes presents no insurmountable problem, particularly as the disarmament process will almost certainly be a gradual one. Some of the resources released from the military sector will be unsuited for direct redeployment to address economic and social problems, so that there will be a transition period during which manpower is retrained and physical assets adapted, to the extent feasible, for civilian operations. For this transition to be as smooth as possible and to involve the minimum of waste through unemployment of resources, it is vital that every effort be made to anticipate the extent and character of the conversion problems that will arise. Furthermore, since the resources released through disarmament measures will be finite, it will be necessary to consider very carefully the alternative uses for these resources in order to maximize their contribution to the solution of economic and social problems both in the national and international contexts. Preparing for conversion is not only of significance in the event of disarmament, but

also important for improving the domestic disarmament climate in that it assures those who are dependent for their livelihood on military production of alternative employment and engages diverse groups and institutions in society in an ongoing disarmament process. The process of conversion will be the final step in the execution of any negotiated disarmament measure. It seems clear, however, that preparation for conversion should be among the first steps on the road to disarmament. *The Group recommends that Governments create the necessary prerequisites, including preparations and, where appropriate, planning, to facilitate the conversion of resources freed by disarmament measures to civilian purposes, especially to meet urgent economic and social needs, in particular, in the developing countries.* One might envisage, *inter alia*, the creation of a core of people within each country with a significant military establishment with knowledge and expertise on conversion issues; the development of contingency conversion plans by plants engaged in specialized military production; the broad involvement of all affected parties in conversion planning, including management, trade unions and national defence research institutes.

4.   Preparations for conversion, particularly if carried out in relation to disarmament measures under negotiation or agreed upon, could foster international confidence: a society that is prepared for conversion is a more credible proponent of disarmament measures. Moreover, the undertaking of such preparations is not costly. For these reasons, the Group feels that it would be beneficial if Governments were to report on their experiences in and preparations for solving the problems of conversion in their respective countries. Such reports would become a generally available body of knowledge on conversion issues and could lead to a fruitful cross-fertilization of ideas on how particular problems can be solved. *The Group therefore recommends that Governments consider making the results of experiences and preparations in their respective countries available by submitting reports from time to time to the General Assembly on possible solutions to conversion problems.*

About the Contributors

Nicole Ball is Director of Analysis at the National Security Archive in Washington D.C. Her latest book is *Security and Economy in the Third World* (Princeton University Press, 1988).

Greg Bischak was Corliss Lamont Research Fellow at the Department of Industrial Engineering and Operations Research Columbia University, New York from 1986 to 1987. He has a PhD in Economics from the New School for Social Research in New York and is a researcher at Employment Research Associates, Lansing, Michigan.

Olav Bjerkholt is an economist, Director of Research in the Norwegian Central Bureau of Statistics, and an adjunct professor of economics at the University of Oslo.

Ådne Cappelen is an economist and a senior research fellow in the Norwegian Central Bureau of Statistics.

Lloyd J. Dumas is presently Professor of Political Economy and Economics at the University of Texas (Dallas), and formerly Associate Professor of Industrial Engineering at Columbia University. He is author of *The Overburdened Economy: Uncovering the Causes of Chronic Unemployment, Inflation and National Decline* (University of California Press, 1986); editor and co-author of *Reversing Economic Decay: The Political Economy of Arms Reduction* (Westview Press and the American Association for the Advancement of Science, 1982). He has written more than 60 articles in books and journals of six disciplines, as well as in the popular press. From 1980-1983, he served on the Committee on Science, Arms Control and National Security of the American Association for the Advancement of Science.

Jonathan M. Feldman is Program Director at the National Commission for Economic Conversion and Disarmament in Washington D.C.

Nils Petter Gleditsch is a sociologist, a senior research fellow at the International Peace Research Institute, Oslo, and editor of the quarterly *Journal of Peace Research*.

Robert Krinsky was Corliss Lamont Research Fellow at the Department of Industrial Engineering and Operations Research, Columbia University, New York from 1986 to 1987. He is currently Program Director of the National Commission for Economic Conversion and Disarmament, Box 15025, Washington D.C., 20003.

Seymour Melman is Professor Emeritus of Industrial Engineering at Columbia University, New York, and Chair of the US National Commission for Economic Conversion and Disarmament.

Lisa R. Peattie is Professor Emeritus and Senior Lecturer at the Department of Urban Studies and Planning, Massachusetts Institute of Technology, Cambridge, Massachusetts.

Mario Pianta was Corliss Lamont Research Fellow at the Department of Industrial Engineering and Operations Research, Columbia University, New York from 1986 to 1987. He is currently a freelance researcher and writer in Rome.

Paul Quigley, MA in Peace Studies, was Corliss Lamont Research Fellow at the Department of Industrial Engineering and Operations Research, Columbia University, New York from 1986 to 1987. He is presently a research officer with Coventry Alternative Employment Research.

Michael G. Renner was Corliss Lamont Research Fellow at the Department of Industrial Engineering and Operations Research, Columbia University, New York from 1986 to 1987. He is currently a researcher at the Worldwatch Institute, Washington D.C.

Steve Schofield is completing a doctorate in arms conversion at the Department of Peace Studies, University of Bradford, UK.

Peter Southwood, PhD (study of the UK defence industry) is a researcher at the Economic and Social Research Council (ESRC) in the UK.

Marek Thee holds degrees in journalism, political science and contemporary history and is Senior Research Emeritus at the International Peace Research Institute, Oslo. He was editor of the *Bulletin of Peace Proposals*, 1968–88. He is recipient of the Lentz International Peace Research Award (1982) and was Hubert H. Humphrey Visiting Professor of International Studies at Macalester College, St. Paul, Minnesota (1984). His recent publications include *Military Technology, Military Strategy and the Arms Race* (London: Croom Helm, and New York: St. Martin's Press, 1986), published under the auspices of the United Nations University, Tokyo.

Inga Thorsson, Sweden's Ambassador to the United Nations, is former Swedish Under-secretary of State and Chairman of the Swedish Delegation to the International Conference on Disarmament held in Geneva. She also chaired the UN study on *The Relationship between Disarmament and Development* finalized in 1981. In September 1983, she was commissioned by the Swedish Foreign Minister to carry out, as a special expert, a national case-study for Sweden on conversion from military to civil production. She is at present Chairman of the Stockholm International Peace Research Institute (SIPRI).

Tom Woodhouse, PhD in Peace Studies, is Chairman of Postgraduate Studies at the Department of Peace Studies, University of Bradford, UK.

Index